THEY CAN'T TOUCH HIM NOW

By James Williamson-Taylor

Blackie & Co.
Publishers Ltd.

First published in 2003

A CIP catalogue record for this title is
available from the British Library

ISBN 1-84470-000-3

Blackie & Co Publishers Ltd
107-111 Fleet Street
LONDON EC4A 2AB

Printed and Bound in Great Britain

ACKNOWLEDGEMENTS

Writing this book needed no imagination just memory, because it's true.

However, getting it to this stage was only possible thanks to my friends who read the initial manuscript and said 'they liked it'.

So following my mother's good advice that 'please' and 'thank you' cost nothing but will take you a long way, I especially need to thank Richard Woolfitt who helped me even though we had never met, Athina Churchill, my agent who believed in me, Josephine Leleu and Margaret Dunkley whose help proved invaluable, and lastly, Philip Whitaker who was the first person in my life to know about Tom, and who said, 'this story needs to be told'.

Preface

In 1958, I was a ten-year-old boy when I was physically molested by a man both inside and outside of the Ritz, one of our local fleapit cinemas.

With no resistance from my parents I had been allowed to go the pictures at night on my own, which is quite unthinkable in today's society. However, then parents worried less about the danger of their children being preyed upon. Children were not escorted everywhere, watched over every second or given great lectures on the dangers of being approached by people they didn't know. Well except for the general warning, 'don't accept sweets from strangers'.

Without what seemed like little thought for anything other than my getting home late, I was given two shillings and off I went. At the prospect of seeing a good war film, I skipped along, oblivious to any possible dangers. I went out an excited young boy and returned a confused and frightened child. Thankfully the man responsible wasn't violent toward me. Had he been, I might now be lying in a grave with no more than a tombstone to show for my short life: lying silent, story untold.

Thankfully I was physically unharmed, but mentally what had happened to me was a struggle to cope with. I was already wrestling with the knowledge that I had been adopted and with the fear I had of my adoptive father, who at times seemed to hate me. His violent outbursts caused me to hate my real mother whom I felt had just abandoned me. At times I would wonder how she could have left me with this man? Now, on top of all this, I felt I had a sexual problem. When I thought things just couldn't get worse I met Tom, a friendly paedophile. I was a young boy and my life was a mess because I was carrying a huge dark secret.

I feel it is time to tell my story and of what can happen to young boys who fall prey to unscrupulous men. Of what can happen when early sexual problems cannot be shared with parents. Of how easy it is to believe those who seem eager to listen and willing to give their time but who are ultimately only interested in satisfying their own physical needs. The question is, do those so-called sympathetic ears belong to a violent person?

I have carried the guilt for my actions for many years and at last I can tell what happened, because Tom is now out of reach and 'They can't touch him now'.

Chapters

THEY CAN'T TOUCH HIM NOW

Chapter One - The Dream

It was dark and it had just stopped raining. The street lamps were on, and their soft white lights reflected like sparkling silver on the wet pavement. I was alone in the street at first, as I walked along. I was a young boy and all I had on was a short vest. I could see a man and a woman walking toward me and as they got closer I started to panic clawing at the bottom of my vest trying to pull it down to cover myself. The closer they got, the more frantic I became. I tried to hide in a doorway but there was no cover as it was too bright. I had no choice but to step back onto the pavement and as I did, I stood there frozen to the spot in a cold sweat, as the couple passed me by. The look on their faces was as though I wasn't there! As usual, I woke up with a start and immediately felt around for the light switch. At first I couldn't find it as I was in a strange room. I was at Bert's, my best man's place. I found the switch on the bedside light and for a moment I lay there thinking about the dream. A dream I used to have regularly as a young boy, a dream I hadn't had for years. It was an unwelcome return and it troubled me.

In the soft yellow light from the lamp on the bedside table the clock showed 6.30 a.m. I got up, lit a cigarette and opened the curtains. It was Saturday the 19th of August 1967, my wedding day, and it was dull, grey and pouring with rain. I sat on the chair by the window in my underpants and shirt, smoking my first cigarette of the day as I watched the raindrops trickle down the dirty glass. The undetectable direction of the tiny rivulets was controlled by the thickness of the grime in their way. I found watching them as they wriggled down the window almost hypnotic and I couldn't help but think that life was a bit like this. Governed by something we can't see, something most people call fate.

Like the raindrop, my journey so far had certainly been unpredictable and definitely not easy. Now at the tender age of nineteen and a half, I was getting married. I had for years stopped thinking about the things that bothered me; it was my way of dealing with my problems. These were things that I either couldn't change or that I had no answer to. Things like my adoption, my early sexual problems, and Tom Granger.

Bert's house was just like our old house, in Morville Street. Even the smell was similar, but unlike us, Bert's family were lucky, as they didn't have to share their house with another family. They also had a comparatively new addition in their home, an inside toilet. I took a deep draw on my cigarette as I watched a paperboy across the road making his deliveries. His black silky bomber jacket and jeans were soaked through and his hair was hanging in wet strands down his face. He hurriedly made his last delivery in the street and cycled off around the corner and I couldn't stop myself thinking of how much things had changed since I was a boy of his age. Of when I had a paper round and when I was little. In my few years I had seen many changes, the worst of which I felt were families being divided as houses became available in new areas or in new towns. The family closeness, physically speaking, was fast disappearing.

Chapter Two - The Family

I was lucky when it came to family closeness as all of Dad's family (the Wilkinsons) lived in Bow, the heart of London's East End. It had huge advantages, especially at Easter and Christmas-time. Then, no one was more welcomed through our front door, than an Aunt bringing my Easter egg or a secretly concealed Christmas present. Dad's family, all had their own rented houses or flats, unlike Mum's family (the Taylors) who were a bit younger than Dad's family and still lived in a flat with their mother in Bethnal Green. The flat was in Seaton Buildings, which has long since been developed into trendy yuppie apartments and no doubt sold for a fortune being so close to the city. But they were far from trendy when my Nan lived there.

Nan's flat had three bedrooms, a lounge and that was it. You may be thinking at this point that I have omitted the bathroom and toilet. I didn't, the architect did! There was no running water or toilet inside, let alone bathroom. Each landing had four flats and, outside of the flats on that landing were four toilets in a row. Then there was a separate room with brown wall tiles and a cold concrete floor. This housed the communal sink, which was huge, about 6 feet by 3 feet by 8 inches deep with two taps over it, cold and cold!

Living in that flat with Nan, was Mum's sister, Sadie and her new husband Ronnie and Mum's youngest unmarried brother Raymond (Ray). Her other brother my Uncle William (Billy) had not long married Evelyn (Eve) and they were living in a flat somewhere nearby. Compared to them we were lucky as we lived in another spin off from the war, 'the shared house'. We shared 49 Morville Street, a terraced house, with another family who we called MacDonald's who lived in the upstairs part of the house. Although it was 1957, life in no. 49 was still pretty much Victorian. The house had a green front door with a black doorknocker in the shape of a lion's claw a black letter box and over the door was a fanlight. The door was recessed in a sheltered porch that had a red tiled step, in front of which on the pavement, was a round black cast iron coalhole cover that led down to the cellar. That served as a source of entrance for me when I got older, if I had gone out without my front door key. The front door opened into a dark and dingy hallway. On sunny days, shafts of light would penetrate the dirty fanlight glass revealing the dull wallpaper, which hung between the picture and dado rails. From dado to skirting board was brown glossy embossed lindcruster wallpaper. The lighting in the hall, other than from the fanlight, came from a solitary light bulb, which was enclosed in a nicotine stained lampshade. The hall floor covering was polished oilcloth whose pattern, due its age, was barely visible, but we did have the odd bit of carpet here and there.

Just about three good paces down the hall to the right was the door to Mum and Dad's bedroom. This was a reasonably good-sized room, with a window opening onto the street.

Further down the hall were the stairs, leading up to the MacDonalds. These were carpeted with a stair runner and although it didn't cover the full width of the steps, it looked pretty impressive with stair rods that had brass ends. The carpeted staircase certainly gave the impression that it led to the better half of the house. Just to the right of the stairs was my bedroom door, again with a fanlight. The door was painted in brown gloss, and had a brass doorknob and no lock. My room was quite a dark room with the window opening to the back of the house.

At the end of the hallway, to the left was a door leading to the cellar, to the right, a short hall to a backyard door, which was the MacDonald's access to the garden. Straight ahead was the door to our small kitchen. Although the kitchen had a good-sized window, it was always quite dark due to the house next door taking most of the light.

The kitchen had a glass panelled door, which opened into the scullery, as we called it, and that had a door for our access to the back garden. The scullery housed our gas cooker, a few cupboards, and a butler sink, with a clip on wooden draining board. The sink, sat under the window, looking out onto the garden. Well when I say garden, in our case I use the word loosely. It was only about 25 feet by the width of the house and it was a mess. At the end of it, was the garden shed, which Dad had built himself. This was where he kept all his tools. It's funny really, but I can never remember seeing my Dad actually buying any tools, yet he seemed to have loads of them. He was a bit of a magpie!

The house at 49 Morville Street offered no luxuries like a bathroom. In fact it was basic to the point that the two families shared the outside toilet, the walls of which were just cement rendered and whitewashed. In the corner of the toilet, there was a nail sticking out of the wall and hanging from that was a loop of string threaded through carefully cut squares of newspaper. Every so often we would sit at the kitchen table cutting up newspaper into squares ready for when the supply ran out.
The wide gap above and below the toilet door was for ventilation but in the winter the cold wind could practically cut off your feet at the ankles. Needless to say, in our house the Victorian bedroom 'gazzunder' (a chamber pot) still had some mileage left in it, or should that be gallonage?

We had no hot running water, so baths were taken once a week in a tin tub in front of the Kitchener, which was a fire-powered, highly inefficient cooker. Sort of a poor man's Aga. On the right hand side of this big black polished box was the fire, which had an open-fronted grate above which was a hatch through which you fed the fire. On the left hand side was the oven. Our fuel was either small bits of wood Dad had brought home from work or coal. When not in use, a regular job of Mum's was to clean it with a liquid polish called Zebra using an assortment of soft clothes and brushes.

So, without the luxury of a bathroom, the likes of which I had never seen let alone been in, I usually ended up in Mum's water after she had finished, was as good as it got. It wasn't perfect but at least I no longer got ridges in my backside from that bloody draining board. For me, real luxury started when I was old enough to take myself off to the Roman Road public baths. There they had heating, huge white towels and, if you spoke politely to the attendant, he would fill the bath good and deep. It was wonderful. While I would hate to do it now due to my chronic aversion to Veruccas, at the time it was just fantastic.

Opposite our house was a prefabricated house, 'a prefab'. It stood in quite a large gardened area where once 3 or 4 terraced houses had stood. Prefabs were a quick and cheap way of providing post-war housing on bombed sites for those left homeless in the Blitz. They were made of asbestos sheets, (before asbestosis) and occupants were told the prefab's life span was a maximum of 10 years. Governments being what they are, that stretched in some cases to as much as 40 years. Unfortunately, if only one terraced house was so badly damaged that it had to be demolished, that site would be too small for a prefab so it was just walled across to stop anyone falling into a great hole that was once someone's coal cellar. Running up the sides of the houses either side of such a gap was a vertical ladder of bricks jutting out where the fallen house had once been keyed in to its neighbour. These perpendicular ladders were very inviting and, on more than one occasion, I remember climbing up them and onto the roof. I could then walk along the entire row of houses throwing down the balls we had lost in our street games. It's funny how in youth there is little fear. There was little more than two inches jutting out on each brick which was just enough for small fingers to grip and for young feet to push up on. I wouldn't do it now, even if I could.

From what Dad told me, most of the German bombing was never accurate, mostly a matter of luck. That was also the case later in the war when the Germans launched the Doodlebug, the colloquial name for the German flying bomb. The unmanned Doodlebug was easily launched from a portable ramp somewhere in Germany and aimed at London. Their fuel was calculated with the idea that when it was somewhere over London it would run out and down it would come. Dad said it was terrifying to hear what he said sounded like a throbbing droning blowtorch, that would suddenly stop, then silence followed by a huge explosion.

The first Doodlebug to fall on London landed in the East End of London, hitting a railway bridge in Grove Road. This is now probably an almost forgotten historic event, despite being commemorated by a blue plaque on the wall of the new bridge.

After the war, there was a lot of work to be done particularly for the skilled and able. Mum and Dad weren't academics but both had worthy, practical skills. Mum was a sewing machinist in a shoe factory called Ce-aks, situated in Bethnal Green, just around the corner to where Nanny Taylor lived. In those days Mum, like a lot of factory workers, wore a wrap around apron and a turban made out of a headscarf. The sewing machines stood either side of aisles above which, fixed to about every fourth, strength giving steel tie bar, hung a huge loud speaker. These were used for the factory announcements, tea breaks, lunch breaks etc. and between these, broadcast loudly to get over the noise of the machines, radio programmes like Housewives Choice or Workers Playtime.

Working in a shoe factory proved to be a big help for Mum because of her disability. Unfortunately, when she was a child she had contracted Polio that left her with a malformed right leg. Her leg and the foot were smaller than the left, and that gave her a prominent limp. I think her limp was exacerbated due to the fact that she was only 5 foot tall and a bit on the plump side. As a child she wore a leg brace, which helped her to walk but did little for her confidence.

It must have been quite terrible for her as a young girl with regard to footwear as all that was on offer was clumpy ugly black orthopaedic shoes. Shoes that looked like they belonged on some ageing nursery Nanny, and not a young girl. I am sure it was her disability that was behind her motivation to work hard. It was thanks to her determination she could afford to buy shoes from work at trade price. Of course, for her to have a pair of shoes that fitted, she had to buy two pairs. A pair of 4's to give her the right shoe and 5's for the left. Even then, her right foot was quite deformed and there were many styles she simply could not wear.

I never once heard her complain about her disability and I expect she had long gone through the 'why me?' phase. When I was very young I didn't really see her as being disabled, she just had a bad limp. Mum was just Mum. It was only when I got older that I started to notice some of the problems her leg gave her, especially in the winter. She would come in from work and her right leg, which had poor circulation, would be blue from the cold. She didn't dare put it near the fire to warm it as this would result in chilblains. I would often look at her poor leg and think to myself if I were given one wish it would be to make her leg normal. Sadly the wish was never granted. One day, when I was out with her she caught me sniggering at someone who had a physical deformity. I can't remember what it was, probably a hump on the back – they were always good for a laugh or so I thought then. My Mum quickly pulled me to one side and pointed to her leg and asked me how would I feel if we were out and someone laughed at her. I think it was the first time I can really remember being made to think in an adult way about something. The thought of someone laughing at Mum repulsed me and I have never laughed at anything like that since.

As I got older, on Saturday mornings I would sometimes go to work with Mum at the factory. She felt it kept me out of harm's way and meant she and Dad could get the hours in without worrying about what I was getting up to. It wasn't long before the owner of the factory suggested to my Mum that, if she wanted, I could do a little job for which he would pay me. The job was sticking the labels on the ends of the shoeboxes. I'll always remember the smell of that glue and how I would manage to get it on my hands. I hated my fingers being so sticky. Still, I worked away and at the end of a morning would be paid two bob (10p). To a lad of 7 years old back then, that was excellent. I suppose it was my first taste of honest work.

Dad's skills were different again. With so much rebuilding necessary after the war he had plenty of work, as he was a Scaffolder. He would come home after work wearing his black donkey jacket, which would be hung behind the kitchen door revealing his bib and brace overalls. Round his waist was his leather belt on which hung two squares of leather, in each a neatly cut hole to hold his scaffolding tools. Apart from these he only used his hands and feet, which are the main tools of any Scaffolder. He wasn't a particularly tall man, about 5'10' and he was quite wiry but incredibly strong. To look at him you would never have guessed his profession.

As far as I know he didn't do an apprenticeship to learn his trade and for a man that could neither read nor write, he did well.

I think it was his sheer determination and willingness to work hard that carried him through most things in his life. He would be out there working 7 days a week throughout the year, no matter what the weather. I remember him telling me that he had known it so cold that the scaffold poles would stick to his hands when he picked them up. He wouldn't use gloves as he always felt they didn't give him a good enough grip. He told me the blokes down below would never appreciate a twenty-foot scaffold pole dropping down on them from 10 storeys up! Who would argue? Of course it was and still is a dangerous profession. Accidents happened that nearly always resulted in a fall and he did have one or two bad ones. Once he fell 30 feet but seemed to do so without injury and on another occasion he fell 50 feet but wasn't so lucky and he ended up in Guys Hospital with broken ribs. He was a dreadful patient and managed to make everyone's life a misery. Those poor nurses would tell him he had to keep still and he would do exactly the opposite. I remember Dad telling me that his worst fall and most lucky escape came during the war. He was working on concrete invasion barges when a cable jammed in the pulley wheel of a crane. Being a Scaffolder and not frightened of heights Dad volunteered to climb up and free the cable. He got to the top, freed the cable and lost his footing. He fell 80 foot and landed in the water in a gap between two recently finished barges. The gap was only about 8 feet, so on that particular occasion he was extremely lucky.

Dad often liked to slip back into the past, and his recollections nearly always started out with
'When we first took you, I worked seven days a week as you 'ad nuffink but the cloves on yer back and you slept in a

drawer as we didn't 'ave a cot'.

When he said took, he didn't mean I was snatched from a pram outside of the local grocer's, of course he meant adopted.

Chapter Three - Michael John Grant

I was born in 1948, in Lewisham Hospital, South London. My biological mother's name was Eileen Patricia Grant, but generally known as Pat. On the column of my birth certificate headed Father's Name there is just a dash and the address is shown as 103, Sibthorpe Road, Woolwich.

Pat had four other children before me, and their names and approximate ages were, Patricia 1941, Stella 1943, Robert in 1945 and Linda 1947. Then there was me, Michael John Grant, born 25th March 1948. From when I was three to nine months old, I was in hospital with chronic gastro-enteritis, something in those days that was a killer of young babies but luckily I survived. I was a fighter, which is just as well in view of what was to come.

While I was in hospital Pat moved away into a flat above a cycle shop in Solebay Street, Mile End and not long after that she moved again, above a café in Three Mill Lane, Bow. It was when she was there that she took up with a man called Alfie Wilkinson, and was introduced to his family including his brother Jim, and his wife Edith. It was likely that some of Alfie's family would not have approved of him living with Pat, especially as she had four children (or so they thought) as she had kept me, her fifth a secret. Then one day I did something really inconvenient. I got better and could come home. This meant Pat had some explaining to do. She dreamed up a story and told everyone that I was her sister's baby whom she was looking after as her sister was dying of cancer. Edith took to me immediately and offered to look after me for a week or two to help out. Pat deliberated carefully on this offer, for all of about 5 seconds, agreed and I was handed over to Jim and Edith in 'wot I lay in'. I say lay as opposed to stood because, due to my long-term hospitalisation at nine months old, I couldn't sit up let alone stand and at first, due to no cot, I slept in a drawer.

Edith was talking to Jim one day and asked him what he thought of the idea that they ask Pat if it might be possible to adopt me? Jim's reply was, according to what he told me in latter years, 'well if that's wot yer want, ask 'er'. Not what I would call a positive demonstration of enthusiasm.

Edith broached the subject the next time she saw Pat who advised her that, as she and her father were my guardians, she would need to speak with her Dad about it. Unfortunately her imaginary sister was too ill to discuss the idea. A few days later she told Edith that she had talked to her Dad and that they had agreed it was a good idea to have me adopted. Pat said that she felt that Edith and Jim were right for the job of bringing me up. Given that Pat didn't really know them from Adam I often wonder how she arrived at this decision. I think it was more a matter of Hobson's choice.

Edith set about contacting the right people to put the wheels in motion and a few weeks later, following a welfare report on Edith, Jim and me, the adoption papers were drawn up. On the 24th of September 1949 the Court hearing was booked and paid for. The cost was a total of £0.15.00 shillings or fifteen bob, five bob for the hearing and ten bob for the Plaintiff. The hearing date was set for Friday the 4th of November 1949 at 10.15 a.m. in front of B.G Nicholson, Registrar in Bow County Court. That was the day that the adoption deed was done and I was signed for like a registered envelope. My first name was changed to the same as my new Dad's, James, followed by Alfred Wilkinson, Dad being James Edward Wilkinson. My life then took a new direction – in a drawer with no more than 'wot I lay in'. It could be said that I had entered the Wilkinson family, Lock, Stock and Drawer! Shortly after this Alfie and Pat split up and she left the area without a word. Mum said she was pushing me in my pram through Roman road market one day and Pat passed by without so much as a glance into my pram or a word to ask how I was doing. That was the last time Pat was seen. There was no going back, I was now well and truly a Wilkinson.

Edith and Jim were happy with their new acquisition, although remember a baby is for life, not just for Christmas! The first problem that was to arise was the fact that Edith loved working and wanted to continue. The only way she could now do so was to place me with a baby-minder and I can remember a succession of these. Some of my earliest recollections were of being delivered to various people to look after me. The best of my minders actually lived next door at number 47 Morville Street, where the Easton's lived, another shared house with Mr and Mrs Easton downstairs and their newly married daughter Alice and her husband James upstairs. James was in the Merchant Navy and I remember there being a photo of him on the sideboard in his flat officers' cap, with a pipe in his mouth. I just loved it in number 47. Alice didn't have children of her own then and she adored me. She would spend endless hours with me playing all sorts of games to stimulate the imagination. We made tents out of a few blankets stretched across kitchen chairs and I was dressed up as an Indian. Alice would also make a train out of kitchen chairs and I would wear one of James's caps and be the train driver and this to me was bliss.

I would be given my breakfast, which was often 'dippy eggs and soldiers'. This was simply soft-boiled eggs with a slice of toast cut into fingers for dipping into the egg. When James was there, Alice had shown me how to turn the remains of the shell upside down, replace it in the eggcup and offer it to him, saying

'Here's your egg Uncle James' trying not to giggle and he would then crack it open to find nothing. He always went along with this act and his huge surprise never failed to crack me up into fits of laughter at my success at this deception.

Ah, such great memories but the saddest thing is, I don't have such memories of being with my adopted parents.

I started school when I was 5 years old and I clearly remember Mum taking me on my first day. I went to Malmesbury Road Junior School, which was an excellent school sharing the grounds with Colborn Road Grammar School for Girls. Impressive stuff. The two schools were separated by a six-foot chain link fence, which went through the middle of the playground, dividing us tots from the girls.

I loved Malmesbury from the day I started to the day I left. I sat next to Jack Fletcher who became my best friend. Jack and I managed to get into all sorts of scrapes but he would always be in more trouble with his parents than I would be with mine. Sadly for him, his parents weren't so easy going. I seemed to get a lot more freedom than he did. We would often go out and play together and simply forget about time. I remember on one occasion when we were boys, we discovered, under some railway arches in Campbell Road, sacks of Army belts and other sorts of military webbing. We ripped open sacks, dived around wearing belts playing all manner of war games. After much fun we headed off home and even though we were much closer to my house than to his, I felt I should go home with him to back up the story we had concocted on what we had been doing. It was dark and we never realized how dirty we were and we were filthy. When Jack's Mum opened the front door, she freaked out. Jack went in through the front door ear first as his Mum firmly gripped it, yanking him in. The door was slammed shut in my face and I could hear his Mum saying,
'That's the last time you go out with him!'

Of course it wasn't.

Chapter Four - My first business

When I was nine, I, just like my mates, wanted pocket money and, thanks to the wisdom of my mother, I had to earn it. I did this by going to the shops in Roman Road after school every day. It was then that I set out on my first business venture, which came up thanks to divine intervention - well sort of. Each day I would pass the church around the corner from where we lived which had been bombed out and of which all that remained was the shell. It was easy to enter and I loved to play in there. One night on my way back from the shops I went in for a nose about. As I looked down at the floor I noticed it was parquet - made from individual wooden blocks that had been laid using some form of tar for the adhesive. These were easily prised up and made great firewood. So slowly but surely, day by day using my Dad's hammer and an old screwdriver, up they came. I spent many afternoons trudging neighbouring streets selling tar-ry blocks for a penny (1d) each from the home made wheelbarrow my Dad had made me.

Life in Bow as a child was great, there was so much to explore and do. We lived quite close to Nestlé's dairy and I used to love sitting on the wall watching the empty bottles going around the automated system after they had been washed ready for re-filling. It was quite a challenge to try and hit them with stones, well at least until someone screamed out, 'Sod off, you little bugger'.

Another great form of entertainment was the Saturday morning pictures at the Odeon, opposite Mile End underground station. This was a highlight of the week and sheer excitement for kids. London was a far safer place then for children. So many kids used to walk there on their own. There were no two-car families in those days with mums dropping off and picking up kids. Back then we walked in much safer streets.

Once you had paid your tanner, slang for sixpence (2.5p in today's decimal money), to get in you were treated to the magical tension of Marvel Man, the hilarity of the KeyStone Cops or the sheer genius of Laurel & Hardy. Of course there was also the singing and dancing Shirley Temple, but I was never keen on her. There were plenty of opportunities to cheer the goodies and hiss at the baddies. In fact the cinema staff discreetly led the cheers and boos encouraging this. Now I think of it, it was probably a clever marketing ploy as all that screaming and shouting made you thirsty so there was always a rush to the usherette when you saw that commercial for Kiora Orange. I expect we all looked quite funny at mid-day as we poured out of the cinema blinking in the bright light.

I was pretty much like any other kid in those days even to the point of once stealing half an orange off a fruit stall in Roman Road market. However, unbeknown to me, a neighbour had seen me do this and I was reported to Mum who questioned me on this. Naturally I got told off but, despite my promises of being good in future, I still went wrong.

One morning before I left for school some of my mates encouraged me to take my dad's air rifle over to the local canals to shoot water rats. I was young and easily led, so off we went - of course playing the hop in the process (the hop being slang for playing truant from school). We were on our way to the canals, air rifle in hand, when we passed the huge open air storage area used by Fitzpatrick Limited, the road laying and building contractors. The huge open-air compound was surrounded by chain-link fencing to enclose the huge piles of bitumen blocks. I looked across and there he was, bending over moving some of the blocks and this was just too tempting for words. I broke the barrel of the gun, the action of which charged the rifle's lungs full of the air necessary to project that small lead pellet some considerable range. I loaded the gun and poked its barrel through the fence and rested it there. I took aim and slowly squeezed the trigger. Bull's eye!! I have never seen anyone leap up so fast. He looked round and screamed out the most foul string of language you have ever heard. Well I had heard it all before as my dad could always be relied on to lay his tongue to language most foul. As I got older I always used to try to justify my father's ability to use the 'F' word so much. Sadly Dad was illiterate and to him the 'F' word was like 'and', 'if' or 'but', and used just as much. In fact, for someone illiterate, he was quite adept at fitting 'F' in the perfect and most effective place in a sentence, or better still in the middle of a word.

To escape from the person I had shot, we fled to the canals where we continued shooting pellets into the water at air bubbles as they rose from the murky depths. We were convinced that water rats were making these bubbles. Our fun however was soon to end when the trusty Old Bill (police) were informed of our activity, probably by Mr Sore Butt. The gang ran at the sight of the police and as they did the rifle was passed back down the line to its owner - me! At the age of nine, running with a rifle up canal banks was not easy and naturally I was the first to be caught. The gun was confiscated, my name and address taken and I was allowed to go.

Later that afternoon, the gang met up in the cellar of one of the gang's house. When I arrived they were all chugging their way through a selection of Player's Weights and Park Drive cigarettes. These were the brands that were cheap, affordable to kids, and were sold in small packets of five without the shopkeepers ever questioning the age of the buyer.

I was terrified as I imagined my dad rolling his tongue round some choice phrases. His swearing ability was matched only by his temper and I was convinced I was dead. I may not have been afraid to climb up that sheer brick wall ladder hanging on the side of a terraced house, or even balancing on a ten-inch water pipe to cross a canal in the days when I couldn't even swim, but when it came to my dad, that is when I learned about fear.

I told my fellow gang members as I leaned forward peering through the smoky cellar I had better go and I left in silence. I shouted 'See yer later' as I pulled the front door closed by the big black knob in the centre of the door. I was standing on the coalhole cover and below my feet came the sound of the gang chatting in whispers. I slowly turned around and I could see Dad coming up the street on his motorbike and sidecar. I felt the fear go straight to the pit of my stomach. Suddenly, I got the idea that the answer was to get the rifle back so that Dad wouldn't know what had happened. Without a minute to waste I trudged to Bow Road police station. I walked straight up to the sergeant's desk, against which I was just about tall enough to get my chin and he said to me, 'What do you want son?' I burst into tears. I just could not speak for sobbing as he took me into the police station, sat me down and coaxed me into telling him what was wrong. I was given a cup of tea and biscuits and promised there was no need to worry. I thought he was so kind and I suddenly felt safe. I thought he was going to give me my dad's rifle back. Instead he organised a bobby to take me home, without the rifle, to explain to dad what had happened to save him killing me. We arrived at our front door and my escort lifted the black knocker. The knock seemed to echo in the hallway beyond and soon I could hear my dad walking up the passage. I was gripped with fear as I slid behind the policeman and when the door opened I peered at my dad as the policeman explained to him what I had done. He told Dad that someone would be round later that evening from C.I.D. to speak with him. I think if I had known what the CID was and how my dad felt inside about me at that moment, I would have happily died on the spot.

Dad said 'OK, we're in tonight' and I was handed over, with the words, 'Go easy on him.'

My Dad thanked the bobby politely as he seemed to listen to his plea. I went in and as the door closed the light faded and suddenly I was travelling down our front passage having received a blow to the back of my head that felt like it had been delivered by a cricket bat. It wasn't, it was my dad's hand.

I regained my balance only to lose it again when that great leathery hand found the back of my head once again. I fell to the floor and screamed,
'Don't hit me again.'
He grabbed the back of my coat and I came off the floor as he turned me to his face. I hung in his hands like a lifeless doll and he was so angry as he shouted at me that I was covered in spit.
'Hit you again,' he spat,
'I'll fucking-well kill you,' he said. I felt the blood drain from my head and I thought I was going to pass out as he threw me to the floor. I followed him into the kitchen and sat in the armchair motionless as I watched him silently make some tea. My sense of survival told me to keep my mouth shut. We didn't have a TV so Dad sat and listened to the radio as he slowly stirred in a spoonful of Nestlé's condensed milk along with two spoonfuls of sugar. He then poured his tea from his mug into his saucer and slowly drank it. Each slurp sounded noisier and I wanted the tea to last forever as it was giving him something to do other than clout me again.

After about an hour of silence save for The Archers on the radio I heard the front door close. It was Mum. Normally if

I was in trouble I would run to her, but I was too scared to move. I knew she would be really mad at me too but at least I knew she would not try to knock seven shades of crap out of me. She walked into the kitchen and Dad said,
'Wanna a cup of tea, Ede?'
'No, not for the moment,'
'I would,' he shouted, 'It might keep you calm while I tell yer wot this little fucker has been up to,' Mum looked at me and I burst into tears again and as she hung her coat up behind the kitchen door she said,
'Why, what's he done?' As Dad told her, she remained calm. It was her way. Thank God she could think about something before lashing out. My Dad's thinking capacity was just about zero, equal to his tolerance level. When he had finished telling her what had gone on, she turned to me and said,
'Well, why did you do it?'
'Well, I was going to school but some of my mates called round and suggested I take the day off and go shooting water rats and...'
'Oh really,' she cut in, 'and what happens when the police come back later tonight and arrest us for not looking after you properly?' I looked at her puzzled and couldn't answer.
'Oh, you don't think that can happen? Let me tell you it can, and then what? You know you are adopted and just because the adoption is legal, it doesn't mean that you can't be taken from us and put into care. Is that what you want?'
I could see Mum was really upset, and that she was genuinely concerned. I felt more terrible than ever for upsetting her so much.

I was in such a state I found it hard to speak sincere words of apology. I just ran to her put my arms around her and begged her not to let them take me away. My entire body shook with sobs and fear. She knew I was sorry but she didn't suddenly put her arms around me with comforting words of there, there. She just said,

'Well, we'll have to see what happens when the police come round tonight. I hope it will be all right, for your sake,' she went on to say. 'Mind you I hope you realize that if this sort of behaviour is ever repeated, what you have done today will be kept on record and that any future trouble you get into with the police, this will count against you.'

I could sense forgiveness and I made a solemn promise that I would never play the hop or do anything like that again.
'Well, let's see what happens when the police get here,' she said and told me to get cleaned up and change my clothes. She rubbed my head and I winced a bit where I had taken a couple of blows from Dad but she didn't notice. While Mum was getting the tea ready I sat and listened to the radio. The house sounded hollow and I was still full of fear at what the police might say when they called round. The clock on the mantelpiece ticked away loudly and the quarter chimes seemed to sound so much louder that night.

We had tea and Mum settled down to read the paper after washing up while Dad went to his shed in the garden as he often did. Normally at this point I would ask if I could go out for half and hour but under the circumstances, I felt to sit quietly would be a wiser thing to do. I just felt that if I sat so quiet Mum wouldn't notice I was there and I wouldn't annoy her. As time ticked by I started to feel sick with worry.

As I sat waiting for the dreaded knock on the door, the warmth of the fire made me feel drowsy and I fell asleep. It was the knock that woke me up and as I looked up I could see Dad sitting there rolling a cigarette. I think he could see the fear on my face and I just wanted either him or Mum to call me over to sit on their laps, but the call didn't come. I was going to have to sit this out on my own. Mum went to the front door and I heard a voice say, 'Mrs Wilkinson?'
'Yes,' she replied.

'Hello, I am Detective Inspector Marsden from Bow Police station. I understand you are expecting us this evening with regard to an incident earlier today involving your son Jimmy and an air rifle. May we come in?'

'Of course,' she answered, 'please come in.' The two police officers entered our front hall and made their way down to our small kitchen.

The first officer was a really tall man with a deep warm voice who put his hand out to my father and introduced himself and his colleague. My Dad took his hand and shook it. Dad may have been shorter but I reckon his hands were as big and I bet tougher too. Dad said,

'Please sit down, d'yer wanna cuppa tea?'

'That would be really nice, thank you.'

Dad looked at me and said,

'Jimmy, put the kettle on.'

I quickly went into the scullery and did as I was told. The officers sat at our kitchen table and Dad remained in his armchair, next to the fire.

'Well, Mr Wilkinson, or can I call you James?' As I reached to fill the kettle I remember thinking, who would call my dad James? Everyone called him Jim. In fact I often wondered why we were given the name James when everyone called him Jim and me Jimmy. For a brief moment I had drifted off in these thoughts until the kettle boiled and I heard the officer saying,

'And that's when we caught him with your rifle.'

My stomach rolled over and I felt sick as I quietly walked back into the kitchen with a tray loaded with the teapot and cups. I gently put them on the table.

Dad told me to sit down and listen as the officer turned to me and asked me to confirm the addresses of the other boys. Even then you never squealed on your mates and I was filled with even more fear of what would happen to me if I told. Thank God the officer made it easy for me by telling me that they already had all the names and addresses but it would be easier if I could just confirm the door numbers. I didn't think that counted as squealing so I nodded as he called out the addresses of my friends. He then asked his colleague to go to the car to get Dad's rifle. I cannot remember Dad being questioned on where he got it, but I guess as it was an air rifle and easily bought without the need for a licence he wasn't really bothered.

The officer did suggest that in future perhaps it should be kept locked up and I wanted to say 'no need'. There was no way I was going to touch it again. I was only too pleased to be getting off as lightly as I did. Maybe the man who I had shot up the backside had not called the police after all. I am certain that there would have been a lot more trouble if he had. The police finally left, having given me a lecture on crime, playing the hop and where all that would lead me. All I can remember is the feeling of relief at how lightly I was getting off. I reckoned the feeling of relief was like leaping out of a plane and seeing your chute open. Mine had opened and all I could now hope for was a soft landing.

The police left and I was sent to bed. I got undressed as quickly as possible into my pyjamas and snuggled down into the safety of my bed. I tried to go to sleep as quickly as possible as I knew even my dad wouldn't wake me to give me a telling off or even worse another wallop but the fear and tension throughout the day followed by relief caused sleep to elude me. The bedroom door opened and it was Mum, thank God.
'Jimmy,' she said, 'Are you still awake?'
'Yes,' I whispered. She stepped over and sat on the edge of the bed, trying not to fall on top of me. Unlike modern divans my bed was a mattress on a sprung frame and a few years of

leaping on it from the top of my chest of drawers had caused it to sag deeply in the middle. I loved my bed as at night it made me feel secure, a bit like sleeping in a hammock.

'Look Jimmy, this is the first and last time you will bring the police to our house. I never want you doing this sort of thing again, OK?'

I have to say that I was so relieved at how easy she was being with me, that when I said 'yes', I really meant it. Mum went on to tell me that if ever I did wrong again and the police came to our door for me she would not let me hide behind her but she would just hand me over to them. She was very much a woman of her word and I knew she meant what she said. I was just so relieved to have all this trouble behind me and I promised myself that I would not do this again. She pushed her fingers through my fair hair then she got up and said, 'Get to sleep, you've got school tomorrow'. I turned over and as the sheer burden of fear left my shoulders I fell into a deep sleep.

The year slipped by as we enjoyed a good summer. Summers as I remember them, were filled with days of blue skies with huge patches of bulbous white clouds, gardens with washing lines loaded with colourful clothes billowing in warm summer breezes. We were well into the school summer holidays and staying occupied and out of trouble was growing harder to do. We used to love going over to Victoria (Vicky) Park where there was plenty of space and plenty to do. I used to love the boating lakes and, if I had the money, I loved to hire a rowing boat. Vicky is a large park but to a small boy, enormous. It had a lido, paddling pools, and even an animal sanctuary.

The gate into Vicky, nearest to the boating lakes, was on a crossroads where a new traffic island had been installed and on one of the corners the council was building a new block of flats. A few of us decided to get onto the site one weekend and explore when there were no workmen about. Much of the building was finished and getting up to the top floor was easy for a scaffolder's son. There were all manner of tools lying around as well as some five-gallon tins of red oxide paint, presumably to be used on the new metal window frames - something councils were then opting for instead of wood. Well, we thought it would be fun to tip the paint off the roof and leg it. We all had a tin each and we removed the lids looked at each other, wondering who would chicken out. On the count of three, the tins had to be tipped on their sides. Five tins, five boys and not one chicken!

I reckon we were down those floors so quickly that we were able to look up as the first trickles of the twenty-five gallons of red paint appeared over the top of the roof. As the volume built up, the paint slowly spread out over the side wall of the building. It was at that point we decided not to hang around and disappeared back in into the park. I spent many hours of fun in Vicky, especially in the lido during the school summer holidays.

Chapter Five - Hop Picking

I had longer summer holidays than most kids as we used to go hop picking for about a month. Hop picking takes place at the end of the summer, which meant each year I would get an extra week or two off school to go off with Mum. Dad would come for weekends, but somehow Mum managed to wangle four weeks off work and would cart me off with her. Although hop picking may be an acquired taste, it was a big annual event for London's East Enders.

In the early days, we would go by train to the hop fields in Kent. There would be me, Mum, Nanny Taylor and a few other kids and of course our dog, Fido. Everything was packed into that huge box, which was put onto a pram and off we'd go. Those in the family that had any means of transport would bring down pots and pans and anything else that was needed but too heavy or bulky to carry on the train.

As time went by and some of the family got a little better off, our trips to the hop fields became easier. My dad's brother, Uncle Steve, was a lorry driver and he would roll up outside our house in his canvas covered lorry, which would already have Nanny Wilkinson aboard. He would jump out of his cab, drop the tail gate and we would be loaded aboard with what bits of furniture and utensils we needed along with good old Fido and off we would go to the next Aunt. Uncle Steve always managed to get so much and so many of us aboard for the trip down to Selling just outside Faversham in Kent. We would arrive at the farm where someone would billet us in our hut. Huts were built in blocks, fifteen to a block and built out of the roughest type of building block imaginable. Each hut was just one room, with a stable door on the front, the top half of which doubled up as the window (there was not a separate window). The hut was about twelve foot square and on the back wall was a bed frame, provided by the farmer.

This was just a simple wooden frame on top of which was nailed half poles, curved side down and about four inches apart, to put the mattress on.

Behind the blocks of huts the farmer would place a pile of dry straw for our use and while mums were unpacking and getting everything ready, us kids would be outside playing in the straw and forging new friendships that would last the season. We didn't know it, but we were playing in our bedding. Our mattresses were just straw-filled palliasses, made out of blue and white mattress ticking. Mum and Nan would take the palliasse to the pile of straw and together they would stuff it full. Then Mum or Nan would roughly stitch the end closed and it would be thrown on the bed frame. I would then be invited to do a bit of rolling which entailed taking off my Wellington boots and rolling about on the mattress to flatten it out. Rolling was quite an important job, as no one liked trying to sleep on a lumpy bed. When my job was done, sheets and blankets would be added, topped with a bedcover. For those who do not suffer with hay fever or have never slept like this you have no idea what you are missing. It is comfortable and warm. The old chest of drawers we had brought with us held our clean clothes and another small cupboard we had brought was in the corner stuffed with food. Nails had been banged into the wooden frame, which went round the top of the walls to hang our pots and pans on. The finishing touch was the hurricane lamp, which was placed on the chest of drawers ready to give us light at night. Electricity did eventually come, but on reflection I think it took away much of the charm of hop picking. The hut was now ready for occupation for the next month.

Opposite each block of huts there were two kitchens shared by each block. Now when I say kitchen, please don't get carried away with ideas on the lines of 'fitted'. On the contrary, the farmer put up a frame made of four upright posts joined together at the top by four more posts to make a frame. The top would have a corrugated tin roof sloping down slightly to the back to drain off the rain. Around three sides would be strung with bale wire and tied upright to the bale wire were twig walls to break the wind and keep out the bad weather. Inside the cooker was made from half of an old steel water tank. The farmer had simply cut an old tank in half, turned it upside down with the open end to the front. One tank did two kitchens. The last thing the farmer would provide was faggots (bundles of branches and twigs bound together with string or bale wire) and this was the fuel for the fires.

Toilets were the dug out latrine-type affairs built around the back of the huts and in a different place each year ready for the next season. They were simply built out of corrugated tin with a wooden door. Inside there was a wooden upturned box placed carefully over the deep hole and in the top was cut a neat hole shaped to fit any bottom. I know it all sounds very primitive - it should do, it was. However, to a child from the East End of London, to get away into the country was brilliant, in fact next to seeing the lights switched on at Southend-on-Sea or Christmas, hop picking was one of the year's best events.

It was all so well organized by mums, nans, aunts, and uncles who had been going hop picking for years. They all knew what they were doing and before you knew it the kitchen fire was alight, water containers were filled from the stand pipes at the back of the huts, pots filled with vegetables were beginning to boil as they sat on top of the now glowing upturned water tank, sorry, oven! Dads or uncles would be turning sausages in huge frying pans to stop them burning. No meal to me would taste as good as those we had on the farm.

Mum always said I was a nervous child and that I was scared of the dark; that was until we went hop picking. I don't wish to glamourise it all but it was a cure for many ailments and it was a holiday where you had to get on. There really wasn't room for squabbles and I can honestly say, I can only really remember one, almost, fight. I have no idea what it was over, but I do remember my mum, with her pronounced limp, storming up to the next block of huts and threatening this woman that if she so much as uttered another word about her then she would tear her bloody head off and feed it to the pigs. I was so shocked as I had never seen my mum like this.

It frightened me as I hated violence and I prayed that the woman would not make a stand, as I couldn't imagine what it would have been like to see my mum actually fighting. Thankfully the woman realized she was in the wrong and she stayed firmly put in her hut. I never knew my mum had it in her. Those stories of Mum protecting her younger sister were obviously true. It was hard to believe that Mum would have needed to do that as, compared to my Mum, Aunt Sadie was built like a barn door. Obviously when Sadie was little she wasn't so big and Mum would have no one picking on her or her brothers.

The farmer allowed us the weekend to settle in and then on Monday morning, it was work. We would all traipse down to the hop fields and I was amazed at the rows and rows of vines growing. They extended up to the bale wire stretching from post to post. There were miles of vines and tons of hops to be picked. In between the rows of vines would stand our hop bin. These were made from wood and sacking. They were simply two crosses of wood, held together by two horizontal pieces of wood nailed to the tops of each cross. This was to stop the crosses collapsing flat to the floor. The horizontal bars were joined together at each end by two one-yard long strips of webbing. Lastly, nailed to each of the two horizontal bars was hessian sacking to form a trough which had a piece of sacking roughly sewn into each end to stop the collected hops from falling out.

In the main hops were picked by the women, and of course, when they wanted to earn some pocket money, the kids too. The men would be the ones to pull down the vines and stretch them over the bins ready for picking. Us pickers, would stand next to the bins (me on my box because I was short) and pick. I am told that when I first started picking, I used to pick the petals off the hops instead of the hop off the vine. This was obviously a source of amusement to the seasoned picker. Pickers were paid so much per bushel picked. As our bins filled, the workers, on the back of the tractors, would come round with their bushel baskets scoop out the hops and then write in our pass book, how many bushels collected. You see, all quite simple really. I learned many things on these holidays and one of them was that hop picking was not something I had to do. In fact I think the novelty wore off after about a day and I would be off with my new friends and cousins to go tree climbing, exploring or scrumping apples. There is no apple in the world that tastes better than an English Cox's Pippin that has been nicked off a tree or scrumped. The whole time for me was wonderful with blissful nights sleeping on my crackling straw bed, top to toe with cousins. We enjoyed dinners that were wholesome and that managed to satisfy even the greatest appetites that had been drummed up on a hard day's play. After such meals we would soon be drifting off to sleep as we listened to the adults around the fire outside as they swapped stories or just gossiped. No one really stayed up too late as the working day was long and there were six of those long days in a week.

Friday night or Saturday morning would see the drift back of the husbands or dads, who had been back home doing their jobs during the week. Saturday saw everyone picking, well everyone except my dad who didn't like picking hops too much. He preferred collecting firewood or water and generally rooting around to see what he could find! You see, he never stole anything; he always found it, usually long before it was lost.

Picking used to finish earlier on Saturdays as it was the last working day of the week. As the last of the hops were scooped from the bins one of the men on the tractor-towed trailer would hand out subs, (an advance on wages). Then pickers would wend their way back to the huts. The older ones, or those who were disabled, like Mum, would grab a lift on the back of the trailer. It didn't take long for the women to have food on the go while the men boiled water, gallons of it, using anything that would neither leak nor melt. Then out would come the dreaded tin bath.

In a conveyor belt system, almost like one of those Mickey Mouse cartoons, one kid after the other would be bathed and dressed ready for dinner by a grandma - or as we called her, Nan - or an aunt, not on cooking duty. Dinner was dished up and we would eat it wearing an old pillowcase or a tea towel as a bib to keep us clean. The whole Saturday process was very much a matter of teamwork and it didn't seem to matter who washed whose kids. It was orderly chaos. With washing up done, next the women were readying themselves for their Saturday night out. We would all walk across the fields to the nearest pub where a great deal of stout, light and bitter and Guinness were consumed. Someone would start to play the piano and all those East End favourites would be sung. The atmosphere was electric. The night would end with the kids sound asleep, cradled in the arms of their mothers, the bigger ones slung over the shoulders of Dad as they all walked back across the fields.

Sadly at the end of the season, when it was time to go home,

I used to find it hard to adjust back to my life as an only child. Although I had quite a few mates who lived in or close by to Morville Street or who were just friends at school, I still used to get dreadfully lonely. It was great when it was summer with long days and short nights and the weather enabled me to get out to play. But I hated the winter because it was long, and time to play outside far shorter. It was during these times that my need for company was greatest and I wished more than ever that I had brothers and sisters. Then I would wish that I hadn't been left behind by my biological mother, whatever the reason. Hop picking was even more important to Mum and me than Dad ever realized. He was a difficult and a quick- tempered man, known for lashing out with his big leathery hands. We always seemed to be tippy-toeing around him, trying not to upset him. I am certain that is why my Mum used to insist on going hop picking every year. It was her chance to have some time without him.

Dad would come down to the farm at weekends, that is, if he wasn't working, so we would have Monday to Friday without him and his unpredictable temper, and those times were great. I think it was the friends I made at hop picking and the absence of Dad's temper that made me love it so much and coming home at the end of the season was never a joy for me.

Chapter Six - The Annual Holiday

The time I grew to dread the most was our annual holiday: camping. We didn't go camping because it was cheap but because Dad always wanted to get away from it all. To him there was no place better than the middle of nowhere, but that is not a very good place to be for a young boy who craves company. When it was time to go away, Dad would roll his home trailer out from behind the shed in our back garden. This would be hooked up to the back of our motorbike and sidecar. He had even made the hooking-up mechanism and he had worked out how to connect it into the bike's lighting system so that the trailer had tail and brake lights. As I said earlier he was no fool; he was just illiterate, which I think was a constant source of frustration for him and which went a long way to contributing to his quick temper. It wasn't until later in life that I worked out for myself what the problem was between Dad and I. I believe it was due to my education and growing ability to see sense and reason. The more I reasoned with him the more frustrated he grew with me because his sense of reason was so poor. This was to manifest itself into more and more explosive situations. I might have been able to reason but he was the parent and breadwinner, of which he so often reminded me by saying what he had done for me. Always beginning with 'when we took yer'. I grew to feel more and more unhappy with my life. I began to wonder why they had adopted me, as at times he seemed to hate me.

His frustration with me would so often culminate in violence. Then when Mum came home from work and saw that I had been beaten or was terribly distressed this would invariably end up in a row between them and I would blame myself for that too. At times I felt this was a dreadful situation for anyone to grow up in and I hated my father for his uncontrolled physical and mental cruelty toward us. It was as though he enjoyed pushing us to the very edge of a precipice and then he would be nice and draw us back to him again. It was hardly surprising that as I got older setting out on holiday with Mum and Dad filled me with dread. He was an explosion just waiting to happen.

Our annual holiday was touring Devon and Cornwall. We used to get there by using the main South West road, which was the A30, long before the days of the Exeter bypass or the M5 motorway. It was a long drive and often done overnight. Thankfully I was at last big enough to ride pillion on the bike rather than being jammed into the small seat in the back of the sidecar behind Mum. For my journey I was dressed up in warm clothes as even English summer nights on the back of a speeding motorbike can be cold.

My ultimate layer of clothing had to be waterproof and was usually one of Mum's raincoats. One year the 'in thing' for ladies' raincoats was pink and plastic. Heaven only knows what villagers must have thought as they saw us passing through late at night. Dad wearing his huge Parka, waterproof trousers and Wellington boots and me sitting behind him wearing a flying hat and goggles, pink raincoat tied round the middle with a piece string. On top of all that Dad and I were tied together with strong cord. This was to stop me falling off if I fell asleep, which I would often do.

We would arrive in Devon in the early hours of the morning and stop at some farm or another. Dad would find the farmer and ask if we could camp in one of his fields for a night or two. The answer was nearly always yes and we would set about unpacking everything and putting up the tent. By now we had advanced considerably to a six-foot tall ridge tent with an extended flysheet that gave us an awning to the front of the tent that acted as our lounge and kitchen area. Before this luxury we used to manage with an old ex-army tent, that was only three foot high, six foot wide at the bottom and about seven foot long. As you can imagine access in and out of this was really awkward especially for Mum. By comparison our new big tent was fantastic and without always wishing to paint too bad a picture of Dad, when he was in a good mood, life wasn't too bad.

I used to love life on a farm and I would always ask the farmer if I could help out. In my time I have helped milk cows by hand, shear sheep and feed pigs. I can remember waking up to great summer days and the smell of breakfast being cooked by Dad on our little petrol primus stoves - yes, petrol. We used to have paraffin stoves, the type you pumped to keep up the pressure. Then Dad found these little stoves powered by petrol. They were really small, only about four or five inches high. About two inches down the stem of the stove was a small collar and on this he would put a small bit of paper soaked in methylated spirit (meths). He'd light the meths, which warmed up the stem and the petrol in it. When it was hot, he'd open the valve at the base of the stem and light the gas jets at the top and - bingo! - we would get a roaring blue flame that needed no pumping. He would then carefully place the two primus stoves into his home made two-ringed cooker. On one ring would be the kettle and on the other a frying pan with sizzling bacon. This was without doubt one of the best ways to wake up in the morning. To sit up in your sleeping bag on a warm summer's morning, looking out of open tent flaps into our awning with Dad cooking bacon and eggs while Mum passed me a mug of tea and a handful of biscuits to dunk. Life wasn't always bad and these were truly blissful times.

After breakfast I would be given a bowl of warm water and I would have a good wash, then off to the farmer. Mum and Dad wouldn't see me again until I was ravenously hungry at lunchtime. The holidays would soon pass, hopefully without too many bad days with Dad. I used to try to keep out of his hair as much as possible as if I was around he would often ask me to help him service or repair the bike. This involved me reading the manual with Dad trying to follow the instructions I was giving him. Of course I was too young to understand what needed to be done. I mean what did I know about tappets, valves and valve collars? My lack of understanding of motorbike mechanics would nearly always result in Dad screaming the most foul abuse at me. I used to shake with fear as I knew that at that point his fuse was well alight and I was liable to get a spanner thrown at me because things were not going right. If he so much as dropped a spanner at the wrong moment I would close my eyes in fear. I used to pray to God to ask him to please help us do this job properly so I could go and play. As time rolled on Dad's temper got worse and I grew more frightened of him.

His great love for the middle of nowhere never changed, which meant we never went to any crowded places. Of course that ruled out all seaside towns, which were completely out of the question. I never got to enjoy a beach or a funfair. We did go camping in the North once, quite close to Blackpool. We were again camping on a farm when Dad suddenly announced that we should go into Blackpool so that I could see the tower. I think this was more out of his attraction for heights than his desire for me to see it. We got on the bike and I was amazed at how big Blackpool's front was and at its trams clanking along full of people.

It was only Dad and I that went up the tower. There was no way Mum was going up there, as she hated heights. Before we got in the lift I managed to sneak a quick look into the tower ballroom at the end of which was the organ called the Mighty Wurlitzer that was played by Reginald Dixon on the radio. We got in the lift and up we went onto the windy viewing platform. It was the highest I had ever been and it didn't worry me at all. I was fascinated at how small everyone looked down below as they ambled along the front.

Dad announced that it was time to go. Not only back down, but away from Blackpool and back to the farm. I think we had been there about an hour and a half and that was to be my experience of a summer holiday by the sea. Still, as my Mum used to say, 'what you don't have, you don't miss'.

I always hated the return trip to London as I used to react badly to the change of air. Compared to the country, London's air was quite polluted and as we got closer to its outskirts I used to feel quite ill. But, after a few days I would soon be back in the swing of things in good old Morville Street and settled into the routine having fun with my mates. Thank goodness for Victoria Park, which was our countryside, even if the air wasn't as clean.

Chapter Seven - The Scouts

One day while playing hopscotch in the street one of the older boys was talking about the scouts. He was excited as he told us that the church hall where they had their meetings even had its own snooker table. He made it sound fun and the idea of becoming a scout interested me enormously. The only problem was, you had to be eleven years old to join and I wasn't quite ten. I was desperate and I didn't want to join the cubs as that was for babies. So I asked Mum and Dad if I could go and they agreed. On Thursday evening I took myself off to Bow Baptist Church in Bow Road, which was the base of 38th Poplar scout troop. It never occurred to me to question why it was the 38th Poplar when we were in Bow. Poplar was another East End of London borough adjoining Bow in the days before it all became Tower Hamlets.

For my age I was quite short, with an angelic face and I certainly didn't look eleven years old. I followed the directions I had been given and I walked along Bow Road for about three quarters of a mile and came to Bow Church, which stood on an island in the middle of the road. To me Bow Church always looked impressive. I carried on in the direction of Stratford East and then on the left hand side I found it, Bow Baptist Church. The church was walled on the side next to the road, with a long row of internal wooden doors taken from the remains of houses that had been bombed out. It looked quite strange to see a fence made of all different coloured wooden doors.

The entrance through these was made from two pairs of doors, which had been nailed onto backing boards and then hinged onto posts. These opened into a courtyard, part of which was an old graveyard. At night the doors were closed, chained and padlocked. I have to say it all looked a little off putting. I walked into the grounds on my own and on my left was a row of tombstones all standing up against the side wall of an adjoining house. I walked down the poorly lit path toward the light coming from an open door, which was the entrance to the hall at the rear of the church. I later discovered that the reason for the unique fencing was the war effort. Many buildings that had iron railings and/or gates had them removed, probably without choice, for the manufacture of ammunition.

Thankfully there were no application forms to fill in and I guess due to the problems of wayward youths in those days, Scout troops were probably a little more flexible in their rules when it came to vetting new applicants. A few questions and I was in. I have to say, joining the scouts was probably one the greatest things that ever happened to me. I couldn't possibly know how much the simple act of turning up that Thursday night would change my life.

Scout nights were Tuesdays and Thursdays and our Scout Master, or Skip as we called him, was another Jim who lived in the house next door to the church with his wife and daughter. I am not sure if the house was tied to the church in some way, but I rather think it was. Skip was strict and he commanded a lot of respect. When he shouted 'Troop On Parade' we all loved the scramble that followed. We stood in our patrols with Patrol Leader in the front and his second at the rear.
Young boys standing to attention with hands pressed hard into our sides and shoulders pushed back almost too far to look smart, patrols were awarded points for just about everything they did and collected on a league table. We all desperately wanted our own patrols to be the best. I am proud to say, that we- 'The Eagles' patrol - were nearly always the top of the league, thanks to our fourteen-year-old Patrol Leader, Peter Chandler.

We mastered the art of forming the straightest possible line and Peter had us in line in height order which, because I was so short compared to the rest, put me at the back of the patrol just in front of the patrol's 'second'. I think knowing that I was under age is what kept me there without complaining. However, I was never happy at being so far from the front. I really wanted to stand behind Peter. He would stand there in his well-pressed uniform looking immaculate. Uniforms in those days comprised of a green beret, worn pulled down over the right eye, khaki shirt and shorts. Our troop colour was red, as defined by our scarves, neatly held in place by a woven leather woggle and bound neatly by a white lanyard. Khaki knee-length socks with elasticated garters complete with green tassels. These were perfectly placed on the outside of each calf. All topped off (or should that be bottomed off?) with well-polished, black shoes. At the head of our patrol stood Peter, hands behind his back with right thumb held in left hand. The pride I felt being part of this elite team was immeasurable.

I did not have a uniform for a few weeks as I had to prove to Mum and Dad that I was going to stick at this before they would make that investment. So there I was each week in my black jeans, white shirt, half-in-half-out and scruffy shoes. But stick it I did and after not too much time, I got my uniform. The shirt I had was second hand and had a sort of fleecy lining, but the rest of my uniform was new. I remember when I finally had the money to buy my uniform, going up to Baden Powell House (scout headquarters), which was situated half way between Stepney Green and Whitechapel underground stations on the District line, to get myself rigged out.

I had my money and I remember buying myself a beret, socks, scarf, woggle, lanyard and garters. After all these years I can still remember the smell of the inside of my beret with its black leather band. I now had my full uniform and I could stand in line and really feel part of the patrol, and that was a great feeling. Peter was my mentor and I soon learned everything he had to teach me. He was always so smart and his shoes always so shiny. I would look down at my own and I realized it was time for change.

As mum worked full time, I soon learned how to press my own uniform and suddenly much to Mum's delight, a shiny polished surface appeared on my shoes. What was this miraculous change happening to little Jimmy? This was just one of many changes to come.

Soon Mum, who was no great one with a needle and thread, was stitching badges onto my shirtsleeves, of which there were many (badges, that is). I went in for everything but my favourite thing was cooking. This was something that would really come in handy at our weekend and summer camps. How to become Mr Popular with a gang of kids big enough to pulverize you? Be able to fill their bellies! I had learned how to open air cook long before I joined the scouts from our family holidays camping. My mum could make porridge on an open fire without ever burning it. Topped with sugar and a knob of butter it was a firm favourite of mine. With my enthusiasm for the scouts it took me no time at all to graduate from being a tenderfoot. I had memorised the Scout Promise and Laws and I was soon up the front of the troop being tested and sworn in. I lived for Tuesdays and Thursdays and my life was transformed.

The rest of the year passed quickly and so did Christmas. I had been given a lot of toys, which were placed in a pillowcase at the end of my bed. I was up at five in the morning, full of excitement opening them. Of course I had long since given up on Father Christmas being real, but I was once a true believer in him, to the point where one year I told

Mum that I had truly seen his hand disappear up the chimney in my bedroom.

The winter of 1958 soon passed and it was time for my first weekend camp. In fact it was our Easter camp, which was always held at Cuffley in Hertfordshire. We all met outside Bow Road underground station where we took the District Line to Mile End and onwards to Kings Cross. Kings Cross station was such an exciting place; full of people rushing about catching trains and the air was mixed with smoke as old steam trains pulled in or out of the station. We would pile into the old corridor carriages that were pulled to Cuffley by one of these old steam engines and there was no greater excitement in a boy's life than to go on a steam train.

We arrived at Cuffley and our many kit-bags, rucksacks and our famous 'troop cart' were unloaded from the train (well, thrown onto the platform). Everything was carried through the ticket barrier, where the collector would count heads by bashing them as they came through the gate. The cart was assembled and the tents and heavy gear were loaded on. Rucksacks and kit bags were carried by all except by those scouts on cart duty, whose kit was on the cart.

I stood there looking at my kit bag, which was just a little smaller than me and wondered how on earth I would manage to carry it. Off we marched to the campsite, which was a long walk for a small boy, but somehow I managed to carry it. After a few of these weekend camps I soon learned that if I dragged back a bit, I could thumb passing cars (there weren't many in those days) for a lift. A small lad with a huge kit bag drew sympathy from most drivers and I was often lucky and I would soon be speeding past the troop sitting in the back of a car. I would always thank my hosts most politely and set about waiting for the troop to arrive. I don't know why, but I was never told off for doing this and hitching was never banned. The troop would roll up and one or two would give me the evil eye for not having had to walk, but that never lasted. In the scouts I never once came up against bullying or anyone horrible. I think that is why I loved it all so much.

Skip would go to the office and pay our camping fees and then we would all set off to our allotted site. Tents would soon be erected, groundsheets laid. Skip would come round and allocate six boys to a tent. The tents had openings front and back, but not all of them had flysheets, which is an additional cover to give the tent extra protection against the rain. Tents without flysheets had a tendency to leak a bit in heavy rain, especially when some idiot would want to get up and have a wee in the night. In doing so he would tread all over us and then probably scrape his shoulder against the sloping roof. If it was raining, where you touched the tent, was where it would leak. Next to farting in the tent, scraping the tent roof in the rain was a good way to find out who your friends were.

I think, thanks to scouting, I have always loved getting up early in the mornings. I have always felt the morning is the best time of the day. As I got older and more experienced in camping I would often be one of the first up and over to the showers for a nice open air cold shower.

I would invariably have the fire alight before the rest were stirring. I loved the smell of the camp fire in the mornings as it took hold. The wood would often be a bit damp and hard to light, but once it was going, brilliant. I am still a lover of open fires. Huge billycans would be filled and placed on the fire ready to make tea and then our daily ration of porridge. Our resident cook was Ted Rouse, who we called 'Wishbone' after the cook in a television program called Rawhide. While the water was getting hot, Ted would be over to those showers and back before it was boiling. No one hangs around in an open air, cold shower for long at Easter time. I would soon become an old hand at scout camping especially at Cuffley, which was our nearest and preferred camp.

Easter 1958 was not only special to me because it was my first scout camp but because my tenth birthday fell on one of the days we were away. My day started out by being given all manner of presents by my chums, in the main stuff they had bought at the site's tuck shop. Then I was dragged out of bed, thrown under the cold shower and allowed to dress, when I eventually found my clothes. Next, just like a salad, I was lightly tossed in a blanket to a great height, eleven times (I had lied about my age to get in remember?), being allowed to bang on the floor each time. This sort of counted as being given the bumps, which is when your dearest friends grab you by your limbs and proceed to throw you into the air, of course not letting go and allowing you to bang your backside on the ground on the way down. Your body is thrown up once for each year plus at least once for luck. You know the luck is working if your mates don't manage to break your back in the process.

I had taken Mum and Dad's birthday cards with me and in one was a ten shilling note, and wow, was I now popular. Later that morning I went over to the tuck shop and bought myself a staff, which was considerably taller than me but I was thrilled with it. The rest of the day passed without further incident regarding my birthday and it ended with songs around a campfire. Each patrol had to perform a sketch and, for anything remotely theatrical, I was always first in line. The Eagles' sketch was simple. Peter, our patrol leader would want to hold a conversation on the telephone to his second, Tony. To do this he would require some volunteers, usually the other patrol leaders, their seconds, and possibly Skip or our ASM (Assistant Scout Master). A long piece of rope was required and the volunteers, eight on this occasion, would be asked to act as telegraph poles holding the line of rope high and taut above their heads. Peter and Tony would hold an end of the rope each and through their imaginary telephones have a conversation, which ran something like this:

'Hello Tony, how are you?'

'I'm all right Peter,'

'What's the weather like there?'

'It's blowing a gale,'

'Really! Here too.'

Peter would then tell the telegraph poles to sway in these gale force winds.

'Is it raining there Tony?'

'Yep,'

'Here too,' Peter would shout and then four of us from The Eagles patrol would run out with wet sponges spraying the telegraph poles with gale swept rain and in fits of laughter in the process.

'You been fishing lately Peter?'

'Yep.'

'How many d'yer catch?'

'Oh,' he would reply as he slowly looked along the line and loudly counted the eight mugs holding the rope, 'I caught eight bigguns today!'. Much hilarity would follow as we had caught out our ASM and the other patrol leaders and seconds. Oh such happy days! It was a wonderful weekend and I loved it. A real bonus was the fact that Skip's wife and little daughter had come along. Skip's wife was really nice to us all and when you are young and away from home it's sort of nice to have a surrogate mum around. We soon became particularly fond of Skip's little daughter and we were very protective of her.

Ours wasn't the first camp they had been to and we were pointedly told about a camp they had been at a couple of years before when Skip's daughter had badly scalded her backside. Someone, having finished cooking breakfast, had left a frying pan full of hot water next to the fire to sit and soak ready to clean it out. Thankfully it had cooled down a bit before Skip's little girl fell backwards and sat right in it. Nevertheless she got badly scalded. Thankfully it was a pan of hot water and not hot fat. Skip showed us the burns to her lower back, which served as a memorable lesson to us all.

Despite these warnings, accidents still happened and that weekend, like an idiot, I was to have one. I was removing a small billycan of boiling water from the fire using a wooden tent peg mallet to pick it up with. Unfortunately for me, the head of the mallet was loose and turned under the weight of the can and the bubbling water spilled all over my right foot. It quickly seeped through lace holes on my shoe and into my sock which thankfully went some way to cooling the water down a bit. I yelled out in pain and quickly pulled my shoe and sock off to reveal a blister coming up the diameter of a fifty pence piece. The ASM was first at the scene and I was rushed to the first aid hut with my foot submerged in a bucket of cold water. The blister eventually stopped rising and the attending medic burst it. The wound was dressed and I, thanks to my trusty staff, managed to hobble around for the rest of the day. The next day as planned we set off for home.

Thanks to my injury I was allowed to sit on the troop's kit cart, towed and pushed as usual by the bigger boys in the troop. What luxury...My journey didn't end at Bow Road Station, as I expected. To avoid another change of trains, Skip and I got out at Mile End station outside of which was a taxi rank. I was taken home by taxi; my first ride in a black cab. It was Easter Monday and it was my Mum who answered the door to Skip's knock. She took one look at me hopping about on the doorstep and asked Skip what had happened as we went in. He explained things to her at the same time apologizing. She did no more than ask him if he would like a cup of tea.

Dad was out in the garden knocking something up in his shed and I was plonked into an armchair. When he walked in, he was holding a pair of wooden stilts he had made me. He took one look at me and said,

'What's 'e done?' Mum told him what had happened, trying to save Skip the embarrassment of having to explain again. I would imagine today a parent would be suing for negligence. I was OK and thankfully nothing more happened.

I was sitting in the kitchen looking at the stilts Dad had made me thinking these were my birthday present and that my birthday was over. Suddenly my Dad said in a fit of generosity that he thought my bike was too small for me and that he was fed up with seeing me on other kids' bikes. It was time for a new bike. My Dad, as part of his unpredictability, would occasionally have a fit of generosity. This would happen mostly when he had accused me of doing something that I hadn't done. When later it transpired that my denials were true and that I had been punished for nothing, buying me something was his way of saying sorry. He would very rarely say 'I am sorry'. That was hard for me, but if anything, it taught me that saying those three little words 'I am sorry' is worth more than any gift in lieu.

On this occasion he was being generous because I had been hurt and it was also my birthday. He said that when I was able to walk properly, we would go up the bike shop in Roman Road and he would buy me a bike and true to his word, he did. About ten days later he came in from work and said, 'Come on we're going out.' I walked out the front door and went with him on his motorbike to Roman Road. We stopped outside the bike shop and I was thrilled that he had remembered his promise and that neither I, nor Mum had had to remind him. We went in and he had a word with the manager. The next thing I remember were the bikes, (that were the right size for me and which were hanging on display frames fixed to the ceiling of the shop) were being brought down for me to try.

Blimey, what did I want, Straight, Cow Horn or Drop handlebars? There were so many to choose from. I kept looking up at the rows of bikes and then I saw it. It was sort of a rusty red and it had straight handlebars. It was lightweight and beautiful.

'Can I have that one please Dad?' The man looked at Dad and his eyebrows rose, as if to say 'yeah, right'. The bike came down, I tried it and it was love at first sight. Sadly for my Dad it was the most expensive bike in the shop at twenty-three pounds and in 1958 that was a lot of money. I also have to say at this point that no matter how rotten my Dad could be at times and no matter how much I was frightened of him, I saw his moments of generosity as moments of his love and I loved it. Thankfully, it also taught me that you couldn't buy love or forgiveness, as he would so often try to do. It is sad when a man would rather part with hard-earned cash than say a few words which are free, although for him obviously, not easy to say.

Dad paid a good deposit on the bike and the rest was on the 'never never' (hire purchase). All I had to do was cycle to the shop once a week to make the payment and get the little receipt sticker stuck in the repayment book. With my new bike and a grin from ear to ear, I was left to cycle home from the shop. When I got back to Morville Street, my mates were out in the street and the attention my new bike drew was fantastic. What a birthday present!

I had to miss scouts for the next two weeks but after that I was back in full swing. I could hardly wait for Tuesday night, to be able to get back to the scouts and this time, to go on my new bike. As soon as I got into the hall I was welcomed by everyone I knew, and in particular by Skip and Peter. It was just so good to be back among my friends. The evening as usual just flew by too quickly for me and before we knew it was time for the end of evening announcements.

Skip did the usual bit about church parade on Sunday and who would be carrying the troop flag and the Union Jack and then he gave out to each patrol leader some leaflets to pass down the line. They contained the details of the coming Summer Camp. The cost is something I cannot remember, probably blocked out by excitement at the time, but the camp was to be held at Pett Level Farm, Pett near Hastings and it was to be for two weeks.

At the end of the announcements Skip shouted out 'Troop, Dismiss' and we all stood smartly to attention, saluted and broke up. There was the usual noise as we all said our goodbyes or rushed up to Skip or our ASM to ask questions about the evening, the announcements or Summer Camp. I rushed over to my friend Tim and asked him if he would be going, but he didn't seem that enthusiastic about the idea and shrugged his shoulders,
'I don't know really, I doubt it'.

I left the hall and rode my bike like the wind back to No. 49. I wanted to get home well before Mum and Dad went to bed so that I could show them my piece of paper and ask if I could go. I thought they were bound to say yes, as they loved the idea of me being in the scouts and I think the change in me was more than obvious and I might add, for the better. I think a lot of the mischief I had got up to until then was more out of boredom and loneliness than from being a bad kid. I got to the door of 49, pulled my key from out of the neck of my shirt on its grubby white tape and put it into the lock. The door flew back with the key still in the lock and I almost hung myself in the process. I quickly rolled my bike down the hall but, fairly quietly as I had become programmed to,

'Shh, the MacDonalds'.

I got down to our kitchen, opened the door and, as usual, Dad was sitting by the fire. Mum was making him a cup of tea in the scullery. I wheeled my bike into the garden and covered it over. I tried to slow myself down as I tried to calmly hang my coat behind the door.

'Dad, Dad,' I said in a hurry, he looked at me,

'Wot?' he said, as he raked out the bottom of the fire in the Kitchener.

'Guess what. In July the scouts are having a summer camp for two weeks, can I go?' As I poured out my request, Mum walked through the scullery door carrying a huge white mug of tea for Dad and a smaller one for herself.

'What do you think Ede?' he said.

'What do I think about what? Jimmy, do you want some tea or would you rather have Ovaltine?' she asked,

'Ovaltine! Yuk, tea please, are there any biscuits?'

'Yes,' and with that she turned and went back into the kitchen.

She quickly returned with my tea and biscuits and said to Dad,

'Now then - what do I think about what?'

'About him going to a summer camp with the scouts?'

'Well depends if he behaves himself I suppose.'

'Of course I'll behave myself. If I do can I go? Can I? Can I?'

'We'll see,' Mum said and that was the end of the matter, for then. But for me, I knew I would be going. I knew I could behave and I knew at the end of the day they wouldn't say no…

Chapter Eight - Stage Debut

Easter holidays were over and I was back at school. My friend Jack was a couple of months younger than me and joining the scouts wasn't his thing. I never really asked him as he was too young and there was no way his parents were going to let him go all the way to Bow Baptist church twice a week. It was far enough for me, but a lot further for Jack. Thanks to the scouts, our nights of mischief together grew far less, of which I am sure his Mum and Dad were glad. School was great and this year I got into drama. I played the King in our school play. I took the script home and, with Mum's help, I soon learned the words. Sadly, due to work commitments, Mum and Dad never came to the school play. On the opening night (or more likely late afternoon!), there I was, on stage dressed in a white satin shirt, black and gold pumpkin shorts, black tights and a gold cardboard crown, a sight to behold. Everything went well and I delivered my lines word perfect. I wasn't shy or frightened and I had discovered something else that I enjoyed very much: the limelight!

Although I was only ten years old, I was becoming more and more sexually aware. Not sexually mature but sexually aware. It surely couldn't have been an early rush of hormones. However, whatever it was for some reason, I was becoming more and more attracted to men and I found myself staring at them at every opportunity. Especially when I could do so without anyone knowing. This growing desire frightened me and I was beginning to wonder more and more what on earth was happening to me.

I remember once during the recent Easter holidays, I was allowed to go on my own to see my Aunt Eve and Uncle Billy (Mum's brother). They had moved from Bethnal Green to another flat in Stangate Street, which was across the road from St Thomas's Hospital, just south of Westminster Bridge.

Although I was only ten years old I was allowed a great deal of freedom, which, on reflection was probably too much for a boy of that age. I think this is the age when boys in particular are so vulnerable to those that prey on them. Thankfully, in those days things seemed a little safer than today, or maybe it was just down to the fact that the media weren't so technically fast at reporting such problems.

There was no problem with my parents for me to make the journey to Westminster Station on my own. Westminster is on the District line, and so were we; therefore the journey was easy. I caught the underground train from Bow Road straight through without the need to change trains. I found the prospect of making the journey really exciting and I felt so grown-up making such trips on my own. I purchased my child's return ticket from the grubby little ticket office at Bow Road underground station and went to the correct platform to board the westbound train. Bow Road was the first station in the westbound direction where the tube train went underground. Half of the platform was in daylight and the other half under cover. The tracks to the next stop, Mile End, were quite straight and without leaning out too far over the edge of the platform you could see Mile End Station in the distance down the long dark tunnel.

The train suddenly came clattering downhill into the station and drew to a halt. The doors automatically opened and without hesitation I got on. Before the doors closed again I was sitting down trying to read my comic but there was no way the excitement of this journey was going to allow me to do that. It seemed like I was getting a huge adrenaline rush just by making this journey. I looked up from flicking through the pages and I couldn't help but notice the man sitting opposite me. He was extremely attractive, with his tousled hair and he was sporting a five o'clock shadow. He was wearing a brown leather bomber jacket and jeans and for some reason I found I was attracted to his good looks. What was even worse, I found my eyes kept drifting southwards down to the fly of his trousers and try as I might I couldn't stop myself from looking. I desperately tried to read my comic but gravity just seemed to pull the comic down and once again I found myself staring at this chap.

Of course, at my age, he probably thought I was a bit weird and took no notice of me, thank goodness. In fact he probably didn't even notice me at all. Although, he might have done had he been the wrong type of man! I could have easily been one of those boys who find themselves in the wrong place at the wrong time. I can now look back and see that for some reason it was not part of the plan of things that I should be harmed, or perhaps I was just Lucky Jim?

The journey was fun and I was soon at my aunt's enjoying myself with my cousins Kathy and Simon. The thought of the journey was soon out of mind and I got on with being a ten-year-old. It was a warm sunny day and I took my cousins over to the local park and we spent some time playing about and enjoying the swings and slides. Sadly the day went all too quickly and it was soon time for me to go home again. Aunt Eve wrapped up a piece of coffee cake for me and off I went. There was no fear of me picking at the cake as I hated coffee cake then, and still do now. The sun was still bright in the sky as I walked back across Westminster Bridge towards Big Ben and the Houses of Parliament, which stood there in front of me looking elegantly dirty, against a backdrop of blue spring sky. When I got to the traffic lights at the other side of the bridge, I crossed the road with eyes fixed on the statue of Queen Boadicea standing there in her chariot with spear in hand. The wheels of her chariot had large curved blades attached to each hub for the sole aim of cutting down the enemy. I was soon safely across the road and entering Westminster station. I walked down the really dark tunnel, which seemed to be even darker having just come out of such bright sunlight. I found the eastbound District line platform and waited for the next train that showed any station on the front of it beyond my destination of Bow Road. Usually they read Barking, Dagenham East or Upminster. The train rolled in and stopped and then with a pisshh, the doors opened. I leapt aboard and had a swing on the straphanging handles, which were just beyond my reach. I would leap up to them hang on and then swing hand over hand down the carriage.

I could see some of the passengers scowling at me so I sat down to behave. I could hear my mum telling me that if I didn't behave, I wouldn't be able to do this again or even worse, there would be no Summer Camp. Suppose one of these people knew my mum, blimey if they told her what I had been up to, that would be it. No camp and no more train journeys. I settled down with my piece of cake in my lap and comic in hand. We had got as far as Aldgate East when two workmen got on the train, obviously going home from work. They were filthy dirty wearing overalls and dirty great boots and you could smell the trench dirt and sweat on them. In those days men dressed like that would stand out of politeness, as they wouldn't want to get the seats dirty. I sat and watched them talk to each other. I couldn't hear what they were saying but once again I found myself staring and wondering what was happening to me? I really didn't understand. I looked away through the window of the train and watched the cables that were fixed to the wall of the tunnel, as they seemed to bounce up and down as we sped along. I found the cables almost mesmerising and soon we were entering Bow Road station and it was time for me to get off. The walk home wasn't too far from the station and took me past Bow Road police station. There was just time for a quick pat of the horses. I was allowed to make many such trips on my own.

Chapter Nine - The Cinema

As usual school had finished and I left via the Malmesbury Road gate saying goodbye to Jack. I rushed home to do my chores going to Roman Road to get Mum's errands and then back out into the street to play with my mates. I was playing when Mum came home at about five pm and as she passed me she called over to me that I was to come in at six o'clock for tea. I shouted 'OK' as she went in the house. Dad got home at his usual time, around five-thirty, and, as I was starving hungry, there was no delaying me going in for tea. What I always tried to do was have tea and then get back out again to play for half an hour or so. Sometimes I could, it depended on Mum's mood. The trouble was getting me to come back in again. Every time she called me I would beg for another two minutes and it was that which made her reluctant to let me out again after tea. Why didn't someone tell me that?

The year was marching on. It was Whitsun and the last school holiday before we broke up for summer. I was under threat to behave myself as now I was old enough to be left to my own devices during the holiday and Mum did not want to hear one word of trouble about me.

The weather was getting warmer and days were growing good and long. During school holidays I was allowed to stay out a little later. I loved playing street games like hopscotch, tin can tommy, or cricket. For cricket we used to jam the stumps into the lifting holes cast into the manhole covers that ran down the centre of our street. Of course, we only used soft balls but I am sure at times the noise we made must have driven the people down the street nuts. Naturally, like all kids, we never realized and if anyone complained they would be in the wrong as far as we were concerned. The week was rolling by and one day one of my mates told me there was a great film on at the Ritz cinema in St Stephen's Road. The film was called The Battle of the River Plate and was about the sinking, or should I perhaps say the scuttling, of the German battleship The Graf Spee. As I was hooked on war films I wanted to go.

In those days films rolled continuously, first a short B movie and then the main feature - the A movie. You would pay, go in, sit down and watch the film until you got to the point where you came in. How many times I went to the flicks (the cinema) with Mum and Dad and I can still hear my Mum say, 'Oh well, let's go, this is where we came in'. We would then get up and go home. It was a weird way to watch a movie as you would often watch the end before the beginning.

I asked my Dad if I could go to the flicks and he said he would ask Mum what she thought. She said it would be OK as long as I came straight home afterward. Of course, what else was I going to do? Dad gave me two bob (two shillings - equal to 10p) and off I went. It was about a fifteen to twenty minute walk to the Ritz from where we lived and I remember running most of the way. The Ritz was a little fleapit cinema sitting at the top of St Stephens Road just off Roman Road and its days as a cinema eventually ended in the late sixties when it was turned into a little wholesale warehouse.

I was now at a point in my life where something was about to happen to me, which up until now has always been a secret. Even now I do not find it easy to speak of, as there is still an element of a ten-year-old boy's shame left inside me.

I purchased my ticket and was shown to my seat by the lady with the torch. I flipped the seat down and was almost immediately drawn into the movie. Battleships were in outright war with each other as their guns blazed in the night sky. The noise was loud and the cinema kept flashing alight as each salvo blazed away. I was mesmerized and I hadn't noticed the man arrive and sit down next to me. I was sitting in a row that was practically empty and he sat there to my right with his legs wide apart, hands resting on his knees. Although I was engrossed in the film I couldn't help but notice that when he moved his left hand from his knee to his thigh I could feel his knuckles against my leg. I was wearing shorts and the first time this happened I took little notice. It was the action movie that had my attention. I could watch a film and be in it to the point that I would take little notice of anything going on around me. However, I became more and more aware of the pressure he was putting against my leg with his hand. His hands had also started to move up and down more. Pressure turned into a gentle stroking motion. My eyes were fixed forward and I didn't dare move. The film was becoming less interesting and my heart raced so fast I thought it was going to burst. I still felt that this was probably a coincidence and after a few minutes I found myself wishing that he meant it.

As he touched my leg more and more I sat there frozen to my seat. This seemed to go on for an age and eventually he got extremely brave and his huge hand gently clasped my small thigh. I thought I was going to burst - not with fear like you would expect but with excitement. It was a very dangerous thing for him to have done as I could have screamed out at any time. Perhaps children generally in this situation do not scream out. Perhaps they just get up and walk away and tell someone. All I know is that I didn't. I just sat there.

The movie went from the flashing guns in a night-time battle to the daylight of the following day and the cinema seemed just a little brighter. I braved a look at the man to my right in this brighter light. He was about thirty years old and he looked quite ordinary except for the fact that he was touching me as he stared ahead as though nothing was happening. I just sat there and copied him, staring at the screen but I could smell him next to me with his faint smell of body odour and the hair cream he had used to slick his hair back. What was I to do? I had never experienced such excitement and I gave no thought at all to the possible danger I was in. Of course we never knew of danger like that. How could I realize that I was at a point where I could have been one of those missing boys later found dead in a park or the canal? Yet no thought of this crossed my mind, just the excitement of it all.

The film, for me, had gone round and I was at the point where I came in and I got up to leave. He swung his legs right to let me out of the row and into the aisle. I walked the uphill slope toward the exit. I did not look round - I didn't dare - and I quickly left the cinema. It was dark and I turned left into St Stephen's Road and then right in Roman Road, so that I could look into the shop windows. My heart had slowed down and I was really confused by all of this. What on earth had I done? What had happened to me? Why didn't it frighten me? Why did I like it? So many questions for such a young head to understand and not one answer to any of them. Well I had one answer - or at least a feeling - it was wrong!

I stopped for a moment outside the toyshop window and I was looking in when suddenly I could see a reflection of someone standing next to me. I slowly looked up into the face of the man who had sat next to me in the Ritz. He had a warm friendly face that as I remember had a look of nervous innocence.

He smiled at me and said, 'Hello' and I smiled back. How crazy can a boy be?Again he said 'Hello' only this time he asked me my name and told me his. He then smiled at me and walked off across the road. He glanced back and I followed him as though he was the Pied Piper of Hamlin. He walked to a new block of flats that had just been built below which were empty shells of what would soon be more shops. He continued to the end of the block where a staircase led down to the courtyard and parking area at the back. We went down and walked along the back wall of the block where there was a row of doors, each one leading to the basement storage area for the shops above. We came to an unlocked door, which he opened and he quietly slipped inside and I like an idiot, followed him. He closed the door and then in the darkness I felt him reach out for me. His hand touched my head and stroked my hair and neck as he gently pulled me toward him. I stood against him and his hands reached down my back as he softly squeezed me into him and I could feel his excitement, and as hard as it is for me to say this, I was excited too. He had sat himself down on the cold concrete floor and held my hand. Maybe it was to stop me running away or just to reassure me I was safe - I have no idea. At first I couldn't really see much, which just seemed to add to the excitement of it all. Soon my eyes adjusted to the little light there was and I could see him sitting there with his trousers around his ankles. He reached out to me and undid my shorts, which also fell to the floor. His knees were bent so he could reach me and his feet were placed between mine.

I felt no fear as he reached up under my armpits and slowly lowered me down onto him. We lay there and my excitement was perhaps equal to that of a teenager experiencing sex for the first time. I had no consideration for anything as I lay there with my head cradled in his arms. He said nothing to me as he enjoyed the feel of my body, as I did of his. He did not have an orgasm he just laid there cuddling me. After a few minutes we dressed and left. I ran home and I never saw him again.

After my experience in the Ritz, I tried to get on with my life as a young boy doing all the things a young boy does, but I was having a problem. I had become aware of a form of excitement that I liked very much and I wanted more of it. I became hungry for the company of my own sex and, what's more, I wanted physical contact. Not because someone had corrupted me but because I liked what had happened to me and I simply wanted more. However, I am sad that I had experienced this at such a young age and in such a sordid way as it meant as a young boy I had to learn how to carry a secret that was to be a great burden for me. It's funny how through life some of us endure the burden of such huge secrets. I still cannot believe that at last I have shared my Ritz experience. Until now, I have always been so ashamed of what happened that night. What is really sad is that this experience led me to want more of what I was clearly too young to have. I was simply too immature to deal with this sort of thing. Perhaps, unknowingly, my need for more physical contact was obvious to those who were around to take advantage of me.

Time soon passed and at school we were breaking up for the summer holidays. I rushed home after school and ran along Malmesbury Road, which was having new paving stones laid along it. Every few yards on the curb side of the road was a pile of sand, which the workmen mixed with limestone and water to make a sort of sloppy mix that was used to set the paving slabs in. I was having a great time running up and down the piles of sand. There it was ahead of me - a small mountain of sand. A dune in the Sahara! I took a great run at it, screaming 'Geronimo' as I leapt; only it wasn't sand but the sloppy mixture. I landed squarely on it on both feet and promptly, sank up to my waist. My new sandals, socks and shorts were in it and so was I, up to my neck! I thought 'Oh shit! The scouts! The summer camp!' I managed to get myself out and got home as quickly as I could. I pulled out my latchkey, and took my shoes and socks off. As I did so it hurt, as the sand and lime were abrasive against my young skin.

I got to the kitchen door and opened it. My mouth dropped

open and fear set in,

'Hello Dad,' I said. He was kneeling down working on a bit of his motorbike, which was sitting on the floor on a piece of newspaper. He looked round at me.

'What the fucking hell's happened to you?' he shouted.

I blurted out what I had done and thought it was temper time, but much to my surprise he just laughed.

'We'd better get that fucking lot off you before your mother gets in,' he said.

I couldn't believe my luck. I think he loved it when I got into that sort of trouble. I think it reminded him of when he was a young boy.

He got me out of my shorts, and told me to stand out in the yard. He put on a huge saucepan of water to boil and came out to try to brush me down. The sloppy mixture had by now dried on it really hurt as he gently brushed me with his leathery hand. I cried out 'That hurts!'

'Wait there,' he said while he poured the hot water into our washing-up bowl. He then picked me up, carried me to the sink and stood me in the bowl of warm soapy water. Slowly, with one of the tea mugs, he poured water down my legs and the sandy mix softened and started to run down into the bowl.

'Your new fucking sandals are a mess!' he said. 'You know what your muvver's like about shoes,' he went on.

'I know Dad, but I was only running up and down the piles of sand. How was I to know that one of them was that sloppy stuff?'

'Well, let's see if we can get all this shit off yer.'

For some reason he found this really funny and although it was sore cleaning me up, we both laughed together, which was something we didn't do too often.

I was scrubbed up and he sent me to my room to put on some clean clothes. When I came back he had put on some more water to heat and then he rinsed my clothes through. They were soon on the line and next he was cleaning my sandals.

'There you are,' he said. I couldn't believe it – they were like new again. 'You had better put 'em away.'

I picked them up and took them to my room. I couldn't believe it, as my Dad was never really like this. For some unknown reason he was in a really good mood. Especially considering he was mending a bit of his motorbike and I had interrupted him, this behaviour was most unusual. Mum came home and Dad said that I had had an accident on the way home from school and fell into a pile of mixture they were using to lay the paving stones in Malmesbury Road. He told her he had washed my shorts out and they were out on the line but there was no other damage. Was this my Dad I asked myself?

'What are you doing?' she asked him, as he still wrestled with the bit of motorbike on the kitchen floor. He actually brought his bike into the kitchen once one winter. He stripped the engine down and got the cylinder head re-bored and then re-assembled it. The house stank of engine oil for days.

'It's Keith's carburettor. It's knackered. I think the jets are worn and he's asked me to look at it for him.'

'Oh,' she said as she went through to the kitchen to get tea ready.

'I think I'll drop it round to him after tea and tell him to get some new jets. That might do it.'

Uncle Keith was Dad's brother-in-law, married to his sister Jane. He was a bit of a character really. He used to work as a cooper in a barrelmakers under one of the railway arches in Rounton Road in Bow - just along from a shroud makers which was owned by Elsie and Doris Waters - the sisters of Jack Warner, of Dixon of Dock Green fame.

We had dinner and afterwards Dad shot round to see Uncle Keith. Mum brought in my shorts and pressed them for me. I said I was sorry, I didn't mean to get in a mess - it was an accident but she never said anything. I think like me, she too was amazed at Dad's good mood.

I was in bed when Dad came in. He went down the hall and he was making more noise than usual. He and Uncle Keith had been to the pub. I hated it when Dad had been drinking, as then you never knew what might happen next. I heard him go through the kitchen door and start to tell my Mum the latest on what Nanny Wilkinson had done to Jane.

'Do you know, Ede,' I heard him say, 'the ole lady (his name for his mum) nicked (stole) their Sunday joint out of the cupboard. Can you believe that?'

His mood was good and I could sleep. I always used to worry about Mum until I knew what mood he was in. I used to hate it if they had arguments and that was always a real possibility if he had sunk a few pints.

The next day was Sunday and I was up bright and early, as I had to get myself ready for church parade. This Sunday I was carrying the troop flag. Mum and Dad were still not up so I took them tea in bed. I hated going into their room. They used to keep a white enamel bucket with a lid on it in their bedroom to pee in, to save them going to the outside toilet. This wasn't emptied daily and the room always had an acrid smell of stale piss in it.

Church parade was over and I came home in a really good mood. After the service we had been stacking piles of newspaper we had been collecting. Old newspaper had a scrap value and so we all collected it avidly as we were saving the money up to buy our own troop van, which was to be for our camping trips.

As I walked back into No. 49 I could smell Sunday lunch cooking. I entered the kitchen and there was Mum sitting at the table with a pile of fresh peas on a newspaper, shelling them. The radio was on and she was listening to Two Way Family Favourites with Jean Metcalfe and Cliff Mitchelmore. Even to this day, when I smell roast lamb cooking, I can still hear that programmer's signature tune, 'With a Song in my Heart', and then the sound of Jean Metcalfe as she announced a request for some soldier in BFPO somewhere or other, with fond love from his dear wife and children. I always thought it must be really sad to hear such a request if you were far away from home and your loved ones.

'Where's Dad?' I asked as I took off my jacket to hang behind the kitchen door.
'He's out in the shed mucking about with an old drill, or something.'
'Oh,' I replied, thinking I should keep out of his way before he roped me into to helping him. Helping Dad could be a recipe for disaster. Mum told me to put my coat away and to change out of my uniform and to come back and help her. I wasn't about to argue; summer camp was getting closer and that was no time to upset anyone. I quickly changed and got back to the kitchen to finish off the job of shelling. The smells coming out of the scullery were mouthwateringly good.

Although my Mum was no great pastry cook, there were few people who could turn out a Sunday roast as well as she could. She could make a Yorkshire pudding that would try to take out the top of the oven and we always had a Yorkshire on Sundays whatever the meat.

Mum still made gravy in those days by pouring some of the green water (the water the cabbage was cooked in) into a baking tin and then placing that on one of the gas rings over a low heat. Then she would take her old spoon, put in some sugar and hold it over one of the other gas rings to heat. Very quickly the sugar would boil, turn black and then catch fire. It was then she would plunge it into the bubbling green water and stir it around. The green water would turn gravy coloured but it would be as thin as water itself. I guess this was a leftover from the war days when getting hold of gravy browning or flour was probably hard.

I could easily finish my meal before Mum and Dad and I would sit there and wait patiently for any leftovers on their plates. There invariably would be and I would then proceed to demolish that as well. I think next to my Mum's cooking, my next favourite meal was, pie and mash. You could buy this in any one of the many pie and mash shops dotted around the East End.

My favourite pie and mash shop was in Roman Road. There were two shops in that road and both called Kellys but, in my opinion, the best was the one nearest to Parnell Road. Outside of the shop was a market stall from which they sold live eels. They would be slithering about in their own slime in huge tin trays. At the end of the stall was a wooden block and the fishmonger was there in his bloodstained striped apron ready to prepare your purchase. I used to like to watch him while Mum queued to get into the shop (pie and mash shops were always busy).

When someone bought an eel it would be fished out from the tray and moved to the block still slithering in the fishmonger's great big hands. He would hold it just below the head and then swiftly chop it off after which the body still wriggled furiously. He would then slit it up the belly, scrape out its guts and then chop it into small pieces all the way along the body, but he would not chop right through. Even chopped in this way, the bits were still wriggling! Yuk! Wrapped in newspaper, this would be taken home by the purchaser and stewed for tea. Double yuk!

When Mum was about to be served I would be called in from watching the entertainment of eel chopping.
'Can I have four please?' I used to ask.

The woman behind the counter used to say, 'As 'e got bleeding 'ollow legs? I'd rather keep 'im for a week than a fortnight?' My Mum used to laugh with an element of pride and I was passed this plate of delectable food. Mum would sit down with two pies and mash. I would always finish before her.

'Fast eating will be your downfall' she used to say as I scraped my spoon around the plate trying to get up the remains of the liquor - liquor being the gravy that comes with the meal and it is green in colour! It's made from the juice of the stewed eels (which were also sold in the shop) mixed with parsley and flour and it was absolutely wonderful.

Chapter Ten - Summer Camp

At last the day arrived for our summer camp. My kit bag was packed and I was in my uniform ready to go. Dad helped me put the kit bag in the sidecar of his motorbike and as I kissed Mum goodbye, I received the usual blessing from her 'Be good or else'. She then pressed two one-pound notes in my hand, which was a lot of money then.

'Blimey, thanks Mum' I said as I gave her a huge hug.

'Look after it,' she said.

'I will, don't worry.'

I hopped on the back of Dad's motorbike for the short trip to Bow Baptist Church where we all met up. I introduced Dad to Skip for the first time and they exchanged pleasantries. It was good really, because my Dad didn't swear once during this exchange of words. I didn't think my Dad could do that so I put it down to the power of the Church! Dad then pulled out my kit bag from the sidecar as though it weighed nothing and passed it to me. Unlike him, I thought it weighed a ton and as I was struggling with the thing, he banged me on the side of the head and told me to behave myself. Shortly afterward a coach turned up to take us to the station.

The journey to Pett Level farm wasn't too bad, but the walk from Pett station was a killer. It was uphill all the way and a real struggle, even with the help of my trusty stave. We arrived at the farm and we were soon checked in. We were allocated a field in which to set up camp and it was exciting as we rolled the kit to our site ready to do so. Our tents were set out on the top of a hill. We were on a plateau and behind our camp was the field's boundary, a huge thorny hedgerow. About fifty yards in front of the tents the field fell away down a steep hill and then it rolled up the other side and into the woods beyond. It was perfect, except for the fact that it was a bit of a slog for those on firewood duty. Still, necessity is the mother of invention and we soon devised different ways of carrying as much firewood as we could between us. My favourite way was two staves tied together to make a stretcher and then loaded with long branches, of which there were plenty lying about on the forest floor. Of course the other duty when we arrived was digging the latrines. We had brought with us two latrine tents and suitable holes had to be dug out. The older members of the troop set about this while we helped pitch tents and unload everything we had brought with us for our stores tent. As we started to unload our troop cart, I could see why it was such a struggle pulling it up that hill.

We were soon settled in and a campfire was lit with the cooking under way of our first meal. Everything was devoured and plates washed up. We had gathered some logs, which were placed around the fire as seats. The sun was setting and the Union Jack was lowered from our makeshift flagpole. This was made out of one of the longer and thinner fallen branches lying on the forest floor. We then got ourselves comfortable around the campfire. Skip then stood up and told us that he felt we had all behaved extremely well on the journey and that he was proud of the 38th. Ordinarily if we had have been told that at school for example, it would have been OK to hear. However, when you are a keen scout and enjoy being part of a great team, you couldn't help but be filled with pride.

He went on to tell us that he was depending on us for good behaviour and reminded us that we represented the whole Scout Association when we were out and about in uniform. We should never forget that. Skip was highly respected by us all and so we paid attention to what he had to say. Not bad for what some might think of as just a bunch of rowdy East End kids.

The first week flew by and the weather was fine.

Unfortunately, my mate Tim didn't come to the camp but I had no shortage of other friends in the troop and a lot of fun was had. Skip's wife and daughter were in their tent, which was a little way away from the rest of us. It gave them a bit of privacy I guess. Skip's wife was sort of mother to us all for two weeks. She would sew buttons, tears in shorts and be the nurse when necessary - this, on top of looking after her own little girl, certainly kept her busy.

At the end of the first week I was sitting on a log by the fire when I could see in the distance two people walking towards us from the direction of the farmhouse. One of them had a limp! It was Mum and Dad. I ran over toward them crying out breathlessly,
'What are you doing here?' and I gave Mum a real hug as I was pleased to see her.
'We thought we would just pop in to see how you were doing.' Pop in! We were just outside Hastings and they had come from Bow...Pop in!!

They came over to our camp and Skip welcomed them. He remembered my dad and said, 'This must be your mum, you look just like her!'
'People are always saying that,' I chirped in, 'but I'm adopted.'
Skip looked a little embarrassed as he asked them if they would like some tea. Dad said he would and they moved over to the campfire area. Mum was given a chair to sit on while Dad found himself a comfortable log. I was sent off on tea duty.

While I was away Mum, Dad and Skip seemed to be having a real good old chat and getting on famously. I brought over the tea and sat down next to Mum.
'I suppose you are wondering why we are here,' she said,
'Is anything wrong?' I asked Mum.

70

'No, not at all. We have brought you a present.'

'Really!' And then Dad produced a package from off the floor behind the log he was sitting on and passed it to me. It wasn't that big, but quite heavy.

'Open it carefully,' Mum said. I did - and as I slowly pulled back the layers of paper, I revealed a fantastic bone-handled sheath knife. Not just an ordinary sheath knife - the handle contained a variety of utensils rather like a Swiss army knife. I was thrilled and my excitement was more than noticeable.

'Is this really mine?' I asked. I was told it was but I had to use it properly or it would be taken from me.

'Blimey. OK,' I replied, eyes still wide in surprise. 'Thanks Mum. Thanks Dad!'

'Well, we'll be off then,' Mum said.

'Won't you stay for some tea?' Skip asked, 'We have got some Angel cake, and you can meet my wife.'

'Well, we don't want to put you to any trouble,' Mum said.

'Trouble! I have got thirty little slaves to do the work! It will be no trouble for me!' said Skip. They walked over to meet Skip's wife and his little daughter.

Everyone dashed around as though we had royalty at the camp. I think everyone enjoyed showing off how well they could do things. It was a good time. It was one of those rare enjoyable times with my Dad, and he didn't swear once and what an effort that must have taken, but it was time for them to go. I walked back to the motorbike and sidecar with them and was warned once again about using the knife properly. There was no worry really because, although I was only ten years old, when it came to the scouts everything I ever did was done with great sincerity. Of course there was time for games and fun but when it was time to be serious, I was, all part of my great love of the Scouts and all it stood for. Mum got in the sidecar and Dad swung down on the kick-start. As always, the bike started first time, and I watched them steadily drive up the farm road. What a great day!

During the second week of camp someone mentioned that they had seen a sign down in the village for a stables advertising horse riding by the hour. I had never sat on a horse, let alone ridden one, and thought the idea was really exciting. I think it comes from all those times I petted the horses at Bow Road Police Station. I asked Skip if some of us could go and he said that as long as we went with a Senior Scout, over fifteen years old, we could. I started badgering the seniors and the best was Ted Rouse - 'Wishbone'. Ted agreed and he took two of us, me and my mate Roland, down to the village the next day. The walk to the stables seemed to take forever. Wishbone went up to someone in charge and we were told how much it was.

Wishbone had money and so did I, but Roland didn't have too much and didn't want to blow most of it on the horses, no matter how much he wanted to ride one. Things weren't so easy for Roland. His Mum had separated from his Dad and his Mum had him and his sister to bring up on her own. It didn't seem fair that Roland had walked all that way not to get on the back of a horse, so I paid something toward it. I liked Roland a lot and he was a good friend. He used to have a terrible stammer and everyone used to take the piss out of him something terrible. I, on the other hand, never forgot my Mum's words about people with afflictions and Roland and I became close pals.

We went off riding for an hour and it was great fun and worth every penny. I wouldn't expect there were too many East End boys that got the chance to get on the back of a horse and ride it for an hour. The walk back to camp was full of excitement as we recalled what we had done. There was the obvious exaggeration of the speed we went which had somehow turned from a steady walk into a gallop. By the time we reached Pett it was hard to tell which one of us was the Lone Ranger! The excitement of it all certainly dulled the ache in the legs from the walk up the steep hill from Pett to the farm. There was another reminder the next day of our horse riding. It's surprising how much you use your legs to stay on a horse and after only one hour how much those leg muscles ache.

Sadly the second week at camp passed too quickly and all too soon we were on our way back home. Tents were dropped and packed away. The campfire's ashes were raked out and the square piece of turf that had been carefully cut out and put in a safe place and regularly watered, was replaced and watered once again.

Latrines were dropped, holes filled and turf again replaced. The store tent was emptied, dropped and packed away. The whole troop was made to stand in line each of us about a yard apart. Then we were told to walk slowly across camp and pick up any small bits of paper, sweet wrappers or hopefully coins that had fallen out of someone's pocket. This was followed by our last act, the lowering of the Union Jack. We all stood in a circle around the flag as it was lowered for the last time. It was really quite sad, as it had been such a great time. In no time at all, the light green patches of grass where the tents had stood would turn back to their rich dark green colour and there would be no trace of our having been there at all.

The trip home wasn't as full of excitement as the trip there, but we were in good spirits nevertheless and there was much recollecting between us of what we had been up to. Skip soon had us all singing some of the usual scout songs like, In the Stores, The Crest of the Wave, and good old Ging Gang Gooly.

We arrived back at Bow Baptist at about five on Saturday afternoon in accordance with what Skip had said on the original information sheet, advising parents of the summer camp. There were quite a few parents there waiting for us and in no time at all a lot of goodbyes were being shouted as scouts peeled off with their parents.

Roland and I were not met so we walked home with our heavy kit bags on our shoulders. We walked along Bow Road as far as Fairfield Road where we crossed over and headed toward home.

'See yer on Tuesday,' I shouted out to him as he carried on toward Campbell Road and home.

I arrived at home and dumped my kit bag on the step. I was really hot as it was a long walk and the bag was heavy. I pulled out my latchkey, opened the door and in I went. The hall seemed even darker than usual, I suppose because I had just spent two weeks in the open air in bright sunshine. I picked up the bag and wrestled with it down the hall trying not to scrape the walls as I went. I dumped it into my room and went on down to the kitchen. Mum was in the scullery and Dad was out. I didn't really give much thought to not being met. It was always like that really.

'Hi Mum,' I called and she just replied,

'Hello Jimmy, where's your kit bag?'

'In my room,' I told her.

'Well get it unpacked quickly and we'll get your clothes washed,' I went straight to my room and unpacked. I changed into my play shorts from my uniform, as that too needed washing and I would need it again for Tuesday.

Chapter Eleven - Goodbye to 49 Morville Street

In no time at all everything was hand washed and on the line. Mum made some tea and as she did Dad walked in.

'Hi Dad,' I said, 'have you been working?'

'No,' he replied, 'I have just been round to see Uncle Steve and Aunt Maria for an hour.'

They lived at 19 Wallingford House off Devon's Road with their three boys, Little Steve, Alex and David. I used to love going round there to visit. It was always such a fun place. The boys were great to play with and my Aunt Maria was always such a laugh. Uncle Steve had met her during the war when he was fighting in Belgium and struck up a romance. There were probably lots of romances started like that as troops marched into European countries liberating them from the clutches of the German army. Mind you, who could blame her for falling in love with him? When he was young he was a double of the actor Robert Mitchum. After the war was over she came to England as a nurse, and soon after that they were married.

It must have been incredibly tough for a Belgian to come to England at such a young age and be thrust into an East End family like the Wilkinson's. What a culture shock! While I am sure her style of cooking would have been completely different to start with, she soon mastered the art of cooking an excellent Sunday roast, which she would produce as well as anyone in the family. Thankfully she retained a lot of her continental recipes and no one in the family could make better soups.

Mum sat at the table and as she poured out the tea said they had some news for me.

'What's that then?' I asked, doing my usual biscuit-dunking trick.

'We might be moving,' she said. I don't know why, but Dad

always left Mum to deliver the important news to me.

'Really where to?' I asked with a mouth full of biscuit.

'We have been offered a flat not far from Nanny Wilkinson, just off Devon's Road.'

'Great, what's it like?'

'Well, it's got two bedrooms, lounge, kitchen and an inside toilet and bathroom, and a small garden.'

'Bathroom!' I exclaimed, 'and toilet inside the house. Blimey, does the bath have hot water?'

'Of course it does,' Mum laughed.

'What out of a tap?'

'Yes.'

'Blimey! When are we moving?' Who could say no to such luxury?

'Well that depends.'

'On what?'

'Well we have been offered the flat by the council. All we have to do now is accept the offer and fix the moving in date.'

In my excitement I hadn't given a thought about all my friends in Morville Street or my school.

'When can I see the flat Mum?' I asked impatiently.

'I've arranged for us to have the key on Monday so we'll go then. If we all like it then we can go back to the council offices afterwards and sign the papers.'

'Great, a new home with a bathroom, blimey, can I go out?'

'You've only just got in.'

'Yeah I know, but I want to see my mates and tell them we're moving.'

'No,' Mum said, 'you can go out, but you don't tell anyone until we have signed the papers, is that understood?'

'OK, I won't say anything.' Now normally, I would dash out and do exactly the opposite to what I had said, but on this occasion I knew Mum meant what she said, so I went out busting at the sides with news, and said nothing.

The next day was Sunday and as usual I went to church

parade. I took Mum and Dad tea in bed, said goodbye, then shot out of the door. On a Sunday morning there were never many people about when I set off for Church. The service wasn't as full as it normally was. I guess a lot of the troop didn't show up because they were done-in after summer camp. Although the service was good, it was the hymns I enjoyed the most, as our priest wasn't that great when it came to exciting sermons. By the time the service was over I was usually starving, so I never hung around after church, it was straight home to lunch. As I cycled into Morville Street I could see Dad in front of the house cleaning his motorbike. The sidecar door was open and the hoover was on the floor next to it attached by a long power lead coming out of our front door.

'Hi Dad. Wanna a hand?'

'If you want,' he said, 'you can hoover the sidecar.'

I grabbed the end of the hoover and in no time at all it was clean.

'OK?' I said, seeking his approval, and he nodded. 'I'm going in to help Mum,' and I went in, always mindful of noise, as it had long been drummed into my head:

'Shh, the MacDonalds'.

I walked down the hall and was greeted by the smell of lunch.

'Wot we got Mum?' I asked.

'Roast pork, roast potatoes, cabbage, carrots and tinned peas and Yorkshire pudding.' she said. The smell alone would stimulate the dullest of appetites. During lunch the radio was on and after Two Way Family Favourites we listened to the Clitheroe Kid. I always used to think Jimmy Clitheroe was so funny. He was always getting his sister's boyfriend Alfie Hall into so much trouble.

I waded through lunch and then Mum washed up. Dad suggested we go to see Nanny Taylor and my absolute favourite aunt, Mum's sister, Sadie, who adored me.

Everything was put away and off we went on Dad's bike. I sat on the pillion seat; Mum in the sidecar.

On the bike it only took ten or fifteen minutes to get to Nan's. Dad parked the bike and I jumped off to run round to lift up the top of the sidecar and open its small door. Mum wasn't thin and not at all agile so getting in and out wasn't really easy for her, but she managed. We walked across the tarmac and into the entrance of Seaton Buildings and up to Nan's floor. I ran up ahead and knocked at the door which was opened by Uncle Ronnie muttering his usual stunning, ''Ello, it's you' as he turned on his heel and went back in. Uncle Ronnie was never a bright sparkling personality, but he had a good heart. I followed him in and there she was sitting in the armchair, full up after lunch, my Aunt Sadie.

'Auntie Sadie,' I shouted as I launched myself at her and she caught me in a sort of bear hug and proceeded to squeeze me and tickle me at the same time until I thought I would burst. She would then give me a huge kiss with the sound of Hmmmwah.. She was a large cuddly woman with a big frizzy hair do.

'Now what have you been up to you little bastard?' she said.

'Oh, nothing much, just summer camp with the scouts and we're moving!'

'To Scotland I hope,' she said with a wry smile.

'Got any biscuits Nan?' I asked and Nan grabbed me from Sadie saying, 'Got any biscuits Nan, what?'

'Please,' and she would bang me in the head,

'That's more like it, come 'ere.' She sat me down with a glass of milk and the biscuit tin.

'I don't know where he puts it!' Mum said, 'I swear that boy's got hollow legs.'

'Ede, he's growing, he needs food,' Nan said with a knowing look.

'But Mum, he bloody eats us out of house and home.'

Nan would just smile at me and sit down to roll herself a fag.

'What's all this about moving then?'

'We've been offered a flat in Violet Road off Devon's Road,' Mum told her.

'Oh,' Nan said, 'D'you want a cup of tea Jim?'

'Yes please Gert,' Dad said. Nan's name was Gertrude and if ever I laughed she would crack me one round the head in fun. So everyone tried to make me laugh when they said Gert. It was sort of a family joke.

'Make some tea will you Sadie,' Nan said. Now tell me about this flat.

'Well,' I said.

'Shut up you and eat your biscuits,' said Nan, and I knew it was time for me to be quiet.

Mum continued, 'We applied about three months ago for a council place as living at 49 isn't ideal. I thought we would have to wait ages but it seems that when I told them the layout of 49 with its outside toilet, the person that was interviewing me asked me a few unusual questions that I hadn't expected. He had noticed my limp as I walked in and he asked me what I had done and I told him about the polio. He asked me if it was more of a problem at certain times of the year and I told him it was worse in the winter as I had such poor circulation. Well, it seems he felt that I should not have to be going to an outside toilet with this problem and pushed our case to the front. A week later I got a letter asking me to go and see the Housing Officer at Poplar town hall. I went on Tuesday and was offered a choice of three places, all of them flats. Two of them were not on the ground floor but the blocks had lifts. The other one thankfully was really suitable and I liked it the best.' Mum then described the place to Nan.

'When are you going back to see it again?' she asked.

'We are picking up the keys tomorrow and we'll go round after Jim gets home from work, he's going to finish early.'

'Well, sounds good to me.' Nan said, 'If you take it, I'll come round and help you clean up the place and get it ready to move into.'

The afternoon continued with Nan clearing the table and then everyone sat round to play the card game Newmarket. They were gambling, but only for coppers. There was always much laughter as my Mum would often win and I would sit and count the winnings. I loved it round Nan's, but it was soon seven in the evening and time to set off home. Nan would wrap me up against the night air, even though it was July, and we would be off. As usual I would kiss Nan and Aunt Sadie goodbye and zoom off down the stairs.

'How's he been?' Nan asked Mum, nodding toward me as I disappeared down the stairs.

'Oh, fine, since he's been in the scouts it's really changed him. He loves it.'

'Good. Let me know when the move is going to be and look after yourselves.'

'Tarra Jim.' She kissed Dad on the cheek,

'See yer Gert,' he said.

They followed me down the stairs and by the time they got down, I had the sidecar top flipped over and the little door open. I was off talking to some kids playing hopscotch.

'Come on Jimmy,' Dad said. I helped Mum into the sidecar and closed the small door and pulled the lid down over her. Dad stood on the kick-starter, swung his weight down and the bike started up and we set off home.

We arrived home in no time at all and I was told to get ready for bed.

'Oohhhh,' I complained, but my pleading look didn't work.

'Jimmy!' Mum said, and that was enough and off I went.

Sometimes I could argue about going to bed and get away with it and be allowed to stay up for another half an hour, but this time I felt I was wasting my time so I just went to bed. I was snuggled and asleep in no time. It had been a busy weekend.

The next day we were on our way to Poplar town hall on the 108 single decker bus. It just took us the length of Fairfield Road up to the town hall, which was on the corner of Bow Road. It wasn't that far to walk really but a bit too far for Mum to do so with comfort. We walked through the huge wooden front doors of the town hall and took the lift up to the housing office. Mum asked for the man handling our file but he was not in for some reason so someone else got it. Mum asked for the key to 5 Devonshire House, Violet Road, Bow. We were given the key without any problems, once Mum had shown the lady some ID and signed for it. Mum said thank you and as we turned to leave the lady said,
'Don't forget Mrs Wilkinson, if you are going to accept this property, you must do so by no later than Wednesday before we close, otherwise the offer expires.'
Mum said that was OK and that she would be back the next day as she felt certain the flat would be fine, and we left.

We crossed Bow Road and waited at the bus stop for a number 86 bus, which would take us to Devon's Road and within a few yards of our new home in Violet Road.

As we walked toward Violet Road, I noticed that in Devon's Road there was a very handy parade of shops, which had every shop you would need for everyday life: a grocer's, two butcher's, a baker's, a greengrocer's, and a fish and chip shop which also sold wet fish, and many more. On the corner of Violet Road there was a derelict shop, which, according to the sign outside, had once been an undertaker's.

Next door to the derelict shop was a bomb site sealed off by a wall and then a small unimpressive block of flats that was Devonshire House. In the front of the block there were two arched entrances, the first led to flats 1 to 4 and the next arch led to number 5 to 8. All of the windows in Devonshire House were Georgian style, which at least gave the building a bit of character.

We walked along to the second archway and up two steps to No.5, which was just inside on the left. Mum put the key in the front door, which opened straight into the lounge. The place smelled of fresh paint and in the corner of the room the painters had left their pots of paint and ladders ready to collect. The lounge was quite a good size for a flat and it had a fireplace over which hung a clothes maiden (a wooden rack for airing clothes) fixed to the ceiling and pulled up and down by rope on squeaky pulleys.

There were two doors off the lounge excluding the front door and two large cupboards. One cupboard fitted into a recess, which was under the stairs leading to flats 6 and 7. The other cupboard was next to the fireplace and housed the big galvanized steel hot water tank. The only way of heating the water in the flat was using the back boiler unit at the rear of the fireplace. When the fire was alight, all you had to do was pull a steel drawer at the top, which closed off the chimney. The heat was then drawn into the back and over a heat exchanger. Quite simple, but not too much fun in the summer when it was hot, assuming you wanted a hot bath.

Opposite the front door was the door to the main bedroom and, like in the lounge, the window opened onto the road outside. This bedroom had a nice little feature in it - a fireplace, which sadly was never to be lit. At the far end of the lounge was the other door, which led into a small square of four doors. Opposite was the bathroom/toilet, to the left the back bedroom and to the right, the kitchen. The back bedroom (my room) was about the same size as the one I was used to, but much brighter as there was no building outside to obstruct the light. The bathroom simply had a bath and a toilet; no hand basin, which at the time I never thought was odd, never having had a bathroom before.

The kitchen was a bit antiquated and even had a copper in the corner. No not a policeman, but a brick and concrete fireplace, above which was a large copper bowl, which gives it its name. This was the means of doing the washing - the idea being to fill it with water, light the fire below and boil the washing. In the corner of the kitchen was a coal cupboard. The back door of the kitchen led into a walled area as wide as the block of flats and about thirty feet deep. This area housed eight small patches of garden and eight washing lines and that was Devonshire House.

'What do you think then Jimmy?' asked Mum. I thought it was fantastic. I mean you have no idea what luxury it was just to have a toilet inside, let alone a bathroom. I loved it and said, 'Can we have a dog?'
'We'll see,' came back Mum's usual reply. It's going to need a lot of cleaning up and some changes but I am sure we can soon get that done. I decided to have another look at the garden and what was over the back wall. It was a huge bomb site and beyond that were the empty remains of two rows of terraced houses flanking the road behind. What a playground!

I got back into the lounge and Dad was there talking with Mum. I heard him ask,
'What do yer think then Ede?'
'I like it Jim,' she said. 'It's near the shops and not too far for Jimmy to get to school.' School! Bloody hell, I thought, how do I get to school. Dad had a quick look round and said, 'Ok, then we'll take it.' The next day the papers were signed and the move arranged, which was to be the following Wednesday on the back of Uncle Steve's lorry.

The day we moved I came home from school and nearly everything was gone. Mum and Dad had obviously worked hard at getting all our stuff over to No.5. Thankfully Dad had managed to get the council to give him a rented lock-up garage. It wasn't too close to Devonshire House, but it proved a great place him to house a lot of his junk from the cellar and garden shed at number 49.

I got home from school as Dad was loading the sidecar up with a pile of bedding. I got on the back of the bike and off we went. It took about twelve minutes to get there. I got off the bike and went in to find Mum and Nanny Taylor cleaning up. My bedroom had furniture in it and the bed was made. The fire was alight, and the water hot. Dad had even chained my pushbike to a down-pipe in the garden.

We all set about doing things and I was given the job of helping Nanny clean the kitchen cupboard out. There was a huge pot of stew on the boil and a bowl on the side full of un-cooked dumplings waiting to be dropped in when we were ready. There was another saucepan full of potatoes ready for boiling. Dinner would be stew and dumplings poured over a mini mountain of mashed potatoes. The smell was memorable and the flat, unlike number 49, was warm.

Everything was soon tidy and clean enough to live in. Nanny asked me if I wanted a bath. 'Really?' I said,
'I don't see why not,' she said. The bath was run and she put some soda crystals in to make the water soft. It was probably my most memorable bath ever. I was allowed to wallow and I sang and splashed until I was wrinkled.

Nanny knocked on the door and asked if I was OK or if I had fallen down the plug 'ole. I hadn't and I came out wearing clean pyjamas sporting an enormous appetite. The bathroom was awash and I had even managed to get the toilet roll wet.

Toilet rolls! What luxury! About half an hour later dinner was served and we all sat and tucked into a brilliant lamb stew. And so life began at No. 5.

I was put to bed by Nan, and it wasn't long before I was fast asleep in between my clean white linen sheets. Sleep came quick and deep after my very first bath in our own bathroom in our own house, which was followed by an ample amount of Mum's stew. No doubt long after I had gone to sleep, Dad took Nanny home again, back to Bethnal Green.

I woke up the next morning and at first wondered where I was. It soon dawned on me it was our new home. I had been given the day off school to give Mum and Dad a chance to sort things out so there was time for me to settle in to our new home and area. I got myself dressed and went into the kitchen, where Mum was making some tea.

'Hello,' she said. 'How'd you sleep?'
'Like a log,' I said with a yawn. She licked her hand and used it to flatten my hair down and told me to go have a wash.
'Wash!' I said, 'I only had a bath last night. I haven't been anywhere to get dirty!'
'Never mind about that - wash,' came her response. I ran some cold water into the bowl in the kitchen sink and Mum poured in some hot from the kettle, as there was no hot water left in the tank. I set about washing my face using the flannel that was lying on the little window ledge next to the sink and then I brushed my teeth. Mum wet my hair by rubbing the wet flannel through it and then combed it.
'That's better,' she said. 'If you go in the lounge I'll bring you in some tea.'
Lounge, I thought, we've never had a lounge before, it had always been the kitchen.

Dad was still in bed as I sat at the table and was given a bowl, a box of cornflakes and a bottle of milk. Mum sat with me drinking her tea and I put some cereal in my bowl along with about half a pint of milk and a dessertspoon full of sugar. It didn't take me long to get through it and ask if I could go out to play.

'Alright,' said Mum, 'but don't wander off too far. If there is anything I need I'll want you to go the shops and get it for me.'

My first thought to this idea was yuk, until I remembered that the shops were just around the corner and I no longer had that walk all the way to Roman Road.
'OK,' I said, 'I'll just hop over the back wall and do some exploring, I won't go far.' I went out through the kitchen dropping my breakfast bowl into the sink as I passed it. I opened the back door, ran up to the back wall, and hopped up onto it. Within seconds I was rooting around in the empty houses over the back of ours. While I was exploring, Dad, who had taken the day off work, got himself up, had some breakfast and got on with taking more stuff round to the garage. He had hooked up his homemade trailer onto the motorbike and bit by bit he got it all round the garage. Mum was busy cleaning out the pantry in the kitchen and lining the shelves with brown paper. The pantry was big enough to store all our food and there was room in the bottom for most of Dad's tools, which he would need before too much longer. Soon he would knock out the copper and make Mum a kitchen unit, which went from the corner where the copper stood right up to the edge of the white butler sink. The job he made of doing this is pretty much indescribable. As a carpenter, Dad made a good scaffolder! He was great at demolishing things but hopeless at anything that required some standard of finish or patience. He bought a sheet of red Formica for the top. Of course he no doubt spent some time rooting around the site where he was working to try to find a

bit lying around that no one wanted. The drawers of the unit were unique, as they didn't have stops on them. This meant you always had to remember not to pull the drawer out too far to avoid tipping its contents all over the floor. It was always the cutlery drawer would catch me out.

I was soon over the back methodically searching all the empty houses but there was nothing of real interest to find. It was strange going through houses that had been left by families for better places. There were remnants of carpet or the odd mirror, which if it could talk would no doubt have had a tale to tell. I thought it best to zip back in to see how Mum was doing. I walked in through the back door and found her in the kitchen still unpacking boxes.
'Where's Dad?' I asked her.
'He's taking stuff round the garage on the bike,' she said and then she asked me if I wanted a drink. I opted for tea.
'Good,' she said, 'put the kettle on will you, oh and you will need to run round the corner and get some milk as we are out.' It was my first run of many thousands around that corner. Mum gave me half a crown and I was there in a flash. I got the milk from the grocers and I was back before the kettle had boiled.
'That was quick,' said Mum,
'Yeah, it's brilliant because it is so close.' Dad must have heard me put the kettle on, as we used to say, as he pulled up outside just as I had made the tea. In he came, wearing his bib and brace, which I called his brace and bit, which amused him, as it's a carpenter's drilling tool and not something you wear. He had on his working boots, and a red tartan shirt.
'How's it going Ede?' he asked.
'Want some tea Dad?' I interrupted. Interrupting was never a problem if I was offering something, but it was a different matter if I wanted something.

Dad nodded and Mum told him that she'd unpacked most of

the stuff for the bedroom and all in all things were pretty straight. It's not surprising it didn't take long - as when it came to furniture and things of luxury we didn't have very much.

The furniture from our kitchen now sat in our lounge where it looked lost as the lounge was so much bigger. Still, Mum got on with it and in no time at all made us a home. I walked into the lounge with a tray of tea and, balanced on top of the three mugs, was the biscuit tin.

'I see you had no trouble finding the biscuit tin then,' Dad grumbled as he sat down in his armchair next to the fireplace.

'Dad, I've been over the back,' I said. 'There's loads of empty houses!'

'Anything in 'em?' he asked,

'No not really,' I told him as I dunked a Bourbon into my mug of tea.

'When you've finished you can help me with the next load for the garage.' I agreed of course and asked if there was much more to go. He told me just one more load then sank the last of his tea and he was on his way out of the front door. I grabbed my coat and followed him. We carried the last few boxes from the alcove just outside the kitchen door through the flat and out to the trailer. Dad loaded and tied them down in his usual way. When Dad tied things down an earthquake wouldn't move them. He walked round the bike and stepped onto the kick-starter and swung down and the bike started easily. I hopped on and we zipped off up Violet Road to Crisp Street where we then turned left over a little hump back railway bridge and then passed Bright and Byron Streets on the right. In between these two streets was a school called Hay Currie Secondary Modern and not far past that was Dad's garage. He had already fitted strong padlocks to the top and bottom of the garage door as well as the handle in the middle that also locked. We had entered the era and the area when it was getting harder and harder to own anything without someone wanting to nick it. Dad had already knocked up some shelves for his tools and had made some sort of roof beams on which lay his collection of 'half-inched' wood. We soon unloaded the trailer, which was also stowed in the garage. The Fort Knox type door was locked up and we went back home. Dad showed me a different way home passing by St Andrew's Hospital.

As we got to the junction of Devon's Road by the Hospital, Dad carried on instead of turning left, showing me how to get to the scouts. The journey wasn't too bad but if I was feeling lazy I could always catch a Number 86, which went from door to door.

At the end of Devon's Road was Bow Road where there was a pie and mash shop, and two fish and chip shops, Samuel's being the best. Dad turned the bike around the granite horse trough that sat in the middle of the road and went back along Devon's Road. He pulled over outside an off-licence, and bought a bottle of Grants whisky.
'Hang on to that,' he told me and I put it inside my jacket.
'Shall we pop in to see Aunt Maria?' he asked. I never needed to be asked twice if I wanted to see my Aunt Maria and I had barely uttered, 'yeah' when we swung off Devon's Road into the small estate on which was Wallingford House, the block of flats where they lived.

Dad stopped the bike by the entrance and I ran in and pressed the button for the lift. After a minute it arrived and the rippled aluminium door slowly opened as Dad ran up the steps and straight in. I stepped in and the first thing I noticed was the smell of pee. I pressed button 3 and up we went. We walked along the landing and Dad knocked at number 19. The door opened and we were greeted by Aunt Maria's usual (but very unusual), East End accent.
'Come in,' she said, telling me that my cousins Little Steve

and Alex and David were still at school.

'What time do you expect Big Steve home?' Dad asked.

'I'm not really sure, he's delivering in Kent today, want a cup of tea Jim?' she asked. 'I have just put on the kettle.'

'Yeah all right,' he said. 'Jimmy, come here.' I went over to him and he stuck his hand down my jacket and pulled out the bottle of scotch I was carrying.

'This is for Steve,' he said.

'You shouldn't have done that Jim,' she said.

'Well he won't take any money so at least he can have a drink on me,' Dad said as we sat down in the small kitchen to drink our tea. I heard the front door open, and it was Uncle Steve. I ran out to greet him and he gave me a hug and said, 'Hello you; are you on your own?'

'Nope – Dad's in the kitchen having some tea with Aunt Maria,' I informed him.

'Good,' he said and he turned me round and we went back to the kitchen. Uncle Steve, to me, was tall, strong and handsome. He delivered steel girders and reinforcing bars for Robertson's, who were based in the East End. He walked into the kitchen and said hello to my dad and asked him how things were going. Dad told him we were pretty well settled in, considering, and that he had dropped him a bottle of scotch round to say thanks for the help.

'You didn't have to do that.'

Dad dismissed his remark with a wave of his hand as we finished our tea. We then left before my cousins got home. We were downstairs in a flash as I raced Dad down to the bike. Uncle Steve shouted down that they would come round and see us soon. Dad just waved in acknowledgement. Once again we were off zooming along Devon's Road over Widow's Son Bridge and left into Violet Road.

Dad parked the bike outside and I pulled my new latchkey out of my shirt and opened the front door.

'That's it,' Mum said. 'That will do for now.'

The place looked quite homely really, much more than number 49 ever had.

'Did you get done round the garage Jim?' she asked. He then told her that he had shown me how to get to the scouts and that we'd dropped a bottle of scotch into Steve's to say thank you.'

'Good,' she said. It was now about four o'clock and I was told to get my stuff ready for school the next day. Life was going to get back to normal quickly. I went into my bedroom and made sure I knew where everything was ready for tomorrow. Mum switched on the TV and sat down while Dad wandered around the room with the 'V' shaped TV aerial trying to get a picture. As he moved around the room he kept asking

'How's that Ede?' With his zero level of patience this sort of thing was a recipe for disaster. If he didn't get it right quickly, we would either have to look at a snowy picture full of ghosting, do it ourselves or even worse watch the aerial whiz across the room as he would throw it, saying, 'Fuck the thing!'

Mum sat there and thankfully said, 'That's it' and he put the aerial down.

'Can I go out?' I asked as I walked back into the lounge.

'Yes, but I want you back in here at five-thirty ready for your tea. No wandering off, d'you hear?'

'Yeah OK,' I said as I shot out through the front door. I walked up to the corner of Violet Road and Devon's Road and watched the traffic coming over Widow's Son Bridge. It was all so different to Morville Street. I was used to living in a quiet street with hardly any traffic and now we were living just off a really busy main road.

On the corner of Violet Road was a tobacconists which sold all sorts of sweets, some toys and fancy goods, run by an old

'Jew-Boy', as my Dad would call him, named Monte. Monte would stand in the shop with his pipe hanging out of his mouth and slowly dribble as he did so, yuk. Next door to Monte's was a shop, which sold baby's clothes and next to that was Praters the greengrocer that was run by an old brother and sister. The brother was a real 'Open All Hours' type character, who always wore a brown carpenter's coat and highly polished boots. His sister, Violet Prater, on the other hand, looked a bit like Katherine Hepburn in her latter years. She wore her hair piled up in a bun and she always wore sort of baggy billowing dresses. The shop was open-fronted and it had a variety of interlocking boxes, which were used for the outside displays. These were covered in imitation grass on which were piled the big displays of seasonal fruits. I used to love the smell of that shop. Next door to Prater's was A. G. Hedges, the butchers.

This was only a small shop and in the window were displayed all manner of delicacies such as faggots, surrounded by tins of pease pudding and hanging on the rails above were saveloys, There were also pigs' and sheep's heads, which were sold whole or by the half. Tripe, great with onions, if you like that sort of thing, sheep's and pigs' hearts, lights (sheep's or pigs' lungs) and a variety of salted joints. These were usually shoulders of pork or pieces of silverside of beef, which had been soaked in a barrel of brine for a few days.

Next door to the butcher's shop was the barber's complete with revolving red and white striped pole. The barbers were Monte and Gus - and Gus was incredible. It was rumoured that he had suffered some sort of shell shock from the war, which resulted in him having the most unbelievable stammer. Those that knew Gus would not talk to him during the haircut, as his efforts to reply were extremely dangerous. When he stammered his eyes rolled back in head, his mouth would rapidly open and close like a goldfish and his whole body shook. I liken this to the comedy routine of the comedian Jack Douglas. Part of Jack's act was to have a huge nervous affliction that would often end up with his beer or whatever he was holding going flying. Gus was a very similar character and there was a great risk of losing an ear due to an ill-timed question. After your haircut the best thing to follow, and a real luxury, were hot towels. These would be kept in a steamer and wrapped around your face in a pile leaving an air vent over your nose so that you could breath. Another favourite was to have Pashana rubbed into your hair and scalp. This was quite stimulating for the scalp but it smelled very strong. If ever I had this treatment, my Dad would say I smelled like the bottom of a whore's handbag.

In total there were about twenty shops on either side of the road and between them one could buy just about everything. I walked to the end of the parade on one side, which ended with an ironmonger that sold paraffin. He was our Esso Blue dealer and had an amazing assortment of things for sale hanging outside - everything from a galvanized dustbin to a yard broom. The next street on the left was a cul-de-sac and on the corner was a Lighthouse - well a hall - which was part of the Lighthouse organisation.

I crossed over the road to the shops on the other side, which funnily enough again started with a tobacconist called Peter's. After the fish and chip shop, which sold the most awful greasy fish and chips along with wet fish counter too, there was a launderette, then another butcher's called Greystone & Son, and the parade ended with a baker's, outside of which was a pedestrian crossing leading you back across to Monte with the dribbling pipe. Yuk! I looked in Monte's shop window and the clock advertising Players Weights said it was almost five-thirty so I legged it back home. I opened the front door and Dad was sitting there in his chair, wearing his string vest, with his feet up on the mantelshelf over the fireplace. I announced that I had been round for a good look at all the shops and said we can get nearly everything we want round there.

Dad was too busy to reply as he was watching a children's programme on the telly called Twizzle. Mum walked in from the kitchen and told me to get washed ready for dinner. As this had to be done in the kitchen it was pretty much a 'spit and a lick' job so I could keep out of her way.
'What's for dinner Mum?' I asked and she gave me one of her stock answers,
'Air pie.'
'Well it don't smell like air pie,' I said. We were having lamb's liver, bacon mashed potatoes and Brussels sprouts with thickening (Mum's home made gravy and only ever served with this dish).

Dinner was quickly over and I was soon in my pyjamas watching telly when there was a knock at the front door, which sort of surprised us a bit as we had only just moved in. It was my Aunt Ellen and Uncle William (Bill), Dad's sister and brother-in-law. They lived close by in Fairfoot Road, in the downstairs half of the house where Nanny Wilkinson lived.
'Come in,' Mum said.
'We've just popped round to see how you are settling in,' Aunt Ellen said.

Aunt Ellen and Uncle Bill were a real seaside postcard couple. She was short and quite fat and he was a little thin man with a bald head. I could always imagine her bullying him like the couple on the post cards, but I am sure she never did.
'We're doing fine considering how long we've been in,' Mum said.
'You have,' she agreed as she took a seat on a kitchen chair.

She was really quite big and used to find sitting on an upright chair more comfortable and probably a lot easier to get up from than an armchair. Uncle Bill said, 'We thought we'd get out for half an hour and walk down to see you all.'

They had not long ago moved into the shared house with Nanny Wilkinson and there were many problems following that arrangement. Even in those days when people got on better with each other, it wasn't wise for everyone to live so close to relatives. Especially if the relative was Nanny Wilkinson! Mum offered them tea and Dad offered something a little stronger. Thankfully Aunt Ellen settled for tea. The TV went off and news and gossip was swapped. I just loved to hear all the family tales but unfortunately I was reminded that it was time for bed; school tomorrow.

'Oh,' I pleaded but it was no good. I kissed Aunt Ellen and Uncle Bill goodnight and went to bed.

I got up the next morning and as usual got myself ready for school. It was really strange after all those years at number 49 eating breakfast in the lounge at number 5. However the difference didn't stop me eating my way through an enormous bowl of cornflakes and cold milk; in fact I think the excitement of it all stimulated my already overgrown appetite. I left the flat, slamming the door and crossed the road and waited for the bus. I waited and waited and eventually it came with the conductor muttering to the people in the queue, sorry the driver didn't turn up for the twenty past!

I jumped on and sat down for the short trip to Bow Road thinking, I could have walked it quicker. I got off, and caught my next bus to St Clements Hospital that was opposite Colborn Road. I was now quite close to school and as I walked down Colborn Road I couldn't help think that the journey had taken forty-five minutes, which is a long time to a ten year old.

It was great to be back at school though and among my friends. I used to have school dinners, but my friend Jack had always gone home to his, as he lived just around the corner. After lunch Jack rushed back to school and we would meet up in the playground and generally muck about.

'How's the new house?' he asked.

'It's a flat, and it's great! The night before last I had a hot bath in our own bathroom, and over the back of our garden we have got a whole street of houses which are empty and great to explore. Why don't we go?'

'When?' he asked,

'Soon,' I said, but now that we were at No. 5, it was much further for Jack to travel and his mum wouldn't be too keen on the idea. It wouldn't have been a problem if we were in No. 49. That was the first time I missed where we lived and sadly not the last. No 5, was indeed convenient in many ways, but I was soon to miss all the friends I had grown up with and the playing in the street, which was no longer possible due to the too busy traffic. I said to Jack that it perhaps would be best to get together on Saturday.

'Let's go to the Odeon Saturday morning and afterwards come back to my place and I'll show you around.' Subject to his mother's consent, he agreed.

The arrangement was made but we had not made allowances for Jack's Mum who had grown extremely cautious when it came to playing out with me. She said it was to do with my magnetic attraction to mischief. Still she did say Jack could go to the flicks and that afterwards he could spend a couple of hours round my house as long as either my Mum or Dad was in. Dad would be around, not that that counted for much and Jack and I did our usual exploring. Our new area did have a lot to offer but it is always hard making new friends and there were no other houses close by, so no local kids to meet. As time rolled by I missed all my mates in Morville Street.

Friday night was bath night, it was also the night we had fish and chips for tea. Mum and Dad got home from work and Dad set about lighting the fire.

'Do you remember where Samuel's the fish shop is?' he asked.

'Of course I do,' I said. 'It's down Devon's Road by the water trough.'

Mum said, 'Would you be really good and go on your bike and get us fish and chips?'

'Of course I will,' I said, rushing to get my bike from the garden. I was given the money and a note of what was required. In no time at all I was whizzing down the other side of Widow's Son bridge. It only took me a few minutes to get to Samuel's and join the long queue. Friday night was fish and chip night for lots of Eastenders. I gave the lady behind the counter my note and I was soon on my bike heading for home. Riding in a tail wind, the smell of the fish and chips would race ahead of me and catch my nose as it passed, which sent a signal to my brain to tell my mouth to water. How obedient was my mouth, as it certainly obliged.

I was ravenous by the time I got home. I dragged my bike up the two steps into our archway and knocked on the door. There was no time to muck about with the latchkey; I had a hot load of fish and chips in my saddlebag that needed devouring. Mum opened the door and the heat would hit you from Dad's highly banked-up fire. With the draw pulled across, to heat the water, the fire would roar down that back vent and sound like a jet engine.

'Everything all right?' Mum asked.

'No problem,' I said. I stood in front of the fire holding my bike as the valuable cargo was unloaded. I then carefully pushed the bike back through to the garden and covered it up. On the way back through to the kitchen I was told to wash my hands, which I did at lightning speed followed by a quick wipe on the tea towel and I was at the table. The meals were there , and mine was my favourite, cod, chips and a wally (pickled cucumber). This was a veritable feast and was accompanied by slices of French bread and butter. The way to round off a meal like this is to place the last few chips into the last slice of bread and then use it to mop the plate. That's the way to eat fish and chips, or as I later called it, a heart attack wrapped in newspaper!

After tea we would watch some television, probably Double Your Money with Hughie Green or Take Your Pick with Michael Miles. These were the two big TV programmes of the day. Hughie Green apparently disliked Michael Miles and there was much rivalry between them in the ratings. On one of Hughie's shows he had a contestant called Monica Rose who was a real East End character and won the hearts of the viewers - so much so that Hughie, who liked her a lot, asked her to co-present with him. She did, and up went his ratings. Poor Michael Miles didn't have a Monica Rose, he just had Bob Danvers-Walker's voice to introduce the prizes and of course there was always the mystery prize in Box 13. This could be as much as a whole year's supply of nylons - big stuff, if you're a woman. After Dad had again mucked about with the aerial to try to improve the picture we would try to watch the box and sit as far away from the roaring fire as possible to avoid leg scorch. Dinner was washed down with a cup of tea, which Dad would still drink by pouring it into the saucer and make the most awful noise as he sucked it up. He did this in order to cool the tea, a revolting habit, which never appealed to me, Thank Goodness.

Chapter Twelve - Life at 5 Devonshire House

As I got older there were more and more things about my father that I didn't like. On top of that I was changing. I was certainly brought up by Edith and Jim but I definitely wasn't theirs. I never really became a real Eastender complete with the 'gawd blimey' accent. I feel I was just someone who lived there. I am a Londoner, that's for sure, but thankfully I never acquired the sort of thick East End accent that Dad had. As I was getting older I was also starting to realize that certain things he did were wrong or even hideous. I was growing to hate his bad language, which made it impossible for me to take friends home. However, Dad had other bad habits like flobbing in the fire! To do this he used to sniff back really hard into the back of his nose to clear the snot and then spit it into the fire. I hated that, it was gross, but it was his house and he could do what he liked in it. I still hate spitting now. I think it is one of the reasons I hate football. It seems that all footballers do is gob all over the place in order to celebrate anything good they do. Not just goals but throw-ons or a good pass. The pitch must be covered in spit. It's no wonder they slide about so much!

Another trick of Dad's, when we were out, was to clear his nose by pressing on one nostril and blowing out of the other. Oh, Dad had so many little qualities like that. He was a real charmer at times. On top of having bad habits, the way he looked and behaved was also something pretty special. I always thought he behaved like old man Steptoe out of the TV programme Steptoe & Son. I was convinced that old man Steptoe, played by Wilfred Bramble, could have easily modelled his character on my dad. Even now I am convinced that somehow old man Steptoe must have known him as to me they were so alike. I, on the other hand, did not look like the hapless son Harold, played by Harry H. Corbet, although

I felt at times I suffered the same amount of embarrassment as he did. I still wince if I ever see the repeats on television.

With dinner and the TV programme finished, the announcement would come: 'Bath!' I am certain that Mum had to run the bath to try to prevent the hot water tank in the cupboard next to the fireplace from exploding. On the top of the tank was this large brass safety valve to let off the steam should the water get too hot. We would sit there and listen to the tank make this dripping sound and then hiss. It took Dad quite a while to find out, after having pulled out the entire contents of the cupboard, that this dripping sound was not the tank leaking but the water inside it boiling.

The hot tap on the bath would be fully opened and the pipes would make a retching sound like a dog about to vomit. Then there would be this rush of boiling water and steam. As you can imagine, completely safe! The bath would be run and by now we had upgraded from soda crystals to bath salts that made the water really soft but the smell was revolting. In I got and it was wonderful, despite the smell.

I always used to lock the door because as I got older I wanted my privacy. My Dad used to think it was great fun to rattle the door and try to come in, threatening to wash me down, which I am sure made my need for privacy abnormally premature. Mum would knock on the door and say, 'Come on Jimmy,' if she couldn't hear the noise of moving water. She would fear I had fallen asleep in the bath. I would reluctantly haul myself out and in no time I'd be dry and in my pyjamas. I would never pull the plug as often Mum would get into my water.

I used to love to sit and watch TV for a while after my bath and, with the combination of tiredness, a full belly and a hot bath, I was soon sitting there nodding off to sleep.

'Come on,' Mum would say and I would reluctantly go to bed.

The next day was Saturday and I was due to meet Jack outside the Odeon. I didn't bother to wait for an 86 bus to Bow Road - I just ran. They were bad enough in the week but at weekends they just weren't worth waiting for. I could see a bus coming along Bow Road and I made my usual mad dash to catch it. All the buses travelling west along Bow Road went past Mile End station - my destination. I was soon sitting upstairs on a Routemaster bus, I used to love sitting up top and in the front. I would wind the windows down with those little chromium plated handles and watch the world pass by. As we approached Mile End it was time to make a move. It wasn't a request stop, so I had no worries there. You had to ring the bell at a request stop - if you didn't the bus would just carry on. Of course, apart from local knowledge, there was no way of knowing this and I expect there has been many a passenger forced to walk back half a mile because they didn't ring the bell. Just the sort of thing you need when you are in a hurry or if it's tipping down with rain!

I hung onto the handrail as I ran down the steps and reached out for that white plastic coated upright pole on the platform at the back of the bus. If the conductor wasn't looking we used to hang onto this and swing out. The things kids would do on buses in those days would give even the hardiest of conductors a heart attack and often result in a clip round the ear or even being put off the bus, but even the threat of that didn't stop us.

I crossed over the great wide road (which had now changed its name from Bow to Mile End Road), at the lights on the crossroads of Burdett Road and Grove Roads. I ran into the hordes of kids waiting for the doors to open and I caught sight of Jack.

101

'Hi-yer,' I shouted out, 'not opened yet then?' Suddenly the doors opened and a flood of kids would pour in and queue at the two ticket offices. It didn't take that long to get our tickets and we were soon heading into the wonderland of children's cinema.

We came out after we had screamed our heads off at the villains and cheered the heroes and we decided to walk to Campbell Road. There were hundreds of kids waiting at the bus stops outside the cinema and even though there were loads of buses using this route we knew it would take a while to get on a bus, so walking would be quicker anyway. We were soon down to Bow Road police station where we crossed the road. We decided to save all of our bus fares and walk the rest of the way home, which, as we chatted away, didn't seem to take very long at all.

We arrived outside No.5 and I pulled out my latchkey.

'Hi,' I shouted out, 'Anyone home?'

Mum called from the kitchen, 'Yes, wipe your feet before you come in, I've just washed the floor.'

Jack followed me in and I showed him my bedroom. Then we went straight through the kitchen and into the yard.

'You hungry Jack?' asked Mum.

'No, not at the moment,' he answered.

'We're going exploring over the back,' I said. 'Can we have a sandwich when we get back?'

'Of course,' Mum said, being extremely polite. 'I am going to the hairdresser so I'll leave you both a sandwich on a plate on the draining board. There's a bottle of Tizer in the larder Jimmy. Make sure Jack has a drink.'

'OK,' I replied and we shot off down the yard and hopped up on the wall and soon disappeared into one of the many houses. Some had a strange feeling about them, almost as though something had been left behind. Probably it was someone who had died in the house - who knows. The feeling was eerie and in those houses we didn't hang around. You

102

could smell the dampness in them and the bits and pieces left behind were there because they probably wouldn't suit the new home.

'I bet these places could tell a tale or two,' I said.

'Yeah, I bet,' Jack said rummaging around in a cupboard. 'Bloody hell, look what I've found,' he called out. He'd found a dartboard, which still had a set of darts stuck in it. We soon had this on a wall in the lounge on a nail that probably once had a mirror hanging on it. The novelty of throwing darts soon wore off and we carried on rooting about.

Time just flew past and I asked Jack if he was hungry. He said he was, so we went back to the flat. I opened the back door and there was Dad having a shave in the sink. The door caught his bum as I shoved it open and he nicked his ear. This resulted in a flash of temper and a whack in the head.

'You fucking idiot!' he shouted at me. Jack was shocked at my Dad's bad language, as his Mum and Dad never swore.

'Sorry,' I said. 'I didn't see you behind the door.'

'Well you fucking-well should have done, it's got glass in it ain't it?' Dad said sticking a bit of toilet paper on the cut.

'Sorry,' I said again. I grabbed the plate with our sandwiches on it and the bottle of Tizer from the larder.

Dad said, 'Where's your mother?'

With a mouthful of cheese and beetroot sandwich, I said, 'She's gone to the hairdresser's' and I carried on eating.

'All right then, tell her I have gone round the garage.' (or 'garidge' as my dad pronounced it!)

Jack and I sat eating and Dad went through the lounge telling us to behave ourselves. I think Jack was terrified of my Dad; that's probably why he never came round our house much. Mind you, I don't blame him really as Dad terrified me too. Jack was used to a quiet life as his parents were so placid.

Dad was gone and we finished our sandwiches and went into

the garden to kick a ball around for a while. We soon got bored with that so I suggested to Jack that we go and have a nose up Knapp Road at the top of which were the gasworks and the cemetery. We went out of the flat and first of all went to the hairdresser's next to the bike shop in Campbell Road to tell Mum that Dad had gone round the garage and that Jack and I were going to have a look around up Knapp Road.

'Why?' she said. 'Look around what?'

I said that Dad had told me there was a cemetery up there and that we could also cut through that way to get back to Jack's house. I would go home with Jack and be back in time for tea.

'OK,' she said and went back to reading her magazine called Weekend as she sat under the dryer, which to me looked like an electric Easter egg.

We left the shop giggling because Jack blew a huge raspberry, which thankfully my mum didn't hear from under her space helmet. We turned into Knapp Road and opposite the primary school I could see my mate and fellow scout, Roland Peters, standing at his front gate. He said hello with his usual stammer and I asked him if he wanted to come along with us.

'We're going to take a short cut through the cemetery,' I said but he couldn't come because his mum was working in one of the shops around the corner and he had to look after his little sister.

'OK,' I said, 'see you on Sunday at church parade.' and Jack and I went on our way.

Much of the cemetery wall had fallen down and beyond the wall it was overgrown to the point that you could hardly see the tombstones. I thought it was sad to see such neglect with headstones fallen over, statues broken and the cemetery in such a mess. It was quite shocking to see how people could leave the graves of their families in such a state. We hopped over the wall although Jack looked a bit hesitant. It was quite a way across the neglected bit to the nearest cleared path and he didn't relish the thought of walking through all those graves. I wasn't heroic by any means but for some reason I wasn't frightened of the dead. It was the living that would beat you up or make your life unpleasant, not the dead.

We got to Jack's place and he ran up the steps and knocked at the door. Unlike me, he didn't have a latchkey. Jack, like we had done, still lived in a shared house - only he lived in the upstairs half. They shared with an old lady whom I never ever saw. She must have been very old as the house was always so quiet and in all my times there I never once saw or heard her. Unlike No. 49, Jack's Dad had built an extension out the back over the downstairs kitchen into which they had installed a bathroom and toilet. So at least Jack didn't have to suffer that dreadful winter wind trying to cut off his ankles.

Jack's Mum was pleased to see him home again, in one piece and reasonably clean. Usually when he went out with me, he and I would end up in a mess.
'Do you want to come in Jimmy?' she asked.
'I'd better not,' I said. 'My Mum will be doing tea soon.'
'OK,' she said and Jack shouted from half way up the stairs, 'See you in school on Monday,' as his mum closed the front door.

I was beginning to feel the aftershock of moving house. No 49 had been home to me for as long as I could remember and I missed all my friends. The great thing about No. 49 was it wasn't a through road and I could play in the street. This meant that whenever I went out there was always someone out there playing. No. 5 didn't have that so it was harder to make friends. I feared that the next few months were going to be tough on me and I was beginning to wonder if having an inside bathroom would be worth it.

Chapter Thirteen – Changing Schools

I soon got bored with the journey to Malmesbury Road School and I started to complain to Mum about it. I said that I just didn't want to make that journey any more and I asked her why I couldn't go to Knapp Road school, which was only a couple of hundred yards from our flat. Why-oh-why didn't someone explain to me what that change would mean to my future? Why didn't someone tell me that such a change might affect my eleven plus results and what sort of school I would be able to go to after that? In fact, why wasn't I told about the eleven plus full stop? No, my cries of 'I am fed up with this journey' were listened to without any such explanations and I was allowed to change schools. I went to Knapp Road school and what a culture shock that was. No longer did I have a different teacher for each subject but one teacher for all subjects. I also found that I was being taught things that I learned the best part of a year before.

I felt my life was suddenly falling apart. I had moved house, lost my friends, changed schools and I was getting more and more unhappy. I was terribly lonely and unhappy at home and that was taking a terrible toll on me. I was starting to experience strange sensations like hearing a hissing noise in my head and seeing double. These sensations often used to happen when I got home from school. The flat was empty and then the problem would start. I used to go out into the garden and hold onto one of the downpipes because I used to feel dizzy, and cry out 'go away'. I would just hold on with my eyes closed hoping it would stop. Mostly it did and I would go back indoors again. I never told my Mum and Dad about this. All I could think about was St Clements Hospital and I was worried I might end up in there. I thought I was going nuts.

On reflection I think my problem was probably caused by

depression brought on as a result of all the changes in my life. I was also getting older and getting a little more independent. I was growing more able to argue my corner using my sense of logic, which was rapidly developing. The biggest problem I had was that I was the second male in a home where logic counted for nothing. I had seen the Armand and Michaela Dennis wildlife programmes when the old lion used to beat the crap out of the young lions if they so much a breathed out of place. My Dad was the old male who felt threatened and so every now and then he would beat the crap out of me. It wasn't fun being the young male.

The next big blow in my life was to fail the eleven plus examination. In what seemed no time at all after that, I was given a choice of two schools to go to. One was St. Paul's Way Secondary Modern in Bow and the other was Hay Currie (H.C.) Secondary Modern in Poplar. I then made an even bigger mistake by choosing the latter and was to hate every single minute there.

Hay Currie was a typical East End post war secondary modern school housed in an old Victorian Building. The architects, in their efforts to give the building character, had plonked a green dome on the top on each corner. If nothing else it certainly stood out in the area and everyone around was aware of Hay Currie and its reputation.It had been built as an island site school, between Bright and Byron Streets, and at each end of the school were terraced houses. There were no grass fields for us to play on; we just had a tarmac playground, which had been lined out for netball and football. This was enclosed by a high wall on which was chain link fencing. All that was missing was the barbed wire. There were no wardens, just cruel inmates who, for the most part, were wrongly described as pupils. H.C. was a mixed school with both male and female thugs!

There was a school uniform, after a fashion, but no one wore it on the basis that most parents couldn't really afford to buy it. And so I was imprisoned there for the next four years. My sentence started after the Easter holidays in 1959 and I was filled with dread as I walked through the gates on the first day. Some of the older boys watched us with a look that said 'You'll do for later' and how right my interpretation of that look was.

First there was the 'morning assembly' when we all sang hymns and prayed. I prayed just to live the day out. At the end of assembly the new kids were told who their teachers were and advised of some of the ground-rules. A boy behind me kept prodding me in the back and saying.

'That doesn't apply to you, you fucking little shit.' I was struck with terror as I felt the blood drain from my head and my legs go weak. I felt light headed but I didn't dare faint. If I did it would draw attention to me. Someone might be blamed for my fainting and then I would have been in even more trouble. I stood locked in fear.

The first morning wasn't too bad mainly thanks to the teacher we had been allocated, Mr Lipton. He was quite young, not very tall with jet-black hair and a big nose. He always wore a nice suit and he was well respected by everyone. His smile alone instilled confidence. I think I owed a lot to that man for my survival at H.C.

I was one of the kids who had school dinners, which were terrible. After dinner I went into the playground with my new friend from class, Tony Keeble. Tony and I sat next to each other and struck up an immediate friendship. I think he was just as scared as I was. We walked out into the playground where there was a small group of boys, or yobs more like, hanging around looking for trouble and we were just what they were looking for. We were dragged into the toilet block, turned upside down and our heads were shoved into filthy toilet pans while they were flushed. If that wasn't terrifying enough, with wet hair dripping down all over us, we were then poled! Outside the toilet block there was a 'lean to' type cover supported by steel upright poles. That's where as many of us that were possible would shelter if it suddenly tipped down with rain. We were picked up, held up against the pole, our legs wrapped around the pole with one crossed over and then under the other. Then it was simply a matter of being lowered down the pole. A position not impossible to get out of, but not easy either, especially when a few yobs are kicking you in the back.

We got our hair dry, went into school for the afternoon and said nothing. I thought that was it. I had heard about school initiations and I thought I had gone through it quite well.

The 'gentleness' of the females in HC was demonstrated one day when Tony and I were walking through the assembly hall on our way to a class and a few yards in front of us walked one of the girls from either the third or fourth year. She was short and fat wearing black tights, a mini skirt, tight jumper and her hair terminally backcombed into a beehive. Her make-up looked as though it had been applied with a trowel. Her mouth was as foul as any sewer, and of a similar size! As we walked past Tony made the fatal mistake of staring at her. I mean, who wouldn't?
'Who the fuck do you think you are looking at?' she said to Tony.
'I don't know, shit ain't labelled!' he replied and we couldn't help but laugh. Even some of her classmates thought it was funny and joined in the fun as they waited to get into class. The walking beehive then calmly came over to Tony and as she did she took a swing at him. Her hand landed on the side of his face and he was knocked clean off his feet. I thought

from the way it sounded his head would surely come off. Poor Tony sprang back up again but it took him a few minutes to get over the shock. We walked off and then we broke into a run and we laughed as Tony shouted out, 'At least I can tell people I have made contact with you, you ugly bitch!'

Things at home between Dad and I were OK sometimes and when they were I loved it, but I knew the good times would never last and that even made the good times miserable. Dad was still a time bomb, a veritable bottle of nitro-glycerine travelling along a bumpy road. You never knew just when it was going to happen but you knew for sure it would. Either at school or at home I always seemed to be waiting for that dreaded moment. Dad's outbursts with me seemed to be getting more frequent and I was having more problems again. The hissing noise attacks in my head were happening more often and the double vision seemed to be getting worse. Although these episodes terrified me, I never dared tell anyone - I hadn't forgotten St Clements. So I received no treatment nor had a proper medical diagnosis. I just got on with it. I was always extremely anxious and I seemed to spend more and more time worrying about when and what I would be subjected to next. On top of this I was also still worried as to why I had this attraction for my own sex.

Things at H.C. had also become much worse for me as I was now being regularly bullied by a boy at school called Robert Tilson. He was a little taller than me, quite podgy and he lived in some flats in Devon's Road, in fact quite near Aunt Maria's. I used to come out of school through a different gate each night to try to avoid him but ultimately there was only one practical route home that I could take and that was Tilson's way home too. There was another way, but it would take us miles out of our way. I say we, because Tilson bullied Tony as well. We used to take diversions through nearby blocks of flats to try to avoid bumping into him. Sometimes it worked but very often it didn't. We used to get our pocket money taken off us if we had any, and he loved to dominate us. Unfortunately for Tilson, every dog has his day and mine was rapidly approaching. He hadn't planned for the fact that ultimately I might rebel and his downfall was just a matter of time.

I was beginning to really hate H.C. but somehow I muddled through the next three months until summer holidays. My only safe haven from H.C. was home, but things there weren't easy either. Dad seemed to be lashing out at me more and more especially if I got things wrong. He would also often accuse me of doing things I hadn't done. He would then proceed not only to tell me what I had done but, through gritted teeth, he would venomously spit out words telling me exactly how I had done it! There was no point in denying whatever it was I had been accused of. He would just say 'You've done this you little fucker and don't you deny it,' followed by, 'This is what you did,' and he would proceed to tell me exactly how I had done what I hadn't done. I would make the same old mistake every time, I would deny it. I would try to use logic to explain how I couldn't have committed this heinous crime, whatever it was.

For example, as already explained, in the kitchen we had a coal cupboard. On the day the coalman would come, Mum would put down newspaper on the floor for him to walk on and she would leave a key with the lady upstairs to let him in. One day Mum forgot to put down the newspaper and as would often happen, Dad got in from work before I came home from school. As I walked through the door he lashed out at me, verbally at first.
'You've had kids in here you fucking little bastard,' he screamed at me.
I just stood there in total shock and filled with terror. I had

just walked through the door from school having been bullied all the way home by Tilson. My home was my sanctuary and now I was realloy frightened. this time of my dad. I said to him, 'I haven't had anyone in here Dad - I have just walked in the door.'

Dad saw this as me just being clever and he whacked me in the head, saying,

'Don't talk to me like I am a fucking idiot - I don't mean just now I mean at fucking lunch time, that's when I fucking well mean,' and he again hit me. Understandably at this point I started to cry, which only seemed to make things worse.

'I haven't had kids in Dad,' I said. I was desperately trying to think of some way to placate him but my eleven-year old head had run out of ideas. He threw me into the armchair and proceeded to tell me in great detail what I had done. He then dragged me back out of the chair and held me up level with his face as my feet dangled from the floor. Our noses were inches apart and he would shout out his theory on what I had done with such venom that my face would be covered in his spit.

'You came home at lunch time.'

'I didn't,' I cried,

'And you brought some of those mates of yours in here, didn't you?' he would scream into my face. 'You played hide and seek in the coal cupboard and walked coaldust all over the place didn't you?' I was still suspended by the front of my shirt with my feet off the floor.

'I didn't, I was at school, and I didn't come home.'

'You fucking little liar,' he screamed at me as he lowered me to the floor and then, out of sheer frustration with me, he smacked me in the face with the back of his leathery old hand. My nose began to bleed as he dragged me into the kitchen.

'You fucking liar!' he kept screaming at me. 'I'll teach you to fucking bring kids in this 'ouse!' By now I was screaming in terror,

'Don't hit me again, I didn't do it, I didn't do anything.'
He released his grip and grabbed me by the hair. He opened the coal cupboard and as if about to shove me in he said 'Now tell the fucking truth you little bas....'

All of the boards that had to be slotted in to hold the coal back when the cupboard was full were in place! The cupboard was brimming full of coal. There wasn't enough room for a cat to get in, let alone me. Even Dad in his own ignorant way soon realized that the coalman had been and that Mum had obviously not put the paper down on the floor.

I stood trembling, with blood running down my face mixed with the salty tears pouring out of my eyes. He released his grip and said still in an accusing tone, albeit much softer, 'Why didn't you tell me the coalman had been?'
I tried to tell him that I didn't know he was coming but my tears and sobs wouldn't let me speak. He walked into the lounge and I went into the bathroom for some toilet roll to clean my face up. I then went into the lounge and sat on a chair. I hated him more than ever at these times and grew to worry more and more when the next time would be.

He kept saying why didn't I tell him, as though it would have made any difference! Like he was listening to me. I don't think so. What he never said was sorry. He just made it sound as though it was my fault. If I had only told him the coalman had been this wouldn't have happened. This was not a time to apply logic; the last thing needed at this point was an eleven-year-old making him look stupid. This was not a time to say, if I had known the coalman had been I would have said immediately and this wouldn't have happened. My nose would still be in shape and I would be happy boy instead of a terrified child. I wouldn't be sitting here with a throat that ached from sobbing and a stomach aching from fear. My Dad could go out of control sometimes to such a degree that I feared for my own safety. Such was the level of his temper.

The moment passed and Dad had calmed down. He had calmed me down before Mum came in. A blind man could have seen the problems etched in my face. Mum walked through that door and as much as I wanted to, I knew I did not dare let on what had happened. I so much wanted her to hold me, but I knew if she did, I would cry, the truth would out and it would probably lead to a row between them. Dad would get violent again and so would my Mum and the argument would be over me and it would be my fault. The hissing noises in my head were getting worse. Much was done by my Dad to make up for that incident. Dad would work at being nice to me and eventually I believed him. I wanted to believe him. I wanted a normal life. I was fed up with going round to the houses of my friends and seeing how natural their parents were and wishing mine were the same. I resented being in a friend's house and not wanting to go home as I bathed in the warmth of someone else's family life, wishing I could stay. I wanted to be loved by my Dad.

Chapter Fourteen - Scotland

A few weeks went by and I was back to trusting Dad once again. I had momentarily stopped worrying about when the next time would be. We were going on our annual camping holiday, only this time to Scotland and with Uncle Billy, Mum's brother, and Aunt Eve and their two children Kathy and Simon. Like us they had a motorbike and sidecar with a trailer on the back. Dad was still into travelling at night but as we were with Billy and Eve we set out in the early afternoon instead of late at night. In those days Scotland took much longer to get to, without the benefit of motorways. We travelled for several hours on England's main artery, the A1, before Dad decided to be fair on all concerned and stop for the night. For the whole journey the weather had been dreadful. I was sitting pillion and as usual was wrapped up like a bundle of rags in anything that would keep me warm and dry. We pulled off the road into a field and set up camp. I really don't think you could do that today somehow, but we used to do it, and for whatever reason, get away with it.

The tents were up and beds were made, all done in terrible conditions. I had to hand it to my dad - he would struggle on in any weather and he always managed to get things done. Dad told me to help him put the waterproof cover back on the trailer to keep out the rain. I was eleven years old and standing there on a really windy night being lashed by rain. I was not strong enough to hold the plastic cover on the trailer as the wind did its best to snatch it from me. A sudden gust of wind whipped it from my cold wet hands and it slapped into Dad's face. He lost his temper and called me a fucking idiot as he struck out at me, hitting me square in the face. I fell over backwards into the mud. I screamed out with the pain as the rain diluted the blood from my nose. I looked down and the blood frightened me even more as I got up and I ran to the tent and he just carried on without me. I opened the flap of the tent and I must have looked like I had just had the absolute crap knocked out of me. I was tired, wet, cold and in pain and I just stood and sobbed, and then it happened. Mum grabbed me along with her coat and purse and off we marched into the night along a field full of corn stubble - a field that was now a quagmire and that was hard for me to walk on, let alone Mum. We passed the trailer, which by now Dad had managed to cover on his own.

'That's it,' she screamed at him, 'you've fucking hit this boy for the last time. We're going home!' Home! I ask you! We were miles from anywhere, the weather was doing its best to annihilate us and Mum and Dad started to have a row. God only knows what Billy and Eve must have thought as they lay in their tent just a few feet away. I screamed in floods of tears telling them to stop. Dad just got angrier and angrier and Mum stood her ground. If ever arguments followed my Dad attacking me, I always blamed myself, especially if it resulted in violence.

Dad's anger was fearful and I thought he would kill us both. His language was terrible with so many 'F' words thankfully being muffled by the wind and rain. In the end Mum realized the impossibility of our situation and dragged me back to the tent. She said that in the morning we would go home, as it was obvious we couldn't go now. Dad then had the time to be nice again, which when necessary he was so good at. He'd once again pushed us all to the very edge and was now throwing us a lifeline to pull us back again. He was suddenly trying to rescue us as we stood on the edge of the abyss he had nearly pushed us into. It wasn't too long before he won Mum over, although the peace never lasted - but for however long it did, it was very welcome.

The next morning the rain had gone and the tents were steaming in the morning sun. Dad was up cooking us breakfast, the cover was off the trailer and already he had repacked much of our chattels ready for the off. Billy and Eve awoke to the smell of hot tea and a cooking breakfast. Dad was steadily stirring a huge saucepan of porridge, which was enough for everyone. No one dared mention anything about last night, save for the weather. Eve said that they had crashed out really quick due to tiredness which was her way of saving him having to apologise for his behaviour and bringing the whole thing up again which was the last thing any of us wanted. The bikes were packed up and we were once again on our way to Scotland.

Our journey took us through Braemar and up the famous 'Devil's Elbow' double road bend and followed on toward Ballater passing through Crathie next to Balmoral Castle, the Queen's summer retreat. The sun was bright and the countryside breathtaking. I couldn't help notice how different it was to the rolling hills of Devon as the bike weaved its path through the woodlands. Every now and then the wooded areas would open into fields and meandering through the middle was the River Dee. It sparkled as it fell over the rocks making its way down to the sea.

Everything was fine and Dad was happy as we trundled along through magnificent countryside. He patted my leg, which told me all was well and I hugged up close to him to keep myself out of the chilly morning air, which was whistling over his shoulders and into my face.

Suddenly there was a sign that said Coilacreich and just beyond that, another saying Camping. The campsite was on the riverside of the road so there was a good chance it would run down to the river. Although I didn't like being in the middle of nowhere, this place was Heaven. Coilacreich was neither town nor village. It was simply an old inn with a few out buildings. Across the road from the inn was one of these old buildings outside of which was an antiquated manual petrol pump. It didn't take me long to befriend the landlord and I was soon helping him to sell his petrol. While he talked to the motorists in his thick Scottish accent, thanks to which most of what he said I couldn't understand, I swung away at the pump handle as I watched the meter to make sure I only gave what was asked for.

We were only about three miles from Ballater so getting food supplies was really easy and made even easier by an enterprising grocer who used to call at the site three days a week in his large van to deliver bread, milk and just about everything else.

We pulled off the road and onto the site, which was on two levels. We went down to the lower level of the campsite and found our spot. The site was undeveloped and quite natural with some old railway carriages on it, which had been purchased ready to convert into permanent holiday homes. Painted green, they blended into the background. It seemed odd, as the last thing you would ever expect to find in a wonderful area like this would be a railway carriage. Dad wandered up to one of them and asked the occupants what you had to do to camp here and who we would have to pay. How he understood them, Heaven only knows and how they understood him was even more of a puzzle. He came back and told us we just set up camp and the owner comes round every day at about teatime to collect the fees. That was all we needed to know. Dad was still being nice, as normally I would be made to help, by unpacking or helping to put up the tent. Instead he told me to take Kathy and Simon down through the woods to check things out. That was a much better prospect and I didn't need to be told twice. We were off and we soon found the path, which led to the toilet. This was built on the same principle as our scouts latrine only more permanent. It was made of wood and not canvas and it had a tin roof, rather like the ones down at hop picking. The inside was clean and it had a wooden seat over a deep hole. The real joy was that it didn't smell because the site was hardly used. We carried on past the toilet for about fifty yards and there in front of us was a short length of two-inch diameter pipe poking out of the ground out of which poured a constant flow of water. It was a natural spring, which served as the water supply for that end of the site. This place was truly idyllic to anyone like my Dad, seeking peace, quiet and seclusion.

Ahead of us was an opening into another clearing and part of the campsite, which again led back into the woods. As we peered out I told Kathy and Simon to be quiet and look. There in the middle of the clearing was a family of rabbits eating and playing about. Kathy couldn't contain her excitement and squealed with delight and that was the end of the rabbits. They zoomed off in every direction back into the cover of the forest. We walked on for a while longer and the path took us through dense ferns, the smell of which was almost overwhelming. On the edge of a clearing there was a pile of pine needles, which attracted my attention, as someone must have piled them there. Not someone, but something, ants; hundreds of thousands of ants. I had never seen an ants' nest before and I never knew they could squirt acid at you. Thankfully I got a long stick and poked at the nest. They went potty, whizzing around all over the place attacking the end of my stick. I dug away and discovered deeper into the nest were their eggs. I had seen enough and left them to it. The way they were working they would soon have it all back together again. Kathy and Simon looked on in horror. We continued into the forest which all seemed so untouched. Then, as the fir trees thinned out, ahead of us was the River Dee. It was full of boulders and rocks over which the river poured its endless flow of sparking fresh and very cool water. The other side of the river was comparatively flat farmland with a few sheep quietly munching their way through the day.

Simon was still very young so I watched him like a hawk just in case he decided to fall into the river. Kathy on the other hand simply sat on a huge boulder contentedly dropping her small handful of pebbles one by one into the water. As they slid through the crystal clear water she excitedly called me to look at the small salmon fry darting about. That little pool was to give us hours and hours of endless fun. It was quite deep compared to the rest of the river, in fact deep enough to swim in, albeit not far. The pool was well protected from the fast flow by a barrier of huge boulders, which even made the water a little warmer.

I thought it was time we returned to tell our parents of our discoveries and in no time we were back. The tents were up and Mum and Aunt Eve were busy preparing some food. First we were given tomato soup in a mug with a thick slice of buttered bread. This was to stave off our hunger until our late lunch, which was well under way. Dad and Uncle Billy had collected a whole stack of firewood as our friendly Scottish neighbour in the railway carriage along the way had told him that fires were allowed as long as we were careful.

We didn't have to create a place for our camp fire; it was already there, tried and tested by those lucky people who had also found this wonderful place. They had carefully placed a circle of large stones to keep the fire in and in no time at all our fire was crackling away. The smell of the burning pine was wonderful.

The holiday went well for a few days until Mum and Dad went to Ballater where they met some people from the site who were resident in one of the railway carriages. They were having trouble with their Bedford Dormobile, an early version of a Caravanette. Dad, as he so often did, offered to try to help them repair it. He told them that he had to get the shopping and drop Mum back at the site but then he would come back to Ballater to see what he could do. He soon found out what the problem was and he made the repair, which got them back to the site. They were extremely grateful to him and invited him in for a wee dram! He had had nothing to eat and the whisky went straight to his head. On top of that they gave him a nice bottle of ten-year-old whisky, to say thank you. Little did they know what they were doing to him - and us. When he came back to the site it was obvious he had downed a few. He parked up the bike and as he sat by the fire Mum asked him where he had been. His reply was almost incoherent, as the whisky had taken hold. Mum mentioned dinner and he mumbled that he'd help her get it ready. He then crouched next to the fire peeling potatoes and in no time was falling asleep over the saucepan, still holding a potato in one hand and the peeler in the other. Mum suggested that he go to bed and she would finish off. Miraculously, for once, he did what he was told and he slept for about three hours. He woke up a different man and God help us, as Mr Nasty was back.

My Aunt Eve had heard enough of my dad talking to us like dirt and spoke up against him. That was her big mistake and Uncle Billy immediately and understandably took her side and that just poured fuel on the fire. Things just got worse and worse from then on and before I knew it, Dad flipped. 'Fuck it, I have had enough,' he said and he started taking down our tent. At this point there was no reasoning with him as he'd made his decision and there was no going back. We were moving. Eve and Billy and the kids went into their tent as we de-camped and took everything that was ours with us. The problem for Eve and Billy was that everything save for their tent was ours. They were left with nothing to cook with or drink from. We moved up to the higher level and there we stayed. Dad had mistakenly left our teapot next to their tent and I was sent down to retrieve it. I felt terribly mean doing this under cover of darkness but Dad was to be obeyed and I lived with him not my Aunt and Uncle.

The next morning Eve and Billy were gone and Dad blamed the whole episode onto them. Mum and I felt terrible but him blaming them let us off the hook and gave us a quiet life and Mr Nice came back again.

The rest of the holiday went well without a single bad word. I even remember Mum having a fit of the giggles about something Dad had said or done. He kept saying 'Wot, wot?' and the more he said 'Wot, wot?', the more she laughed and the more we all laughed. Sadly, moments like that were few and far between.

It was to be many months before we saw Billy and Eve again. You would think that they would never forgive Dad for what he had done to them. However, the love a brother has for his sister will overcome everything, if necessary, and Billy obviously felt that by allowing this rift to continue he was in a worse position to watch her to make sure Dad didn't abuse her too much.

It was Christmas Eve 1959 when Eve and Billy arrived with the kids to bring me my Christmas present. I was the excuse. I was the bridge they needed to get them over the river of trouble. I opened the door and was really pleased to see them. 'It's Aunt Eve,' I shouted out and she came in followed by Uncle Billy, Kathy and Simon. Time had healed everything and miraculously nothing was said about the holiday, well not that I heard. The evening went well and somehow Uncle Billy managed to talk to Dad about everything but their holiday from hell. I am sure Dad never felt there was anything to apologise for so he made his usual effort to make them welcome. It was also arranged that they would come back the next day and have Christmas lunch with us. Eve would bring all the things she had bought and between them she and Mum would produce a wonderful Christmas lunch.

Billy and Dad would first go round the Widow's Son pub just around the corner to meet up with Dad's brothers for a pre-Christmas drink. This was often a disaster as Dad would invariably come back drunk and not want his lunch but just have some more to drink and then fall asleep. Mum and I would then quietly eat lunch so as not to wake up the sleeping dragon.

They came back, not drunk but sober as Dad was on one of his best behaviour trips. He was doing what he was good at. He was being nice to get back into our confidence again; to get us to believe all was well and for us to put our guard down and then, wham, Mr Nasty would come back. This was how life was with him, normally, but not this Christmas lunch. I particularly remember this lunch as we all sat down together like normal people. It was fun as crackers were pulled and then, lashings of food was brought in on plates piled high. Afterwards we even had Christmas pudding with custard and then the adults plonked themselves in front of the TV and we kids set about opening our presents. It was like being part of a real big happy family.

The festive season passed and we entered 1960 the usual way. My Mum and Dad had gone out with the family to a pub. I was at home alone watching Andy Stewart and Kenneth McKeller on the television doing their usual New Year's Eve programme after which I would take myself off to bed. I hated New Year's Eve. Still it was a new decade. The 'swinging sixties' - only I was too young to do much swinging.

The school holidays were over and I was back at H.C. trying to dodge Tilson as usual. I had my favourite subjects and Music was one. Our music teacher was Mr Browning who had a young round face, thick black wavy hair and manicured nails that you could hear click on the keys as he played the piano. He was so kind and he had a great way about him when it came to getting a bunch of grubby East End kids interested in classical music. I took up the recorder and I also joined the school choir. I loved singing even though that too became something to be ridiculed over. The school's upper echelon of bullies thought being in the choir was definitely a bit on the sissy side - something else I had to pay for.

Chapter Fifteen – Enter Tom Granger

The scouts had really proved to be my salvation. It was a place I could go where I could be among boys of my own age and older, who were caring and who didn't bully smaller boys, but instead, helped them. Where you didn't have to be tough to survive and where you could be yourself. I had worked hard at learning what I needed and I soon got my first promotion. I became the Second in the Eagles patrol. I now had a stripe on my shirtsleeve as well as a goodly bunch of badges.

It was at one of our troop meetings on a Thursday night, after we had enjoyed a really good evening, that we were introduced to a visitor. Mr Granger, Mr Tom Granger and we were not told who he was, or why he was there. It was the end of the evening, when everything had been put away in its place and shortly afterwards we were dismissed. He watched us, as we put on our coats ready to go. There was the usual shouting 'g'nite' to each other and the hall was cleared. We saw the office light go on and Mr Granger walk in with Skip.

The next time I saw Mr Granger was on the Sunday at church parade. He was standing next to Skip in the front row. He was a tall man, about fifty years old with thin greying hair that was combed back and stuck down with Brylcream (hair cream). He had a kind face which distracted you from noticing that his ears stuck out and that he had quite a big nose. He stood there in his beige reversible raincoat and highly polished black shoes.

The service went as usual as we sat there in a full church listening to the sermon. You could hear a pin drop as our vicar skilfully told us about the necessity of kindness. He talked of Bob-a-Job week, which was approaching and how it was important to do what jobs we were given with a good heart. He told us that the work was more about kindness than earning money. To me it was a competition as to who could earn the most in the troop. We left for home and I didn't hang around as there was a roast dinner waiting for me. The rest of the weekend went by in its usual quiet fashion. How I missed all my mates in Morville Street. There just seemed nothing to do in Violet Road and no one to do it with. School on Monday was its usual grim self and Tuesday was only marginally better thanks to the thought of scouts that night.

I arrived at Bow Baptist and locked up my bike to the fencing and went in. There was Skip standing talking to a few of the boys and the mysterious Mr Granger was there once again. I, along with many others I am sure, was beginning to wonder what all this was about. The evening went well with its usual mixture of games and learning of knots or first aid. As usual, half way through Wishbone made evening tea that was served with a choice of biscuits for a small fee of three pence. Skip sat chatting to Mr Granger when suddenly Skip blew his whistle and there was silence.

'Right,' he shouted, 'form straight lines in your patrols,' and we all scurried about putting cups in the washing-up bowl and rushing to his instruction.
'Atten-shun,' he shouted and there was an exact row of right shoe leather joining left. He walked down the four patrols, inspecting us and then he returned to the front.
'At-eeze,' he called and we returned to the more relaxed 'at ease' position.
'I have something to tell you. I want you all to sit down.' We looked at each other as we sat down on the floor cross legged and still in our straight lines.

'There is no easy way for me to say this to you so I shall just have to be blunt and come to the point. Due to a change in our circumstances I have decided that it is necessary to leave the 38th.' The gasps of breath and grunts of disapproval among us were loud. We then sat in stunned silence as Skip went on to say, 'As many of you know, I do actually have a job and I have been offered promotion. But accepting it means moving away from Bow up to Northampton. As a family we have discussed the advantages this promotion will bring and after much thought we all agreed that it will be in our best interest that I should accept and we should make the move. I am sure most of you will understand that this has not been an easy decision for us to make, as among so many things we will miss the 38th the most.'

This ragged bunch of dedicated kids sat in silence as Skip delivered his stunning news. I could feel an enormous lump in my throat and am sure there were many others equally as shattered by this news as I was.
'I hope you do not feel that I am letting you down. I have tried my best to make the 38th the best troop in the East End and I think with your help and support we have done that.'
You could have heard a pin drop.

'You have all been introduced to Mr Granger and I want you to know that he has been appointed as your new Scout Master in agreement with both the Church and Baden Powell House. I want you to give him your loyal support the same as you have done me.'
In a way I felt sorry for Tom Granger, as Skip's shoes would be hard to fill. One of the patrol leaders chirped up, 'When will you be leaving, Skip?'
'At the end of the month,' he said, which meant there was much planning to be done. During the next couple of troop meetings we all asked our questions and we began to accept the idea of Skip leaving. Tom Granger was now in uniform and easing himself into his new job well. He was no fool and knew well how to handle this situation.

By the end of the month, Tom was our new Skip and we had learned to follow our new leader. He had quickly realised that to many of us the scouts was a real lifeline and Skip's coming departure was not going to be easy. Still, we had busied ourselves planning his surprise farewell party and a splendid gift to say thank you was also organised, thanks mainly to Tom Granger. On one of the nights when our departing Skip was not at the troop meeting, Tom Granger suggested that an ideal departing gift would be a crystal bowl. If we agreed he would arrange to have it engraved with 'Good Luck from all at the 38th Poplar'. We all agreed.

The dreaded night arrived and at the end of the evening when we were standing neatly in our patrols, we were called to attention and told to about turn facing the back of the hall. Then our beloved departing Skip marched in. He stood, took the salute and we were again instructed to about face. His wife and daughter stood in front of us next to Tom Granger and Skip walked to the front to join them. As he 'did, our patrol leaders led us into 'For he's a Jolly Good Fellow' and we all clapped loudly. It was plain to see Skip was really moved by this. Tables had been placed at the front of the hall where the Church dignitaries sat and at the middle of the top table were three seats for Skip, his wife and his little daughter.

The time had come that we had all dreaded. Our new Scout Master stood and first called 'Troop, attention,' That was his first official command and, as slick as we could, the order was obeyed. Followed by 'At ease', and we relaxed.

The job of presenting our gift and giving a short thank you speech fell to 'Wishbone' Ted Rouse and he did the job well. I remember he finished his speech with the words, 'The 38th Poplar is a well-respected troop, thanks only to your efforts, we all owe you a lot and hope that this small gift will always remind you of us.' He handed over the gift and took his place back in the troop as we all applauded. Skip opened the box and it was easy to see he was having an effort to hold back his tears. The evening went well and we enjoyed tucking into the buffet. There had been enough fuss and speeches and now it was time for him to go.

Skip (our new one) called the troop to order and we did so at ease, facing front. 'Attention' was ordered and we stood there in the neatest possible lines. Our departing leader and his family had made their way to the doors at the back of the hall. 'Troop about face. Salute!' and we did as our departing Skip returned the salute. As he went out of that door, a new era marched in.

One of Skip's first major acts was his decision that it was time we actually got that van we had been saving up for. The newspaper collecting had really slowed down and Skip re-motivated us. Soon we were collecting mountains of newspapers and it was being sold, as soon as we had enough to sell. I don't know how much money was handed over to Skip when he took over the 38th but it didn't seem to take long to announce that we had enough money to buy a van, as well as tax and insure it. We were thrilled. On reflection I think that Tom Granger probably put a good chunk of his own money into the pot to get us to this point so quickly.

We were once again rapidly approaching Easter and our Easter weekend camp at Cuffley. A few days before our departure, we arrived for one of our troop meetings and there it was standing in the courtyard of the church, a bull-nose Ford van with *38th Poplar Scouts* painted on the side of it. It had been well polished up and looked brilliant to the inexperienced eye. It was getting on a bit and was not without its fair share of wear and tear. It was hardly the latest model with its three forward gears and one reverse that made a dreadful noise when it was engaged. Still it worked and it was ours.

Preparations were made for our camp and for the first time we all travelled in style, by that I mean no one had kit to carry. Our new (but old) van was driven by Skip's brother-in-law, and, with some careful loading, it took all the tents, pots and pans, kit bags and rucksacks. We followed afterwards by train and it was so civilised, but I also missed the excitement of us all piling into a London Underground train with all this kit and all the noise we used to make doing it, the train guard watching as we fought to get everything in before he could close the doors. Some of the commuters smiled at a bunch of polite but excited boys struggling with kit bags bigger than themselves, others buried their faces in the morning paper, trying to ignore our giggles. We played to those that were smiling with delight at our antics as we passed about sweets and clowned about. It gave us a warm feeling that we were making someone's otherwise dull morning a bit brighter.

Having, as usual, caught a steam train from Kings Cross station, we arrived at Cuffley in Hertfordshire. It was quite a march from the station to the campsite but with the luxury of not having to carry kit, we got into it and soon arrived in good spirits. Skip went to the office to book us in and soon re-appeared with one of the site's managers who led him to a wooden hut. The door was opened and there it all was a mini mountain of our gear. I am sure the luxury of no longer having to lug kit earned our new Skip a lot of Brownie points and also went a long way to earning him the respect that he would soon come to deserve. The troop's cart was assembled and as much as possible loaded on it. The rest went on our backs or was carried between us. Many assisted in just getting the cart to our allocated site and in no time at all tents were being erected.

We formed the usual shape with our tents only this time, instead of Skip having a large tent for himself and his family set in the centre, to one side was a small one man tent. It was a really good one. Made of thick waxy canvas. It had a sewn-in groundsheet and a small bell tent-type end to it, which I had not seen before. The sewn-in groundsheet was a real boon to us and meant the days of the loose groundsheet were numbered, thank goodness. Loose groundsheets were a real pain, as so often bedding would end up on the grass because the groundsheet had moved. Also clothes, bedding and shoes would nearly always be wet from the dew as it rose during the night.

Skip had a great sense of humour. We first saw this on the day we put up a rope swing, which stretched across the stream on site. It was a hot day, which was unusual for Easter. We had all been on a nature trail and we were hot. It was suggested that we rig up a Bosun's chair across the stream so that we could practise rescuing someone from a sinking ship. Well the chair was never erected but a really good swing was. There was side-splitting hilarity as scout after scout didn't make it across or just hadn't let go at the right time, eventually losing momentum, hanging in the middle of the stream, where, in the end, there was only one winner, gravity! One by one all but Skip, who laughed with tears running down his face, and a few Senior Scouts ended up in the stream, which by now had got really muddy. We were all in a terrible state but what a day.

We were marched off to the showers to get cleaned up while Skip and the Seniors got on with dinner. What pleasure it was dressing in clean clothes and sitting down to a really good meal of sausages, mash and beans. Everything was cleared away and pots were once again stacked back in the store.

The day came to an end and the Union Jack was lowered as we stood in a circle around the pole and Skip led us in a prayer. He thanked God for the great day we had been given and asked him to watch over us this night. We saluted and returned to the campfire, which now seemed to burn brighter in the night sky. We were soon singing our usual camp songs and then it was time for bed. I lay in my sleeping bag and reflected on the day thinking that Skip had certainly proved himself as a good leader. He was a much softer man than the last Skip and he seemed much more openly caring about as. The weekend went really well and Easter Monday came too soon as it was the time when we had to pack up camp.

It didn't take long and soon everything was bundled on the cart and we headed back to the site HQ. There it was, our bull-nose van complete with driver, ready to get all the gear back to Bow Baptist. It didn't take us long to load it up and it was soon chugging off down the road. We all marched off to Cuffley station to catch the train home.

Chapter Sixteen - A New Dog

I got home to No. 5 and things were pretty quiet, strangely so. Dad was sitting in his chair watching television and Mum was at the table eating a tangerine.

'Good weekend?' she asked.

'Yeah fantastic, we had such a laugh and the van made such a difference. It was great not having to carry everything from the station to the camp.'

'Oh, good,' she said, 'put the kettle, on will you Jimmy.' Bloody hell I thought, what sort of a welcome is this?. I went into the kitchen to put on the kettle. I opened the kitchen door and was welcomed by some sharp claws and something that had its needle sharp teeth biting into my scout socks.

'What the bloody hell is...' I started to say and as I looked down I was stopped in my tracks.

'Mum there's a dog in the kitchen!' I picked him up and ran back into the lounge. 'Mum look, there's a puppy in the kitchen.'

'Yes, I know,' she said in a matter of fact tone. 'He's yours.' I couldn't believe it. I had been on about getting a dog and here he was: Prince!

He was a black and white mutt, a mongrel or, as my Dad called them, pie shop dogs. I always thought he meant dogs that lived in pie shops but he said he meant dogs that provided pie shops with meat, Yuk. Yuk. Not this mongrel! Prince was mine.

'We thought you might like a dog for your birthday,' Mum said. Dad just sat there smiling.

'Really, he's really mine, blimey. Come on boy, come on,' I called him and he followed me everywhere I went. This was one of the good times, not because I had got what I wanted, but there was no time better with my dad than when he gave me something, well except a bloody nose.

One night that week we went over to see Nanny Taylor as she had called Mum at work and asked us to go over. As we walked through the door there was something quite different about the place. The kitchen table was clear of all the sauce bottles that normally stood there like a small forest in the centre. There were no pots and pans beside the stove; in fact, the place looked unfamiliarly tidy. Mum was more aware of this than I. As usual I was focused on food and asked Auntie Sadie if I could have a biscuit. She did her usual grabbing hold of me and planting a big smacker on my face as she went 'Hmmwa! How are you, you little bastard, been behaving yourself?'

If the world had been available to her, my Auntie Sadie would have given it to me, but it wasn't, so I settled for a Wagon Wheel instead. A Wagon Wheel was a huge chocolate-covered biscuit made of layers of biscuit, sponge, cream and jam. An important thing to know about a Wagon Wheel is that it was too big for even the biggest mouth to take in whole. Furthermore, it could have safely carried a guarantee that it would put a smile on any hungry young child's face, provided they liked chocolate.

'What's going on?' Mum asked Aunt Sadie.
'At long last we have been offered a house by the council,' she said
'Where is it?' Mum enquired.
'Dagenham,' Sadie told her, with a broad smile on her face.
'You won't believe this,' she went on to say, 'but the address is 128 Grange Road, which is off Parsloes Avenue and near to your old school.'
'Really!' said Mum. At this point Nanny interrupted with 'Want a cup of tea Jim?'

'Yes please Gert,' he said and you could hear from the tone of Nan's voice that she wasn't happy that Aunt Sadie hadn't already offered us tea before getting carried away on tales of moving. Having lived with Nanny for many years, Aunt Sadie was more than receptive to her tone of voice so she quickly put the kettle on, giving Mum a look that said, whoops! The tea was made and soon we were all sitting down with huge mugs of tea and ready to listen.

Aunt Sadie told us about the offer of the house and what it was like as Nanny sat in her favourite armchair rolling herself, Aunt Sadie and Dad, cigarettes. She had a little hand-held cigarette rolling machine that, when loaded properly, as you shut it, a finished licked down, roll-up would pop out of a slot in the lid. Nan had on more than one occasion tried to show me how to use it, but my efforts always came out like lumpy cigars invariably with the paper inside out. The paper not being inside out was important to the process as it meant that the glue strip was on the correct side to stick the thing together. Nanny was really adept and could churn roll ups out on her little machine really quickly. Not only was she quick, but she could make them really thin, which meant that her tobacco went that much further.

I assume to some, the idea of either my Nan or my Aunt rolling fags, may not conjure up a great picture . However, I had grown up with it and at that age, I saw nothing unusual in the way they lived.

The evening passed pleasantly and it was agreed that Mum and Dad would go with Aunt Sadie and Uncle Ronnie to see the house at the weekend. Nanny would stay at home and babysit my cousins Janice, Barry, Peter and Fred. Although Janice was the oldest child she wasn't actually Uncle Ronnie's and Aunt Sadie's daughter. Barry, Peter and Fred were their natural children but Janice was sort of fostered but never properly adopted by them. For some reason unknown to me Janice was the daughter of my Aunt Eve's brother and lived with Aunt Sadie and Uncle Ronnie, I guess because he couldn't cope. Aunt Eve, of course, is the wife of Aunt Sadie's oldest brother, my Uncle Billy. Just like in the TV programme Dallas, all we need at this point is for someone who had died to pop up in the shower and announce that all this is just a dream. I didn't really know much more about the situation with Janice than that and I always felt that my Aunt Sadie was good for doing what she did for her. Aunt Sadie treated her as though she were her own and although life wasn't exactly easy, I am sure life for Janice was infinitely better than what it might have been had she been placed in a home, or fostered by complete strangers. Sadie had quite a capacity to manage and, considering their living conditions, she managed extremely well.

It was Sunday when Aunt Sadie and Uncle Ronnie turned up outside our house. We were ready and were soon off on our way to Dagenham. The new house was at the top of what was locally known as a Banjo. This was a row of houses either side of a wide pathway, which opened at one end into a circle around which the houses continued. It was so named because of its shape. The house had been decorated to council standards and compared to what they had been living in, was luxurious. It had three bedrooms, bathroom, kitchen lounge and a dining room, which could be closed off with folding doors. The dining room in later years became Nanny's bedroom when, because of her bad heart, she was no longer able to climb the stairs.

The garden was large and as they had never had a garden before they didn't know how to look after it and it became a real tip. The dog they would soon acquire helped take care of that for them as it dug holes all over the place.

Their move, as far as I remember, went well and soon we were doing our usual regular visits to Dagenham instead of Bethnal Green. Uncle Raymond, Mum's youngest brother was still living with Nan although you wouldn't have thought so. Whenever we went round there he always seemed to be in bed. I suppose as we nearly always visited on a Sunday afternoon, he was probably getting over his big lunch and recovering from the night before. Nobody once questioned him about being in bed, and, no matter how much noise we made, he would sleep through it. Mum always said 'Uncle Raymond could sleep through a bomb going off.' Judging by the noise we could sometimes make, I think she was right.

Chapter Seventeen - The Death of Prince

I was back at H.C. and I hated being there more than usual. It seemed so much harder to go back there especially after having had such a good weekend among nice people. The kids in school seemed so different. There was so much violence and mindless aggression. This was particularly evident one day as I was walking through the assembly hall to get to my next lesson. I walked past a queue of kids outside a classroom. Someone coming toward me shoved me into the queue as they passed and I fell into a fifth year boy who towered above me.

'Sorry,' I said, 'someone pushed me,' and with that he pulled me up by the upper arms and then kneed me in the balls. The pain was excruciating and by far the worst I had ever encountered and I was in agony as he let me fall to the floor. As I lay there clutching what was probably the remains of my testicles, his classroom door opened and he casually stepped over me and walked in. I managed to haul myself up and then, holding my balls, I ran like the hunchback of Notre Dame through the assembly hall and back to my form class. I collapsed outside the classroom door screaming in pain and someone called for Mr. Lipton. I lay there holding where my balls had once been as it now felt like they were up in my throat, and preventing me from telling him what had happened. My mouth opened and nothing came out. One of the kids told him that they had seen me get kneed by one of the older kids. This in itself was a dangerous thing to do as squealing carried a terrible punishment. However, the boy blurted out what had happened in the shock of the moment and gave no real thought to his own future. I was picked up and carried into Mr Lipton's empty classroom. I still couldn't speak, although the pain was easing a little.

This was one of many mindless and violent incidents that resulted in my Mum coming up to see the Headmaster. The boy in question was not expelled and I eventually recovered, although it was ages before the bruising subsided. I hated H.C. so much that I decided to try to change schools. I didn't think to discuss this first with Mum and Dad.. They hadn't really seemed that bothered about how unhappy I was at school, so I didn't think there was much point in talking to them.

One lunchtime, I went to St Paul's Way school (my other choice when I had left Knapp Road) and made an appointment to see the Headmaster. When asked by the school secretary what it was about, I told her that I was being bullied at school and that I hated Hay Currie because of it. I told them that I thought I was supposed to be going to school to learn and that I didn't think I was learning very much just getting knocked around a lot. Therefore, I felt it was best all round if I changed schools. I was told to go back to school and they would look into it for me. I walked back to H.C. feeling so much better. The thought of changing schools was exciting. The excitement didn't last though, as I before I had stepped outside of the gates of St Paul's feeling much better, one head was talking to the other. As if I didn't have enough troubles with the kids at H.C, I now had trouble with the school itself. I got back to my class to a message that the Headmaster wanted to see me. It wasn't until I got through his door that I found out that what I had done was not good. It was only when he had stopped shouting and slamming his cane down on his desk that I realised how wrong I had been to take matters into my own hands. It finished with him telling me to get out and I was relieved that I didn't get six of the best on each hand. I was terrified as I left his office quietly closing the door behind me.

A couple of days later Mum got a letter from the school asking her to go and see the Headmaster. The whole thing came out and it was the first she had heard about it. I didn't dare tell her what I had done. I was in enough trouble at school, I couldn't cope with trouble at home at the same time. My Mum was really angry with me, for not telling her before doing what I had done. Needless to say, I did not leave H.C. I had to stay there and put up with the bullying and I never once said a word about it again.

139

Life at No. 5 had got quieter and I was managing to get home from school without bumping into Tilson. One day I got home and as I opened the front door there was no Prince to greet me. I found him lying on the kitchen floor just panting, as he lay there really ill. Dad came home and I told him about the dog and when Mum got home she went around the corner and called a vet; a veterinary practice was one of the things we didn't have nearby! It wasn't long before the vet turned up and told us that he was sure that Prince had distemper and there was nothing he could do but to put him to sleep.

No one had to tell me what 'put him to sleep' meant. I remembered Mum telling me long ago that when Fido's back legs gave out and he could no longer walk the vet came and Fido had to be put to sleep. My eyes filled to the point of overflowing as I looked at this poor little animal lying there so sick. The vet said he would come back in an hour to see if there was any improvement. There wasn't any, even though Dad had tried to get a little brandy into Prince by pouring it into the side of his mouth. It was an agonising thirty minutes but at least there was no need for the vet to put him to sleep because the poor little thing just slipped away. I was devastated. The vet came back and Dad told him what had happened and he took Prince away. I went to bed and cried myself to sleep. The world seemed so cruel to me. I was really feeling sorry for myself, big time. 'Why?' I kept asking. 'Why me? I mean what have I done?' I always thought when something went dreadfully wrong that it was somehow my fault, and that I was being punished.

A few days later I was back at school and things were back to normal. Tony and I were still trying to dodge Tilson and hating each day at H.C. One morning after assembly we went back to our form classroom and were given details of a school holiday. It was going to be skiing in Switzerland and the cost for ten days was twenty-six pounds. I liked the kids in my class and if Mr. Lipton were going it would be brilliant because he was so fair and he had a great sense of humour. So, after school I ran home with duffel bag on my back and leaflet in hand. I did my usual chores and as usual Dad got home first. There was no point in giving him the leaflet. I knew he couldn't read and to humiliate him only made him angry so I told him about it and waited for Mum to get home to show her.

That night there was a discussion and it was agreed I could go. The payment terms for the trip were simply that the parents could pay so much a week but the full amount had to be paid up by a certain date. Payments were being made and the total was mounting up. I was trying to be on my best behaviour, a condition applied by Mum. I was going skiing!

A couple of months passed by and Dad kept complaining about terrible stomach pains. He'd had tests and the doctor said that he had to go on a special diet, which he hated and did not follow. It got to the point where it was decided that he probably had ulcers and they would have to operate.

Unfortunately Dad working on a building site meant there was no sick pay. The date was set for his operation and he went into St Andrews Hospital. Not only did my poor Mum have to contend with my Dad, who was the world's most difficult patient, but she also had to contend with telling me that they would now not be able to afford to finish off paying for my school holiday. I said it didn't matter and what had been paid-in was refunded.

His operation was done in the morning and later that day, we waited outside the ward for visiting time. Dad was in bed sleeping off the remains of the anaesthetic - well sleeping for a while anyway. We went in and had barely sat down next to his bed when I heard the sister call out to someone,

'Only two by a bed.' I looked around and could see three people around someone's bed. Things were so strict. Dad looked terrible and he woke up and immediately started to complain about the pain he was in. He told Mum that no one could possibly understand his pain and she stroked his forehead and told me to go out so that someone else could come in. I walked down the ward and, as I opened the door to get out, I could see Uncle Steve and Aunt Maria sitting there.

'Hello,' I said, 'Dad's awake and Mum said I had to come out to let someone else go in. They only allow two by a bed.' Uncle Steve went in and I sat with Aunt Maria. Then Mum came out telling Aunt Maria to go in while she went and talked to Dad's surgeon. I was left outside on my own with that horrible hospital smell that I hated. Eventually I heard the hand bell ring to signal the end of visiting and I shot back in to say goodbye to Dad. By now Mum was back with him and he was looking a little bit better with some colour in his face but he was still complaining about the pain. Mum told him that she had spoken with his surgeon who said that they found no reason for this pain he was having. There were no ulcers, which was really a good thing but it only annoyed Dad.

'D'you mean they've cut me open and found fuck all? D'you mean I've been through all this for nothing?' Mum tried to reason with him but it was no good. The bell rang again and a real bossy sister came round and told us in no uncertain terms it was time to go. 'That's it fuck off and leave me here; it's all right for you ain't it,' he spat in his usual angry fashion and he had done it again. We left and we felt terrible, almost as though it was our fault he was there. The walk out through the ward was terrible as we listened to Dad as he gave one of the nurses a mouthful of bad language.

The whole performance with Dad was repeated the next night, only worse as he was now fully awake, the anaesthetic having left his system. He was even angrier this time, and there was simply no reasoning with him. His behaviour upset everyone especially me. It seemed he hated us for being well. The half hour didn't go fast enough and I was so glad to walk out of that ward.

We got home and Mum gave me some tea. We settled down and it was almost time to go to bed when there was a knock at the front door. Mum opened it and it was Dad! He had walked home from St Andrews, which was about three-quarters of a mile. He was holding his stomach and saying that they were fucking trying to kill him. He had pulled out his drip, got dressed and walked home. He was in a dreadful temper and a lot of pain. Mum got him onto his armchair but he was too ill and in far too much pain to be comfortable.

It only took about half an hour before the police arrived at the front door. Mum opened it and they asked if Mr Wilkinson was here.
'Yes,' she said, you had better come in. Dad was sitting in his chair doubled up in pain and almost immediately after that the ambulance arrived.
'I'm not fucking going back in that fucking hospital,' he said.
'Look Jim,' the policeman said, 'you have got a lot of those nurses in trouble over this. If you don't go back they'll lose their jobs. You surely don't want that do you?' Dad, being completely reasonable, told him to 'fuck off' and said to the policeman, 'If you feel so fucking sorry for the fucking nurses, why don't you get in my fucking bed and let them fucking try to fucking well kill you instead.' The air was as blue as the policeman's uniform. The ambulance driver, who had patiently listened to Dad, told him that if he didn't get him back into the hospital within the hour he wouldn't have to worry about the nurses killing him because he would be dead anyway. His wound was bleeding from the walk and needed attention. Dad capitulated nicely, just like the sentenced prisoner on his walk to the gas chamber.

143

This whole incident put many staff on the carpet and Dad, who was never exactly Mr. Popular among the nurses, became to them just a matter of duty, and you could hear the difference in the way they talked to him, compared to the other patients. There were no more niceties from them and, to be honest, I didn't blame them.

The next few days were a nightmare with Dad. He managed to upset everyone and going to see him was terrible. He would moan about everything in his best foul-mouthed way. No matter how understanding we tried to be, he insisted no one could possibly know what he was going through and because we couldn't understand he hated us for that too. There we were once again stuck between the rock and the hard place.

It took about ten days for Dad's wound to heal enough for them to let him out and I bet the nurses were counting the hours. I certainly wasn't looking forward to him coming home at all. Living at home with Mum had been great, with just the two of us, and she was a different person. She was more relaxed and so was I without that awful feeling of constantly worrying when Dad was next going to be nasty again. At first Dad was OK as he was so happy to be home, but it didn't take long for him to get back to his old self. Mum would go to work and I would be back at school. I would come home and he would start on me about anything and nothing. This would invariably end in tears! Mine. Mum would come in and I was filled with a mixture of relief and dread. Relief because she would take some of the brunt of his anger and dread because I didn't want her to. I used to blame myself as what I saw as his hatred of me would result in row between them.

I was getting to the age when I would try to reason things out. To me there had to be a reason for everything. Yet no matter how much I thought about it, I could never find a reason for Dad's sometimes, hateful manner. I started to think that he resented my ability to read and write but if that was the case, why did resentment manifest itself into hatred? Why did he hate me like this? I would ask myself that question over and over again. Why did he adopt me? It seemed obvious to me that he didn't want me. At times I felt I would have been better off in a children's home than trapped in a house with a man that would lash out at me for no apparent reason. Life was just getting worse and worse. Things at school were bad and things at home were bad. What was I to do?

It wasn't that long before Dad was back at work and better for it. Things at home were better now that they were both working, well for a while anyway. Mum had changed her job and was now working in the dry cleaner's around the corner. It was great for her and she was really happy with the work. No more long bus journeys to the shoe factory, which had moved location to a building behind the Metropolitan Hospital up Kingsland Road. Mum and the manageress of the shop got on famously together. There was much laughter between them and you could see the difference in my mum for this move.

Chapter Eighteen – My Twelfth Birthday

It was my twelfth birthday and my body was starting to go through the expected changes - only I wasn't expecting them. I was getting strong sexual urges but these were still for my own sex, which frightened and worried me. I felt I didn't dare tell anyone so I kept it to myself, and so welcome to the hell of puberty. Mum and Dad had never really made a fuss about my birthday. I got the usual two cards. One from Mum and one from Dad (written out by Mum) and in each was a one-pound note. The day passed and so I entered my thirteenth year.

It was Friday night and I was more than happy that the weekend was here. Two days with no school. I got home and there was Dad sitting by the fire, which he had stoked right up to heat the water. I said hello, but he didn't reply, he just sat there watching the TV. I sensed that he was in a funny mood so I just went through to my bedroom to get changed into my old jeans. I then went out into the garden to muck about for a while until I was called in to go as usual to Samuel's to get the fish and chips. Mum had come home from the dry cleaner's and opened the back door and shouted
'Jimmy we are not having fish tonight; we're having pork chops for a change.'
I guess about thirty minutes had passed before I was called in for my tea. It was later than usual and when I went in; you could cut the atmosphere with a knife. There was definitely something wrong. I washed my hands in the kitchen sink and helped Mum serve up and I went and sat down at the table and Dad joined me after he put his roll-up behind his ear. Mum walked in with two plates and put them in front of us. Tea looked perfect. I started to tuck in when my Dad suddenly said, 'I don't fucking want that!' and pushed his away.
I froze with a mouth full of what suddenly felt like un-chewable pork.

'What would you like?' Mum said in a calm tone. 'I've got a bit of rump steak. Would you like me to cook that?'

What a way to talk to my Mum! He could be a real pig at times. I always thought she should have offered him a smack round the head with a cricket bat. He said,

'I don't care what you cook, but I don't want that.' So she went back into the kitchen and cooked him the steak. Mum was as usual trying to placate him for the sake of peace and quiet but her efforts just made him even angrier. The evening developed into a row. Things got terrifyingly loud and I was frightened and just kept asking them to stop it. I was screaming and crying when suddenly Dad lashed out at me with a blow to the head, which sent me flying. Mum went mad, I had never seen her so angry. I cried,

'No, oh no, stop, stop, please stop!' but it was no use as tempers had taken hold, and control no longer existed.

'That's it,' Mum shouted.

'That's the last fucking time you lay your hands on that boy,' she said and rushed to the kitchen. She walked back into the lounge with a bread knife.

'I'll fucking swing for you if you so much as touch him again,' she said and she went for Dad big time. He picked up a chair to defend himself as Mum had every intention of running him through. It was horrifying to watch this.

'Living with you is just a fucking nightmare, I fucking hate it here,' she said and with that she threw the knife at him.

It was almost like time froze for a second and then she rushed back to the kitchen, locking the door behind her. Dad rushed to the door in what seemed a moment of panic as he realised that things had gone too far. She ignored his calls for her to open the door and instead she put wet tea towels at the bottom of the door to seal it and she turned on the gas taps.

'Fucking 'ell Ede what are you doing?' he screamed through the door.

'Mind your own fucking business, just go a-fucking-way.'

'Open this fucking door or I'll break it down,' Dad shouted. I thought if he did then there would be more fighting and more violence and I couldn't stand it. I ran out of the house, sobbing, 'I'm leaving home, I hate it here.' I hoped and prayed that my action would divert his attention from Mum but it didn't. I ran round to my Aunt Jane's, Dad's sister who lived the nearest to us. I begged her to come and save Mum, but she knew better. She knew her brother only too well and what he could be like. I thought she didn't care, but she knew that if she had gone round it would have only made things ten times worse. She gave me a cuddle and a cup of tea, which I was far too upset to drink. I just sat there shaking and I felt terribly sick. I kept asking myself why are they doing this to me. I sat there in her front room dazed and in shock.

'You must go back home Jimmy,' she said. 'I promise you everything will be all right. Sometimes Mums and Dads have arguments; it's part of life.' Somehow I calmed down and went back home.

It was dark when I pulled the latchkey out of my shirt to open the door. I went in with enormous trepidation. Mum and Dad were sitting opposite each other and things seemed to be OK. The whole incident was smoothed over and I was bought another dog as a consolation prize. Enter Prince II. There were no apologies, as I guess they felt they didn't need to apologise to me. They never really knew the damage they were doing to me, damage that would stay with me forever. The weekend passed without any more fuss and things seemed better.

Life in our house seemed full of huge ups and downs and for someone so young that took a lot of coping with, as did my sexuality. I was still looking at men; I was desperately lonely and once again about to be introduced to the misery of loss. It was a couple of weeks later when I came home from school to find Prince II unconscious on the kitchen floor. I couldn't believe it. I sat on the floor and holding him in my arms, crying out 'Why? Why? Why is it always me?' I was still sitting in the kitchen when Dad walked in from work. He came in and saw me sitting on the floor holding the dog. My face was streaked with tears and as he leaned down to take him from me. He was obviously dead.

We took Prince into the garden and Dad dug a hole that was deep enough to bury him in. Mum came home just as we were about to lower poor Prince in the hole.
'Ede,' he said, 'I reckon he had that distemper.'
'Probably,' Mum said. She put her arm around me and said, 'It sometimes happens with young dogs Jimmy. At least he didn't suffer any terrible pain.'

Not like the pain I was feeling at that moment. I had this huge lump in my throat as I watched Dad carefully replace the earth and scatter the leftover soil over the garden.
Mum kept me off school the next day and I stayed in the shop with her. The day passed enjoyably with Mum and feeling much better, I asked if I could go to the scouts. I think she was relieved that I wanted to get on with things and agreed. I got ready and straight after tea jumped on my bike and cycled to Bow Baptist. I was the first to arrive and Skip was setting out some stuff on the table at the end of the hall.
'Hello Jim,' he said. 'How are you?' and the way he asked he sounded like he really meant it. I told him what had happened and he said that we would all pray for our pets tonight and especially for poor Prince. I thought that was really kind.

About a week later Dad came home from work and told me he had a surprise for me. 'Where? What is it I said?'
'It's out the window,' he said, pointing. I rushed over but could see nothing.
'Look,' he said.
'There, the car.' It was a maroon Hillman Minx, which he had

bought from the local council. Apparently, they were selling off two staff cars. Dad bought one and Uncle Steve bought the other.

'Seventy quid - what do you think?' he said. I blurted out my usual excited

'Brilliant!' and I went outside with him. He proudly unlocked the door and I got in.

It didn't take him long to pass his test, mostly thanks to Mum's efforts in teaching him the Highway Code, which he learned parrot fashion. Of course having had a motorbike for years made it all much easier for him. The motorbike and sidecar were sold but he kept the trailer. No more sitting on the back of a motorbike for hours on end - it was now luxury all the way.

It was about three months later when we were due to go to summer camp that Skip announced that his brother-in-law wouldn't be able to drive the van for us any more. This was due to his heavy work commitments.

'Don't worry,' I said, 'I am sure my Dad will drive it there for us. I will ask him and tell you on Thursday.' Skip said that was a good idea but rather felt that the question would be better posed by him and so after Scouts he walked home with me. We chatted to each other as we walked along Bow Road and, when we turned into Devon's Road, Skip stopped at Samuel's fish and chip shop and bought us a bag of chips each. They tasted great out of the newspaper and soaked in vinegar.

Skip was such a kind and sofly spoken man, unlike my dad. I never felt Skip was suddenly going to go nuts for no reason at all and I felt totally at ease with him. We soon arrived at No. 5 and I opened the door. Dad was sitting in his usual place and Mum was sitting at the table reading the paper.

'Dad, Mum, I've brought Skip home, he wants to ask you a

question.'

'Come in Skip,' I said. He entered our lounge and went straight over and shook Dad's hand.

'Hello Mr and Mrs Wilkinson,' he said. 'I hope I am not disturbing you?'

'No not at all,' Mum said (looking in my direction!) 'Is there anything wrong?'

'No, good Lord, no,' Skip said, 'nothing at all.'

'Would you like a cup of tea?' Mum asked. 'Let me take your coat.'

'Yes, tea would be lovely,' he replied as Mum hung his coat behind the door. I was then dispatched to put the kettle on. All the usual pleasantries were exchanged and Mum asked how I was doing at the Scouts.

'He's mad about the Scouts,' she said.

'Yes I know.'

Then she asked him how he was enjoying being Scout Master.

'They're a great bunch of kids,' he said. 'Really enthusiastic; not what I expected to find in Bow.'

I walked in with the teapot on a tray and Mum got the best cups and saucers out of the cupboard. As she poured out the tea, Skip went on to tell them about the problem we had with our driver.

'As we are so stuck, Jimmy suggested that you might be willing to drive our van down to summer camp for us, Mr Wilkinson, do you think you might be able to help us out?'

Dad had been out-manoeuvred and without hesitation said, 'Yes of course, I'll take the van down for you.'

Skip stayed for about half an hour while they discussed where and when and, before you knew it, Skip was shaking Dad's hand as he thanked him for getting us out of a hole. Mum passed him his coat and Skip said good night.

'Where have you got to get to?' Dad asked him.

'Kempton Road, by the Aberdeen,' Skip said. The Aberdeen

was the crossroads of Grove Road and Roman Road and quite an awkward trip from us by public transport.

Dad said, 'It'll take me a few minutes to run you home and a lot longer for you to walk or catch a bus.' Skip said he couldn't put Dad through that trouble but Dad insisted. I was asked if I wanted to go and I was at the car door before Dad was out of his chair. It did only take a few minutes to get Skip home and he thanked us as he went in his house. We were back home in no time at all and I was teeth brushed and into bed. I remember lying there with the doors partly open and I could hear Mum say to Dad what a nice man she thought Tom Granger was. I agreed, and drifted off to sleep.

Chapter Nineteen – My first interest in Tom

It was time for the scout summer camp, this year to be held at Chalfont St Giles in Buckinghamshire. Dad and Mum collected our loaded van the day before we were due to set out. He found the site, eventually, thanks to Mum's navigation. Although being navigator with Dad was torture and, if you got it wrong, it was air colour change time. Still they made it there and back. We arrived the next day and found everything in the store, which was quickly emptied and our camp set up.

Mum and Dad had long owned their big tent and had given me their old army tent. The trouble was it was too heavy for me to carry, so I hadn't been able to use it. But now the troop had its own van this was no longer the case. My tent was set up at one end of the row of tents and Skip's at the other.

It was great having my own tent and I would often ask one of the boys if they wanted to share with me. This offer was usually leapt at because two in a tent was so much better than four. For my part, I loved it because it was like having a brother. I would often wake up in the night and just listen to my tent mate sleeping. It was wonderful and it was just how I imagined having a brother would be. I would quietly cuddle up to him and drift back to sleep. Having my own tent gave camping with the scouts a completely new perspective.

The summer camp went well and time just flew by. During the last few days a hike had been arranged for the whole troop with the plan that it would take the whole morning. I wasn't keen to go so I volunteered for camp watch and cooking duty. The hike was led by our ASM and, as I needed adult supervision, Skip remained behind with me. As the troop marched off, I set about tidying the site. Then I suggested to Skip that perhaps we should go and get some wood for the fire

We walked to the nearby woods and set about gathering fallen branches and the dead wood that was just lying around on the floor. As we did, Skip pointed out different trees to me, showing me how to tell them apart by their leaves. I looked ahead and I could see a large branch that had fallen on the floor and walked over to get it. As I did I looked around to call Skip for help, and I could see he was relieving himself against a tree. I desperately tried to make my looking in his direction as unobvious as possible, but he must have noted my glances, which told him all he needed to know. I was curious, and therefore I was probably a safe bet. It was probably more than likely that at that point he started to plan an opportunity to get me on my own.

We returned to camp carrying as much wood as possible between us and the fire was lit and lunch prepared when the troop returned. They had marched for five miles and most of the troop, through tiredness, were quiet. They had enjoyed it but were shattered. Many of the boys never got the chance to walk that far in the countryside so for them it was particularly exhausting. Soon lunch was on the go and everything was bubbling away nicely. Skip and I had prepared loads of vegetables to go with the tins of stewed steak, which would be served with a good helping of boiled potatoes. The food went down well and soon ravenously hungry bellies were filled.
'I can see you got a load of wood,' someone said as they munched on a chunk of bread. 'Yep,' I casually replied as I dipped my bread in my stew and even though nothing had happened I could feel my face uncontrollably colouring up from my own thoughts.

Summer camp ended, we set off home and Mum and Dad, as planned, picked up the gear to take it back to Bow Baptist. I was now twelve-and-a-half years old and thinking more and more about the fact that I wanted male company. The problem for me was that somehow I knew wanting it was wrong and that I should not be thinking this way. I tried to leave such thoughts back in the woods.

Chapter Twenty – Goodbye 1960

A few weeks soon rolled by and it was September and time for hop picking. In the last three years things had really changed. We didn't go in Uncle Steve's old lorry but Dad loaded the trailer up, hooked it onto the back of the car and off we went. The farm was much the same but the people were different. They were fewer in number and the friendliness of it all was starting to fade.

The families were smaller as some of the family members were now opting to go elsewhere. A lot of them had started to go to the new holiday camps run by Billy Butlin. Butlin's Holiday camps were incredibly popular at that time because they were affordable and incredible value for money. The camps were well organised and crammed with people eager to have fun. Fun with a capital 'F' was the name of the game. The staff, who were carefully chosen to entertain and run the camp, were known as Redcoats and Butlin's became a great springboard for many well-known entertainers.

Some of my friends, who had been to Butlin's, when they came home, would be full of tales of what it was like. Competitions like Knobbly Knees, Glamorous Granny and Miss Butlin's, the Donkey Derby and so much more. I longed to join in the fun but there was no way that Dad would ever have gone. He was still very much into the middle-of-nowhere holidays and even for those, things were different. More people could afford cars and traffic was getting heavier. Things were certainly changing and even poor old London was suffering by it. We started getting what was called Smog. Not fogs, but much much worse. The Smog was pollution-based and so thick that it could almost be chewed and was caused mainly by coal fires, factories and cars.

When a Smog descended over London it was quick and used to catch everyone off guard and everything would grind to a halt. Buses were led along their routes by their conductors carrying a burning newspaper, if they didn't have a torch, which they invariably didn't. Of course the burning paper only conributed to the problem. The yellowy coloured smog could rip your voice out in a few minutes, and the safest thing to do was breathe through your scarf. Always having an eye open to make a few bob, I used to do just that in the Smogs. We didn't live that far from the docks and if I stood in the street on the corner of Devon's Road and Violet Road, it was only a matter of minutes before a lorry, doing all of two miles per hour, would stop to ask the way to East India Dock Road. I would offer to lead it to its destination, for which I was paid maybe half a crown.

Apart from Butlin's, one of the other major changes that was to affect hop picking was automation. This would bring a great change to the industry and those who used to go each year. Sadly the coming seasons of hand-picked hops were numbered. Soon the huts would be empty save for just a few of the older family members who would just work in the barns pulling the leaves out of the hoppers full of the hops which had been stripped from their vines by machines. Such is progress!

I enjoyed the dwindling season never-the-less and was sad when it came to a close. It was great to be with Mum during the week without Dad around as she was so different when he wasn't there. She would laugh more and seemed much more willing to show me affection. The weekends, when Dad was there, were sometimes OK but he never changed from being like a bottle of nitro in transport. Thanks to this separation, rows were few and far between. Mum was saying goodbye to some people when Dad walked round the end of our row of huts. He had parked the car and trailer round the back and was ready to take us home. As if that wasn't bad enough it also meant it was time for me to go back to H.C. and that thought filled me with real dread. Little did I also know that this would be my last year for picking hops.

The next three months seemed to flash past and once again Christmas was here. Mum had made plans for an excellent Christmas for us. Uncle Billy and Aunt Eve and her Dad were coming and of course, their kids Kathy and Simon. There would be eight of us to seat for lunch so Dad put our dining table into the middle of the lounge and he pulled the leaves out from either end so it was big enough for all of us to sit round.

I was in the kitchen, Mum had the radio on and we were singing carols together. I was preparing the Brussels and carrots as she was basting the turkey, which was looking rich, wearing its golden brown skin and a huge lump of stuffing hanging out of its bum. The smell of food filled the flat as Dad sat down in front of the television, having poured out a large glass of scotch for himself. That was usually a sign of impending trouble as often when he's had a drink or three we would get to meet, 'Mr Nasty'. At times like that he could either give you the world or split your lip.

The pips signalling noon sounded from Mum's radio, and there was a knock on the front door. I ran through in excitement to open it and Simon was the first to pile through followed by the rest of our guests. There were the usual greetings as Mum came from the kitchen wiping her hands on her pinafore and Dad asked the men if they would like a drink. I took the kids into the garden where we played, while Mum and Eve made sure everything was up to speed in the kitchen.

Dad had got a taste for the Scotch and it didn't take him long to suggest that they go round the corner to the Widow's Son to meet up for a quick Christmas drink with his brothers and sisters - the annual tradition. I had long learned that this could be fatal. I went back in with the kids and there was only Mum and Eve in the flat. Mum told me the television was on and asked if would I mind if she and Eve joined Dad for half and hour. I was coming up for thirteen years old, and felt I could well cope by now, so I said

'Why not, but you won't be too long will you? I mean what about dinner?' s

Mum told me everything was under control and as soon as they got back dinner would be ready to serve up. I guess they were gone for about forty-five minutes and, as Mum had said, dinner was ready. She immediately set about serving up. Unfortunately, Dad had sunk quite a few whiskies before going to the Widow's and he was quite pissed when he came back, as were Uncle Billy and Aunt Eve's Dad. Apparently Dad had been drinking light and bitter followed by whisky chasers.

The fire was banked up well and Aunt Eve's Dad promptly fell head first into it. He was so pissed he didn't feel it. Dad pulled him out again but not before the bars in the front of the fire that held it all in place had burned into his neck and face. Thanks to Dad's quick reaction it wasn't as bad as it could have been. Mum taped a huge piece of gauze round his neck and put burn cream on his chin and we all sat down for lunch. Dad at this point said he didn't want any lunch and went to bed. This for me was normal as Dad usually got pissed before Christmas lunch and Mum and I would sit and eat without him. This was Dad's way of making Christmas memorable. A week later it was New Year's Eve and Mum, Dad, Aunt Eve and Uncle Billy had gone out to spend it at some Workingmen's Club and I was once again at home with Kathy and Simon who were in bed, leaving me in front of the television with the Scots again. And so entered 1961.

159

Chapter Twenty One – Tilson's End

The holidays were over and I was back at H.C. Things were at last going to change and Tilson was to get his comeuppance. I was walking home from school one day after Tilson had told me that he was going to throttle me for refusing to do something he expressly wanted me to do. I remember walking along with Tony and we were chatting away when suddenly Tilson came up from behind and leapt on my back, putting his arm around my neck. I had by now grown a fair bit taller than my adversary and he was not prepared for what happened next. I lost my temper. I held on to the arm around my neck that was choking me, leant forward and I flipped him over my shoulder. He landed on the floor in front of me and was obviously dazed and shocked. Then I fell on him with a knee either side of him, pinning his arms down by his sides. Then came the ultimate pleasure. I grabbed his ears and proceeded to bang his head on the ground telling him in Dad fashion, 'If you so fucking much as come near me and Tony again, I'll fucking well kill you, is that under-fucking-stood?'

The sharp gravel on the floor had broken the skin on the back of Tilson's head and by now he was shitting himself.

'Yes, yes,' he screamed out and I let him go. That was the end of his bullying days as far as we were concerned and life at H.C. became just a little better because of it.

Roland Peters had by now left the scouts and my other mate Tim had also gone. I, on the other hand, was heading for promotion again. Our Patrol Leader, Peter Chandler had gone into the Senior Scouts and the Eagles needed a new Leader. While I was the patrol's Second it didn't guarantee me promotion. At the next troop meeting I was interviewed by Skip and the ASM. Then, at the end of the evening, one of the announcements was that Peter Chandler was joining the Seniors and that the new Patrol Leader for the Eagles was to be me. The elation in my heart was unbelievable. I was almost thirteen years old and I was Patrol Leader! The evening ended in the usual way and I bombed home on my bike to tell Mum and Dad. My excitement was incredible - you would have thought I had won the pools!

Life in the Scouts just got better for me and I would often find myself reflecting on my thoughts about my time with Tom in the woods. Nothing happened but my imagination ran riot. Once again hormones were surging through my body causing the expected physical changes. I could not wait to mature and have pubic hair like some of the boys I had seen in the showers at scout camps. I found this along with hairy chests, legs and especially the five o' clock shadow so attractive. As I was growing older, I found myself getting more and more physically attracted to these boys, which excited me and I didn't know how to deal with my thoughts. I had never heard of homosexuality, save for the stories about queer bashing and I didn't properly understand what that was about either. The whole thing was becoming a real worry to me so I thought it best just to keep quiet about it. How could I say anything and if I did, who to?

My thirteenth birthday arrived and Mum and Dad's gift was a Fidelity portable tape recorder. In those days, portable meant it could be moved from room to room providing you were strong enough to carry it. Tape recorders were reel to reel, as cassettes were a long way off from being invented.

Mum said I could have some friends round and she even bought me a birthday cake in the shape of the number thirteen. I invited the kids that I liked from my class including Jean Winter on whom I had a bit of a crush. The evening at home went down just about as well as the Titanic.

We all decided after a polite amount of time to go off to one of the girls' homes to play my recording of Top of the Pops. The recording was real high quality, as you can imagine. I had recorded Alan Freeman on Sunday afternoon - 'Hello pop pickers!' - via the microphone pushed against the radio's speaker. It was interesting to listen to, especially the bit in the middle of the number one, which was my Dad screaming at me,

'Turn that fucking rubbish down!' My embarrassment was quickly eased when we all fell about laughing. What a way to remember your thirteenth birthday.

It was soon Easter camp time and we were off to Cuffley again. Dad did the honours driving the van, for which I was grateful. I was even more grateful for the fact that somehow he kept out of contact with the Scouts. I will admit that while most of the boys were either from or lived in the East End, I didn't want them exposed to his bad language. We arrived at Cuffley in our usual excited fashion with much chattering and laughter. The storeroom was opened and our mountain of gear soon loaded onto the troop cart. We were allocated our favourite site, which had its own built-in campfire surrounded by a circle of logs to sit on. This year was to be special as the site had organised a campfire to which every troop attending camp was invited. There would be much singing and many comedy sketches. These were always great fun because they were carried out with so much enthusiasm. It was impossible not to enjoy them.

The cart was unloaded and I dragged my heavy tent into position at the end of the row of tents. Skip was wandering around, hands on hips, searching for his tent and there was obviously a problem. His tent wasn't there. It had not been loaded, left behind by my Dad, no doubt. It wasn't reasonable to expect Skip to kip in with the boys and I was the only one with my own tent. I offered him my tent and said I would bunk in with the others.

'There's no need for that,' he said. 'There's room in your tent for two isn't there?'

'Of course,' I said.

'Good then, that's settled.' What still amazes me is how no one was suspicious of what he was up to. I suppose in those days no one thought twice about things like that. People were more trusting.

The day went well and everyone was tired from gasping in that clean fresh air for a change, something that wasn't too plentiful in Bow. It was getting dark and the younger ones were packed off to bed. I and the other Patrol Leaders, with Skip and the ASM, sat by the fire as the night grew darker and the fire seemed to burn brighter. I tipped the remains of my mug of cocoa on the fire and said I was going to bed. I got to the tent, opened the flap and lifted up the heavy insect net to slide inside. I left the flaps open and the netting tied up for Tom and I got undressed. It was never easy getting undressed in my tent, it being only three foot tall, but I was soon snuggled down into my sleeping bag.

I could hear Skip talking quietly with the ASM, I guessed about what we were going to do tomorrow and as the warmth built up in my sleeping bag, I could feel myself drifting off to sleep. Suddenly I heard the tent flap being untied ready to close once Skip had got in. The flickering light from the remains of the fire barely penetrated the thick canvas walls and we were in almost total darkness as the flaps closed behind him. I lay there as Skip did his best to get undressed in my small tent without trampling all over me. I could hear him roll up his clothes and put them into his rucksack in the corner. Then he unzipped his sleeping bag and slid in, but I didn't hear the zip close up again. My eyes adjusted to what little light there was and I could just about see his outline as he lay there on his right side facing me. His arm then stretched out above my head onto my pillow and he gently eased his arm under my head and I was cradled there. His hand then curled around my neck and fell on my chest. He must have surely felt my heart racing, which it was doing, so fast, I thought it would spring from my chest. He never moved again.

What he had done appeared innocent and I am sure he was more than aware of what he could get away with in the guise of innocence. He was leaving things to me. It was up to me if I wanted to take this further, but I was also very scared. In a childish innocent way I turned to face Skip with my eyes closed and I could smell his clean body close to mine. He used Old Spice deodorant and I liked the smell. I let my right hand fall against his chest and he did not stop me from finding my way around. I was happy to touch him and I was at last doing what I wanted to do. I felt no fear with Skip, in fact quite the opposite, I felt really safe. Every so often he would move away a bit as he was obviously close to a climax. Although then I had no idea what a climax was or for that matter what happened when a man had one.

Eventually his control could last no longer and with the handkerchief in his free hand he captured the results of his pleasure. He had obviously seen the need to remain clean and as we were in a tent he could hardly tell me what was going on. During all this he never touched me and I was still too young to achieve an orgasm myself. At that point in time I didn't feel I needed to, as I was thirteen years old and at last I was extremely happy. He left his arm under my head and in a short while I was fast asleep. It was for me more wonderful than you can imagine and to think Skip and I were to share a tent for another three nights.

During the afternoon of the next day Skip and I were alone together for just a short while and I was able to ask him if he minded what had happened. He was surprised at my question and wanted to know why I felt that he should mind. I told him that I was puzzled why he kept moving my hand away. The penny dropped and he told me about what happens at the ultimate point of excitement.

'You must have been taught that in school,' he said.

'No, we're doing sex later this year.'

'Ah that explains it,' he said, as he smiled. 'Then you will soon know all' and the subject was left as Skip could see someone walking over toward us. They suggested that I throw a log on the fire and put on a billy for tea. The weekend was a real landmark for me. I had at last found out what it was like to lay with a man; what it was like to arouse him and feel his and my own excitement. I had so often dreamed of it but it was a hundred times more exciting than I had imagined. Of course, it went without saying that this act was to remain a secret. A secret kept until now.

I was lucky as, thankfully, Tom Granger was such a kind and gentle man. He might well have taken advantage of the situation presented to him but I never felt he did. When I needed it, he showed me the love my father was unwilling or unable to show me. He was willing to listen and when I was with him he allowed me to talk and relax without the fear of a sudden bout of violent temper. For the first time in my short thirteen years I had found true kindness and love. Sadly, the one thing Tom could not and did not tell me about was homosexuality. Unfortunately for him, his youth had been spent in times when it was kept hidden. He simply did not know about such things as he had led such a secluded and secretive life.

Over the next few months Tom would occasionally come to our house, especially if he needed to talk to Dad about driving the troop van. While he was there, Mum would always invite him to stay for a meal. Tom had told me that he lived on his own and when I told Mum I think she felt sorry for him, but there was no need really. He was a great cook and quite used to his own company. He became a friend of the family but he never allowed this friendship to get too intense. I think he felt it necessary to cultivate this friendship in order that they would trust him with me. His strategy worked a treat for they surely did trust him and as far as I know, there was never a hint of suspicion over his sexuality. Why would there be? Tom was as normal looking and sounding as the next man. One day I was talking to Mum and Dad about the scouts and Tom came up in the conversation. Mum told Dad that Tom had said that he'd once been engaged to be married but sadly his fiancée had unexpectedly died. I never questioned Tom on this so I never found out if this was true or just part of his attempts to camouflage his life style.

Easter 1961 was over and I was once again back at H.C. However, I was getting older and I understood the school a little better. I was also developing a sharp wit and was able to diffuse some of the uncomfortable situations I found myself in. I still hated the school but I was a little more adept at dealing with its problems.

Chapter Twenty Two - Rechtub's Yob (Butcher's Boy)

I came home from school one day, dumped my stuff in my bedroom and went around the corner to see Mum in her shop. I opened the shop door and Lilly, (or Lil as mum called her); Mum's Manageress, was sitting behind the little reception desk pinning cleaning tickets on a pile of clothes someone had just dropped in. Lil was a real character, tall and thin with long, wavy jet-black hair. She and Mum wore nylon overalls and Lil always well made-up. However, I think her real trademark was her dangly earrings. She must have had dozens of pairs. I always thought she looked a bit gypsy-ish.

Mum was at the back of the shop putting the clothes that had been cleaned and pressed into clear plastic bags and hanging them on the rails in the order of the numbers on their tickets. 'Hi Mum,' I called. 'How was school?' she said and I stuck my fingers down my throat, which said it all.
'Will you go over to Greystones and pick up the meat he has got put to one side for me? It's paid for,' she said. 'Oh and you might be interested to know that old man Greystone is advertising for a 'Saturday Boy.''

I crossed the road and sure enough stuck on the inside of the Greystone & Son window was a piece of paper: Saturday Boy Wanted, Apply Within. I went in and said,
'Hello, I've come for Mum's meat.' I didn't have to explain who I was, as Mr Greystone knew me well enough. He went into the fridge and came out with a carrier bag with Mum's name written on it.
'There you are Jimmy,' he said.
'I was also wondering about the job as Saturday Boy,' I told him.
'OK,' he said, and just then a lorry pulled up outside the shop to make a delivery. 'Come and see me tomorrow after school

and we'll talk about it then. Is that all right?'

'Great,' I replied and turned to leave the shop - as I did, I ducked under a huge box of eggs the deliveryman was carrying.

I took the meat home, put it in the pantry and then went into my bedroom. I put my tape recorder on and I was lying on my bed listening to some music when Dad walked in through the door.

'Jimmy,' he said, 'when you go to scouts tonight don't forget to ask Tom about summer camp. Does he want me to take the kit? Oh, and also tell him that I think the van is on its last knockings and that he should perhaps think about getting another one.'

'OK, I expect we'll soon be given a piece of paper with the summer camp details on it, but I'll ask him anyway.' With that Dad closed the door and went into the lounge.

I was getting dressed in my uniform when I heard Mum come in and go into the kitchen to prepare tea.

'Jimmy,' she called

'Just a minute,' I shouted back and I finished dressing and went to see what she wanted.

'Just take this cup of tea in to Dad will you,' she said, passing me his big cup. I went into the lounge and Dad was squatting on the floor in front of the fire.

'Here you are Dad,' I said.

'Here you are,' he said, and passed me a small black puppy, as he took his mug of tea.

'One of the blokes at work said it's the last one left and did I know of anyone who wants a dog. Do you want her?' he asked.

'Yeah,' I said, but then I thought about Prince I & II. 'Dad, can we get her inoculated against distemper?'

'She's already had her first jab; she has to go back for the last one in a couple of weeks.'

'I think I'll call her Lassie,' I said and Lassie it was. I rushed her in to show Mum who obviously already knew as she was cooking her some nice beef mincemeat for her tea. I was really excited about Lassie and thrilled that she had been inoculated against distemper. Two dogs were enough to lose to that disease.

I wasn't too keen to go to scouts now that Lassie was at home. I had my tea and played with her for a while but she wasn't too playful as she had a full belly of food and just wanted to sleep, so I grabbed my coat, got my bike and went. 'I won't be late home,' I said. 'I'll ask Skip about summer camp Dad, and tell him what you said about the van.' I pushed my bike through the lounge and quietly closed the front door behind me.

It only took me a few minutes to get to the top of Campbell Road and as I did, I could see Tom walking quickly along the pavement on the other side of Bow road. I called out to him, crossed at the crossing then walked with him to the church. I told him about Lassie and he was quite pleased. I also told him what Dad had said about the van.
'I thought as much,' Tom said. 'We shall have to see if we can get another van before summer camp. I want us to go to Pett Level this year. I'll give you dates later.' We marched along together and I was happy. I just loved being with Tom.
'How would you like to come to my house this Sunday for lunch?' he said.
'Really?' I said. 'Yeah I'd love to. I'll ask Mum when I get in tonight. I am sure it will be OK.'
'Good, now all we have to think about is how to raise the money we are going to need for another van.'

We arrived at Bow Baptist and went straight in. The hall was cold but soon warmed up with us lot in it. Everyone arrived and as usual we had a good night. Skip handed out the leaflets on summer camp and said to me that it would be really helpful if my Dad could drive the van for us this year. 'I'll ask him Skip,' I said. 'I am sure it won't be a problem.'

I was keen to get home to Lassie and unusually I was one of the first to leave the hall. I shouted goodnight to everyone but Skip had gone into the office with the priest. It was only a matter of just a few minutes before I was home, out of my uniform and on the floor playing with Lassie. She was a funny little thing with a jet black, very shiny coat which, Mum said, made her look like a seal.

I told Dad that I had spoken with Skip about the van and gave Mum the piece of paper with the dates for summer camp. I also told him that Skip would be really grateful if he would drive the kit down there for us.
We are going back to Pett Level again,' I said, 'Oh, and by the way Skip asked me if I would like to go to his house this Sunday for dinner after church parade. Will that be OK?'

'I don't see why not,' Mum said. 'I hope he's got a big oven; he'll need it to feed you!' 'OK, I'll tell him on Thursday,' I replied and it was as easy as that.

Dad had made Lassie a little bed and she was going to sleep in the kitchen. The floor had been tiled and Dad told me that it wouldn't matter if she pissed and shitted every where as on the tiled floor it would be easy for me to clean it up. Yuk, I thought, I hope she doesn't. She did. It was all over the place and all over her. I got it and her cleaned up and got myself off to school.

As Mum worked just around the corner she could pop home every so often to make sure Lass was all right and let her out for a wee. Thankfully Lassie soon settled in and was no trouble at all.

I got home from H.C. I made a fuss of Lassie for a couple of minutes and then zipped straight round to Greystones about the Saturday job. I walked in the shop and old man Greystone greeted me and ushered me into his little office.

'Thank you for coming back Jimmy,' he said to me. 'I assume you would still like the Saturday job?' he said. Old man Greystone was a kindly old chap - the typical old butcher type with a blue and white striped apron and a straw boater. He had grey hair and a curly grey, handlebar moustache. He looked like he had fallen off a Bisto box, Ah!

'Yes I would. What would I have to do?' He told me about the job and said that it could be a bit messy. I would be required to learn how to 'prepare meat', by that he meant gut chickens, yuk. I would also have to help clean the shop at the end of the afternoon and deliver the local orders. It would be my responsibility to collect money from the customers and he told me that if I were polite, I would probably get good tips and that really appealed to me. He went on to say that he would give me a trial period to see how I got on and would pay me a pound to work from eight am to five pm. Although they never closed for lunch I would be allowed a one-hour lunch break. On top of all that, if I did well and worked hard, he said he would also give me a small meat allowance.

'OK', I said, 'when shall I start?'

'How about this Saturday, eight o'clock and don't be late!'

'I won't be. Thanks Mr Greystone,' I replied and left.

I went straight over to Mum's shop and caught her just before she closed.

'I've got the job,' I said proudly.

'Well done! When do you start?'

'This Saturday and I get a pound for the day, plus tips and he said if I do well he will also give me a small meat allowance.'

Lil came up to me with a wiggle and a sparkling smile and said,

'With that sort of money, you will no doubt be looking for a wife! Will I do?'

'Do for what?' I said, and with that she laughed and called me a cheeky sod and clipped me round the ear.

We got in and Dad was in the garden building himself a workbench from some heavy timber he had brought home from work. Mum got straight on with tea and I took Lassie into the garden to play. We had stuffed sheep's hearts and roast potatoes for tea and although I would eat the hearts, I didn't like them much. Mum used to trim the gristly bits off and fill them with sage and onion stuffing. They would then be baked in the oven with the roast potatoes and when ready served with vegetables and gravy. It may not sound too appealing but they weren't that bad. I spent the evening after dinner playing with Lassie until it was time for bed.

The next day Tony knocked at the door for me to go to school. I opened it and invited him in while I finished getting ready. He played with Lassie and said that he wished he could have a dog, but his Mum wasn't too keen on the idea. I was soon ready. I put Lassie in the kitchen and we made the usual walk to school. We went straight into our form class and Mr Lipton was standing in front ready to call out the register.

'Good, nearly all of you are here today. I have something to tell you, please remain seated. At the end of this term I shall be leaving to teach in another school.'
We all sat in shock. There wasn't one of us that did not like him as our teacher.

He went on to tell us that he had enjoyed his time at H.C. and particular being our form teacher, but this was a great opportunity for him and he felt sure we would all understand that. We didn't understand it at all. He was someone you could run to when you had a problem. How on earth would we manage with what H.C. had to offer without him? Like it or not, we were going to find out.

During the day we decided to have a collection so that we could have a farewell party and buy him a gift. Jean Winter was appointed co-ordinator and it was agreed that this should be a closely kept secret so as not to spoil the surprise. The next weeks were going to be really dull as it would be impossible not to feel sad over what was soon to happen. The only thought worse than Mr Lipton leaving was, who was to be his replacement. Oh God, not Mr Tetley, the Science teacher, we don't want him I thought. He was a tyrant and everyone, but everyone, respected him because of George, his thick plastic beach shoe, which was kept in his top drawer. He never ever had the slightest hesitation in introducing George to the arse of any boy who was the slightest bit out of line in his class. I once met George myself for talking when I shouldn't have been. The trick was not to move before George said hello otherwise the greeting process would be repeated. It would be the end if we got Tetley as our form teacher.

I got home from school and Mum was in the kitchen getting dinner ready. It was Thursday, half-day closing, for most of the shops in the area. I told her about Mr Lipton leaving and that we were going to have a collection. Now that I had my Saturday job I didn't have to ask for money and I liked the thought of being independent.

That evening I had got myself ready for scouts as usual before tea. Dad came home but he wasn't in a good mood really. He wasn't interested in what I had to say about Mr Lipton and just kept asking my Mum for things, and she just got them. Where's my slippers Ede? Make us a cup of tea Ede, what's for tea Ede? and so it went on. I had long learned to recognise the signs of an impending outburst of temper so I just kept my head down out of the way. We had tea and I let Lassie out before I went to scouts. I quietly rolled my bike through the lounge and just said, 'See you later.'

I hated leaving Mum with him when he was like that.

I got to the scout hall and went straight to the kitchen to put on the urn and lay the cups out for our break. A few of the boys had arrived and were just chatting. Skip walked into the kitchen and said that he would like to have a word with my Dad and asked me if I thought it would be OK if he went round to see him after we had finished. I knew Dad was not in a great mood but he would never let Skip see that, so I told him that I thought it would be fine.

Skip shouted the order 'Troop, on parade!' and patrols were formed in the usual neat rows. I headed the Eagles and would give a last quick look back to make sure we were in a straight line. All was well. We enjoyed a typical evening full of fun and learning at the end of which were the announcements. One of the most important ones was that we needed a new van and that Skip thought he had found one. He was investigating it and he'd let us know in a few days how he'd got on. The only problem was, we were a bit short of cash but he felt we could get over that. I was walking home with him and said I'd asked about Sunday dinner and that is was OK.
'Good,' he said.
We just chatted about all sorts of things on the walk home and I told Tom about my Saturday job, but mainly we talked about the problems we were having with the van. We arrived at No. 5 and I put the key in the door. Dad was still sitting in his chair and I said, 'Dad, Skip's here to talk about the van.'

Mum got up and put the kettle on and she asked Skip to sit down.
'How's it going Jim,' he said.
'Not bad,' Dad said as he slipped his feet down from the mantelpiece.
'Everything all right with work?' Skip was working hard at making conversation. Dad told him that the job he was on

was about to finish and he was going to look for more work the next day. Maybe that's why he wasn't too happy. They chatted for a couple of minutes and Mum came in with a cup of tea and some biscuits.

'It's very nice of you to ask Jimmy over for Sunday dinner. I have to warn you he eats well.'

'I have ordered a side of beef, I think there might be enough,' he smiled

Mum passed him his tea and Tom took a couple of biscuits and everything seemed so relaxed. The earlier tension I had detected seemed to have faded away.

'Jim,' he said, 'about the van. I take your point, about it being on its last legs. We can't have it being unreliable so I have been looking around for another one. I think I have found a not too old Black Mariah, which is being sold off by Bow Road police station. The mileage is high but it's been well looked after. It's big enough to carry the kit and on some of the smaller camps when we have fewer of them, the boys as well. Would you be prepared to have a look at it for us?'

Now Dad was never happier, when he was doing something for someone else.

'Course,' he said. 'When?'

'I have arranged we can take it out for a short test on Saturday, would that be possible?' 'Well as I said, the job I am on is almost done; there's no overtime so Saturday shouldn't be a problem.'

'Good,' said Skip.

'Can I come too?' I said.

Mum said, 'Haven't you forgotten something?'

Skip and Dad looked at me for the answer.

'Oh, yeah, I forgot, I've gotta work,' I said with more than a bit of pride in my voice.

'That's settled then Jim,' said Skip. 'I'll meet you at Bow Road Police station at ten-thirty Saturday morning. I'll ring them tomorrow so they know to expect us.'

'No problem,' Dad replied.

'Well, I had better be making a move,' said Skip, and Dad insisted he run him home.

'Can I come?' I asked but before Dad could answer, Mum cut in,

'No - school for you tomorrow and it is late enough already.'

Friday passed quite quickly and I must admit I spent a fair bit of the day daydreaming about Sunday and wondering what it was going to be like. School was over and I was rushing home full of excitement. I had Lassie at home, I was working on Saturday and Sunday I would be at Tom's. It was indeed an exciting and busy time of my life.

I did my usual bit by cycling down to Samuel's for our fish and chips tea, watched a bit of television and at nine-thirty Mum said C'mon, work tomorrow, bed!I was thirteen and this was a big change indeed.

Saturday morning was here and my alarm clock went off. The two bells on the top of it were loud enough to wake the dead and in no time at all I was up, dressed and on my way round to work. It was five minutes to eight when I walked through the door and the first thing they did was fit me out with a white coat and apron which swamped me. After a few instructions I was soon working away out in the back of the shop.

There was a lot to do, which mainly involved gallons of hot water as throughout the day I would slowly and methodically give the shop and the walk-in fridge and freezer its weekly super clean. All of the required hot water was provided by an old, but very efficient gas copper, which was also used to make dripping. It was a busy day and by the afternoon I was starting to tire as I began my second delivery round. It was the thought of the tips that gave me the energy I needed. The day soon passed and I was off home again with my wages, tips and meat allowance.

Dad had kept his meeting with Skip and when I got home from work one of the first questions I asked was how was the van? He told me that he felt it would do fine and that he had left it to Skip to do the negotiations. I don't think Dad felt particularly comfortable hanging around in Bow road nick.
'Great,' I said. 'I hope we get it. It sounds as though it will be much better.'
I went to bed that night with more than an element of excitement about the next day. At first I found it hard to sleep but I eventually drifted off.

Next day I was up washed and dressed for church parade before Mum and Dad were even awake. I took them both tea in bed as I left and reminded them I was at Skip's for lunch and that I wouldn't be home too late. Mum sort of grunted OK and off I went. I didn't cycle to church as I expected Skip and I might go back to his place by bus.

Our parade went well and I particularly remember the sermon. Sometimes they could be quite boring but this one was fascinating. There had been a picture in the newspapers of a snowy wasteland area somewhere in Greenland I think. There in front of us all was this picture, which had been enlarged and placed on a big wooden easel. We were asked what we could see. All I could see was a mixture of snow and rocks, a mish mash of black and white. We were asked to look away and then take another look. I did, and to my amazement there it was, a picture of Christ! I was really surprised and stared in amazement. Then for the benefit of those who still could not see this our vicar placed a paper overlay on the picture just outlining Christ's face and then all could see. It was either a fascinating piece of nature or a divine message, who knows. At the end of the service I was both excited and hungry. Skip and I left saying goodbye to everyone and set out back along Bow Road.

We crossed over the road and hopped on a No. 26 bus to Mile End. I asked Tom on the bus what he had decided about the new van. He told me that he had agreed a good price, probably better because he had said it was for us, and that we were going to buy it. Thankfully one of the coppers knew someone that would take our old van off our hands and give us a fair price. We could have the van for next Saturday and Tom told me to ask Dad if he would get it down to the church. I told him that I couldn't imagine that would be a problem and that I would ask him when I got home.

We soon arrived outside Mile End tube station and set out on the walk up Grove Road spanned by the famous railway bridge that had been hit by the first doodlebug (flying bomb) in World War II. It was about ten minutes in all and we were outside the door of No. 23 Kempton Road, Tom's place. We went in and my first observation was that the house was clean but it had a smell of age about it. We went upstairs to Tom's half of the house and I walked into the kitchen. Tom made me so much at home - I just loved it. I felt so grown up and at last I was able to talk or listen to music without my Dad interrupting with his 'what's that fucking rubbish that you're listening to?' Tom quickly set about getting lunch underway.

He had thought ahead as he had pre-cooked the chicken so it was just a matter of par-boiling the potatoes and then roasting them. Tom asked me to lay the fire in the lounge and I joyfully set about the task. The fire was laid and I returned to the kitchen to find Tom busying himself. I just sat there at that small drop-leaf kitchen table where we would hold endless hours of conversation. We just talked about everything and I talked mainly about my Dad. I told Tom how difficult he could be and how afraid of him I was. I had never told anyone this before and Tom listened well. He never once said anything to give the impression that he thought my Dad was wrong or that I was right, he just listened. It was so good to be able to let out all my troubles to a caring ear..

Lunch was plentiful, well cooked and soon over and we went into the lounge. Tom asked me to light the fire. I did and it was soon roaring away in the hearth as we settled down on the sofa to listen to records. Tom had quite a collection of classical music and I fell in love with Swan Lake and the sounds of Spain. I was allowed to put my feet up on the sofa with my head on Tom's lap. He would stroke my head and life was tranquil. What a place, what a life after living with the constant fear of my Dad's unpredictability. It is no wonder I loved 23 Kempton Road so much, yet I knew this love was wrong.

It was still quite early in the year and quite chilly. Tom's heavy lounge curtains shut out the fading light of day, and the glow of the fire became even more inviting. After a while we would move to the floor on cushions to get closer to the fire and its warmth. With just the flickering light from the flames the room was incredibly cosy. Tom would loosen the top of his trousers saying that he was quite full from lunch and the scene was set. It was incredible that I could enjoy the safety of a home with no fears and no worries. The saddest thing was we never talked about sex or sexuality. I wished we had, but it just never happened. What happened between us was left up to me. I do not know what a typical paedophile is, but somehow I would like to think Tom was not one. Although heaven only knows what would have happened then had the press and the law got hold of him. The attitude then to homosexuals was antiquated and it would have probably resulted in something as civilized as him being stoned, and I don't mean with Wacky Baccy. Our secret was more than safe with me and there was no question of me ever telling anyone. In my own way I loved Tom very much. I loved his kindness, sense of humour and more than anything his generosity with his time. He was so patient, never lost his cool with me and enjoyed sharing his tales of travel with me. Where he and my father were concerned, I could never understand how two men could be so different. I was always getting clobbered by my Dad as he was always so impatient with me and if I didn't get whatever he wanted me to do right, then I had to watch out. With Tom it wasn't like that and in a way made me resent my Dad even more. I started to feel that if one man could be like this, why couldn't all men? Tom spent hours talking about his adventures while travelling in Poland and Spain, of meeting friendly villagers and of young men playing guitars, eating and drinking wine. It all sounded so idyllic and far from Bow. I think that was when I decided I wanted to travel. Time at 23 always went too quickly and I never once tried to outstay my welcome. I hated going home but I knew taking liberties with my freedom from home would put my time at 23 in danger, so I followed the rules. It was time for me to go and I did so giving Tom my usual hug and telling him how much I had enjoyed my time.

Chapter Twenty Three - The dissolving coat

It was Whitsun, the last day of half term and the weekend of our Whitsun weekend camp. The class was decorated and the food laid out. We had blindfolded Mr Lipton who went along with it all without question. He was led into the class and the blindfold removed and he was quite touched by our efforts. The card was presented by Gwen, which we had all signed and he was presented with a Parker pen as our farewell gift. Someone got up and read out a speech for which Mr Lipton said he would give ten out of ten for sincerity but the grammar was doubtful. Someone blew a raspberry and there was much laughter. Then it came to our departing teacher to say something.

We all sat and listened, as he seemed to struggle to say something to us without showing his emotions. He managed to get through his thank you speech and we all waded into the buffet and soft drinks. It was good to sit and ask him about what he was going to do at his new school and if it was as tough as H.C. To me it sounded great and I felt like asking him to take me with him. Who's going to be our new form teacher when we get back? someone asked.
'Mr Tetley of course,' he said casually as he bit into his piece of cake. There was a stony silence and then he roared with laughter as he looked at our ashen faces.
'Sorry, I have no idea. I think they are interviewing people now but they can't find anyone who is stupid enough to look after you lot,' he said with a big grin on his face. His humour made the whole event easier to handle. I would have hated it if he had been miserable. Tearful goodbyes were said and I left school feeling sad but this time for a very different reason.

I got home and as usual let Lassie out and went around the corner to see Mum. As I passed I waved across to Greystones shouting

'Watcha.'

Mr Greystone gave me a big wave signalling me to go over to the shop.

'Jimmy,' he said, 'as you will not be here tomorrow, is there a chance you could do some deliveries tonight?'

'Course, no problem, I'll just pop and see Mum and then come back.'

'Good,' he replied, with some relief in his voice. 'I'll have everything ready for you in a few minutes. It's only the local stuff so it shouldn't take you long.'

'Ok, see yer,' I replied and I shot back over the road to Mum's shop - Perkins the dry cleaner's.

Mum was sitting in her usual place at the back of the shop and as I walked in there was much hilarity between her and Lil. Mum was crying with laughter and as her laugh was really infectious, I found myself laughing at nothing. I asked them what the hell they were laughing at and it seemed ages before Mum could calm down enough to tell me.

It was all about a rather strange woman who lived in the area. She was always scurrying about the place and always wore the same coat, summer and winter. It was black with a wide collar made of fake fur, stretching out almost to the edge of each shoulder. She never did it up but just walked around holding the front left side over the front right side. That meant we rarely got to see her right hand as it was always hidden under her coat. In winter she wore fingertip-less gloves and a headscarf. Her hair was greasy and she wore short Wellington boots on her feet. On top of all of this she had a terrible smell about her.

Mum told me that she had brought her coat in to be cleaned. If you could have seen this woman you would find it hard to understand why she would wish to do this or even harder to believe why Mum or Lil had agreed to accept the garment. I am sure much against the Perkins financial policy; the garment was put into the dry cleaning machine on its own. For a while Mum and Lil watched it go round and then got on with their work. When the machine's cycle had finished and it was time to take it out, all that was left of the coat was the collar (without the fur), the sleeves and front panels. My Mum was desperately trying to tell me this tale but her tears and even more laughter made it almost impossible to relate. The chemicals had dissolved it.

With me being the boring rational one, I asked 'What are you going to tell her when she comes in to collect it?'
With that my Mum slipped the coat onto Lil and as it hung there Mum almost wet herself with laughter as she tried to say, 'What do you think we should say?'
We all laughed again and when the hilarity finally faded we left the shop and Lil locked the door. Her long jangly earrings rattled as she said goodbye, still giggling away. On our way home Mum and I went into the grocer's next door to buy some ham off the bone for Dad's sandwiches the next day. Mum always got Dad ham sliced off the bone and the grocer was always fascinated by the way she would insist on as much fat as possible.
'Blimey Ede,' he said, 'most of my customers complain about the fat - you are the only customer that complains about the lean!' But then that's my Dad for you - always different.

As we left the shop I told Mum that Mr Greystone had asked me to do some deliveries for him and that I wouldn't be home for tea for about an hour. It wasn't a problem for her and, as I wasn't working for him the next day I didn't mind either. The next day I was off to Whitsun Camp and good old Cuffley. So Mum left me with the usual,
'You be careful on that bike' and I shot back over the road. The basket on the front had been loaded up and I was given

the list of deliveries and how much to collect. I zoomed out of the shop in my usual noisy fashion.

The deliveries took me about forty-five minutes and I had been given about five bob in tips. I got back to the shop as they were washing up the meat trays out of the shop window. 'Thanks for that Jimmy,' he said. 'That takes some of the pressure off us tomorrow.'
'S'OK,' I said, in my usual cheery tone. He gave me a small packet of meat, telling me, 'That's for your Mum and this is for you.'
He gave me ten bob and said, 'enjoy your weekend at camp.' I looked at the ten bob and simply said,
'Bloody 'ell! 'Oliday money! Fanks!' He slapped me on the back of the head as I left the shop.
'Look after yourself,' he shouted. I was dead chuffed, as old man Greystone had taken a real shine to me, and I liked him a lot. His son on the other hand was a different kettle of fish, as I would find out.

I got home and couldn't wait to tell Mum and Dad about my tips and what I'd been given. Dad was busy mucking about with the fire (Friday night is bath night) and Mum was in the kitchen, feeding Lassie.
'Did you hear what Greystone had given me Mum?' I asked, as I gave her the small packet wrapped in butcher's white paper to her.
'Hiya Lass,' I cried out and was greeted with the usual licking as she leapt at me in her enthusiastic way. Mum unwrapped the packet to reveal about four slices of lamb's liver. She said it was really nice of him and that it would do for tea tomorrow. She then gave me the money I needed for my trip to Samuel's. I got my bike out and did my usual slow and careful pass through the lounge.
'I won't be long,' I shouted.
'Don't be,' Dad said. 'While you're out I'll dig out your tent

for tomorrow.'

'OK,' I said and thought to myself, what's wrong with him, why is he being so friendly?

I was soon home again with cod and chips three times, two pickled onions and two wallys. The plates were on the table and the lounge was lovely and warm from Dad's fire and we were soon tucking into tea. I cleared the table and Dad asked me what I saw outside when I came in. By now I was playing with Lassie and just replied nothing.

'Nothing?' he said. 'Then someone must have stolen it.'
I went to the window looked out and said, 'What?'

'That fucking great van outside that's what,' he said. I wiped the condensation off the window and I could then see painted on the side of the van '38th Poplar Scouts'.

'Bloody hell,' I said, 'is that ours?'

'Yes,' he said, 'I am taking you to camp tomorrow.'

'What do you mean to camp?' He went on to tell me that Skip had told him that as there were only twelve going to the Whitsun camp we could all go in the van, kit on the top and us inside.

'Can I see inside?' I asked and without a reply Dad just threw the keys at me and I was out of the door. It was huge inside and it knocked spots off our old one.

The next day I was up and packed. I had put my new rucksack in the back of the van (no more struggling with that grotty kit bag) and then I made tea. Mum was up and getting ready for work. Dad was outside checking the oil, water, battery water, brake fluid, you name it. If nothing else he was thorough when it came to pre-journey checks. Just as well really, with us lot aboard. Mum gave me the usual instructions before we left along with some money. I gave Lassie a big hug and told her to be good while I was away. Not that that counted for much as Lassie had developed this passion for destruction. If she were allowed in the bedroom she would get on the bed and try to make a nest out of the bedding. As she sort of ran with her front legs to gather up the bedding as her nest material, she used to manage to put her claws right though the sheets.

We went through a lot of sheets because of that dog but Mum loved her and to her it didn't matter too much. Mind you Lass had also developed a liking for bath towels, socks and even beetroot! Mum once plated our Sunday tea of salad with all the usual bits including beetroot, out on the kitchen unit. She then went into the lounge for something and when she got back to the kitchen Lass had managed to nick the beetroot off the plates. Beautiful as she was, Lass had become a bit of a pain. Still, I gave her 'the you be good' instruction nevertheless.

We were off and it only took us a few minutes to pull into the drive at Bow Baptist Church where everyone was waiting. There was much excitement at our new van and the gear was loaded with a great deal of enthusiasm. Dad did his usual bit of ensuring that everything was tied on the roof rack properly and we were once again off to Cuffley, only this time in luxury. It was great but it was the end of an era as no more were we to travel on a steam train from Kings Cross Station, lugging loads of kit with us.

We arrived at the camp and Tom did his usual bit in the office, paying our fees. We borrowed one of the campsite's carts to get our kit from van to site and as we loaded the last lot on, Dad shouted,
'See you on Monday!' and was on his way home again.

Everyone did their bit and the more experienced scouts showed the ropes to the younger members of the troop. Camp was set and once again I enjoyed the privacy afforded me by having my own tent. Tom had his tent this time and our numbers meant that I could safely offer, if I wanted to, for one of the others to share tent with me. The wonderful Peter Chandler, who was now in the Senior Scouts, was with us and I asked him if he would like to share. He said OK and casually tossed his kit in my tent. As the day wore on I have to say I grew more and more excited at the prospect of sharing a tent with someone I had admired so much for so long.

The camp was great and we had the usual round of fun mixed with learning. One of my favourite things was First Aid and it was always a laugh making stretchers out of our staves with coats. These lessons would nearly always end up with stretcher races. The new boys were always elected as patients and we would run like mad. This invariably used to frighten the life out of the patient but never enough to put them off scouting. It was such a great life and the day would close with the usual, albeit smaller, campfire and then bed.

I was one of the last to turn in, leaving Skip with Jim and Peter sitting round the fire. The night was clear and the moon lit up the smoke as it curled up into the night air. I crawled into the tent and in no time I had done my usual contortion trick of getting undressed and into my sleeping bag. I lay there listening to their deep voices quietly talking by the fire, too low to make out what was being said but probably planning for tomorrow.

I was still awake when Peter came into the tent. He undressed with the flap open to give him a little light from the dying remains of the fire. I could see the silhouette of his beautiful body and then he closed the tent flap and we were in total darkness. He crawled along found the opening of his sleeping bag and slipped in. I lay there and I couldn't believe I was actually next to him. Peter, the boy I had admired so much, was actually beside me. I tried to think what I should do and if I should do it, but my racing heart almost made it impossible to think properly. I knew what I wanted to do but how did I dare go about it? He was lying on his left side with his back to me and I just lay there waiting. Pure excitement kept me awake for what I thought was long enough for him to have gone to sleep. When I felt it was safe I did no more than lay my right arm across him as he lay there in his half open sleeping bag. My hand softly fell onto his chest and I could feel his soft chest hair. Then I was totally surprised as he rolled toward me onto his back and just lay there silently. I was now no longer sure if he was actually asleep but I just couldn't stop myself feeling his smooth young skin as it stretched across his firm chest. Everything that followed was extremely slow, totally silent and in complete darkness. The excitement was mutual, as Peter was not asleep.

The next morning I awoke and Peter was up, the fire was alight and water was on the boil. Tent flaps opened and bleary-eyed scouts stepped out into the dewy morning wearing the screwed-up clothes they had had on the day before. It was time for the showers, open air and cold. I have to say that one of the things about scout camps that I never got used to or liked very much were cold showers. Still in the overall picture of things it was a small price to pay. Breakfast was the usual porridge oats and tea. After that we decided that we should take a walk into Cuffley itself. The village was small with just a couple of shops to look around. I bought Mum and Dad a postcard and did my usual wish you were here bit, although I never really meant it.

After lunch we would often take the new lads on a nature walk to show them how to recognise the trees by their leaves. We were allowed a fair bit of free time too and I used to love to walk through the woods on my own. There is nothing like the fresh smell of an English wood as the sun streams down through the trees drying out the dampness.

The day was rounded off with a dinner of good old English sausages, mashed potatoes and peas with loads of bread to mop up the gravy. The younger ones would be packed off to bed and I was left with Ted by the fire as both Peter and Skip had gone to bed. I loved to sit by the fire and chat away with Ted as he was such a great bloke and easy to be with. The last log was disappearing and we doused the flames with the remains of our cocoa and a little water from the billycan. Both satisfied the fire was safe, we went to bed.

I crawled into the tent and as I held the flap open I could see Peter was lying there on his back, asleep, or so it looked. I got myself undressed and into bed without trampling on him and for a while I lay there, as quiet as I could. I just listened to his breathing and again I couldn't resist the temptation of him lying next to me. Although I was almost certain he was awake I still put my arm across his chest as I had done the night before. I felt he just wanted to enjoy the pleasure but without acknowledging I was there. Perhaps because he was older than me, the thoughts he had of pleasure and responsibility wrestled with his conscience. That night, pleasure won the battle but not the war. I was left with an indelible memory of an act never to be repeated again nor mentioned.

The next day about teatime as arranged, Dad pulled up in our new van and we loaded up our gear and left for home. Peter didn't even look at me, which hurt, as I so wanted him to. So I consoled myself with the fact that he must have been asleep, but of course in my heart I knew he wasn't.

We got home and there was Lassie waiting to greet me with one of her major licking sessions. Mum had saved me a plate of Sunday lunch, which was soon being heated up on a plate on top of a saucepan full of boiling water. The taste was nowhere as good as it was when it first came out of the oven, but it was still more than good enough for me. The day had been long and I was soon in bed thinking about Peter and the weekend, and what a weekend it had been. I was thirteen years old and at last I had been able to feel the body of the incredibly handsome Peter. I lay there and I could feel my face redden at the excitement of just thinking about what had happened. Fresh air and not much rest soon caught up with me and I drifted away into a deep sleep.

Chapter Twenty Four – Tom popped the question

Life back at No. 5 was undergoing some major changes. We'd even had a telephone installed and it was fantastic - especially as a lot of the family already had telephones. It was particularly good to be able to speak with those who had moved away from Bow. We hadn't completely modernised though as we still didn't have a washing machine. We still took everything around the corner to the launderette, except for our sheets and pillowcases, which went off to what we called the Best Wash, which was simply a laundry service. All that had to be done was put the dirty washing into a pillowcase onto which was tied a pre-printed card detailing the contents. This was dropped off at the launderette, where it was collected by the cleaning company and delivered back in a couple of days, wrapped in paper, clean and starched. This for Mum was a great service, as in particular she hated ironing. Ironing was soon something I had to master, especially if I wanted to look half decent going to school.

I still had several chores to do and one of them was taking the dirty washing to the launderette. All I had to do was load it into the machine, pay the attendant, who was Tony Keeble's mum, and she would wash, tumble dry and fold it for us. The problem was, I had now reached that age when boys get easily embarrassed. The thought of people seeing me put my Mum's underwear in a washing machine was definitely no longer something I wanted to experience and I made this very clear to Mum one day. Even though she told me I was being daft, I said that I didn't mind getting the fish and chips no matter what the weather, but my launderette days were over and it was agreed. I was almost thirteen-and-a-half years old and I was beginning to experience some really strange things and one of them, at last, was pubic hair. One day it wasn't there and the next it just seem to happen. After my Friday night bath I was wiping under my arms and a few strands had appeared. Although I wanted it so badly I found this sudden appearance fascinating. I had seen Dad's hairy armpits for years but I never thought about me having them one day. I think the worst bit about this physical change is how it makes you feel, with hormones coursing through your body at a rate of knots. It seemed that every morning I would wake up to find something about me had changed. For a start, I was getting taller and my feet and legs used to ache something terrible. I told my Mum about this one day and I was told it was growing pains.

'What are growing pains?' I asked.

'Just something boys get at your age and it's nothing to worry about,' she said. It was all right for Mum to say 'nothing to worry about' but it was me that was having the pains. I had decided that as I ached the most when I went to bed it was obviously at night when I did all my growing. I had also noticed that Tony, who was a little older than me, had started growing hair on his top lip. I was so envious and I asked if I could have a razor so I would be ready when it happened to me. This request was greeted by a laugh and a firm no!

Once again I was back at H.C and we were busy breaking in our new form teacher, who didn't stay long. In fact we had a number of new form teachers, none of whom wanted us, or the school for that matter. That only re-affirmed my thoughts that H.C. was the pits.

Thankfully the school term between Whitsun and summer was short and soon I would be enjoying another six-week break. Well, not so much enjoying but more trying to keep myself occupied. Vicky Park, now that I was older, was far less interesting and to be honest, a lot of the time I didn't know what to do with myself. I was too old for kid's stuff and too young for the adult stuff. I was stuck in the middle. Still, at least two nights a week, thanks to the scouts, I seemed to have something to do and, more importantly, something to look forward to. It was about now that Tom was to take a real big risk as far as I was concerned. By now I'd had several Sunday lunches and afternoons at his house and my parents didn't mind one bit. I think if the truth were known, they were probably glad to have me off their hands, as I always seemed so bored with nothing to do.

That week after our Tuesday night meeting Tom asked me if I would join the Summer Camp Committee. He said he would very much like me to help out as he felt I made a great contribution to the troop. He told me that he had arranged for the committee to meet at his place on Saturday afternoon at about five-thirty and wondered if I would be able to go after I had finished work. I told him I didn't see a problem although I would probably be a bit smelly as to be there by five-thirty there wouldn't be time for me to get a bath. I must say that the smell of a butcher's shop tends to get in your clothes and in your hair and even into your skin. Tom told me not to worry as I could grab a bath at his place. He then suggested that perhaps after the meeting, which he only expected to last an hour, we could go to the cinema. Now that idea really appealed to me. He said, after the cinema I could jump a bus home easy enough but, ideally, he would need me to go back to his place again on Sunday morning to help him again. He would still need to prepare the cost for the camp per person, and do information sheets.

'I wonder if your Dad will be able to drive the kit down this year?' he asked.

'I don't know, I'll ask him tonight when I get in.' I said. 'I don't imagine there will be a problem. Where are you thinking we should go?'

'I was thinking we could go back to Pett Level again and if Jim will do this for us it will make it so much easier for the boys. It is such a long walk from the station to the farm with all that kit. Perhaps you can let us know what he says when you come round on Saturday.' With that he gave me a piece of paper with the proposed dates for the camp written on it. He then went on to say that it shouldn't take too long for us to get all the paperwork done and he asked me what time on Sunday morning I felt I could get back to his place. Before I could answer he went on to say that after we had finished he would cook us Sunday lunch if I would like. I had barely taken in what he had said and before I had thought about it he then suggested that it might actually be a lot easier if I stayed over at his place for the night...

I was silent and Tom waited for me to reply. My thoughts were 'you bet I would like to stop over.' I loved my time at Tom's place. He treated me like an adult and I loved that. He didn't swear, didn't threaten me, didn't pick on me and when he asked me to do something, if I couldn't do it or got it wrong, he never got angry or gave me a whack round the head, which is what Dad would invariably do. BUT, a stay overnight! Whew! I was just a couple of months past my thirteenth birthday. How would my parents react to this? I was sure they trusted Tom and I couldn't think why they should say no, but suppose they did. Suppose they thought it was funny and asked me if Tom had ever touched me. How would I deal with that? I knew I could easily say that he hadn't but I knew my face would give me away. These thoughts raced through my mind for what seemed an age. I finally answered Tom and told him that it certainly makes sense not to have to get home on a Saturday night by bus only to have to get back the next morning again by bus. I told Tom that I would ask them when I got home and I would let him know on Thursday if it would be OK. I think I felt guilty about all this because I knew that the request for my stopover was not in any way innocent on his part and certainly not on mine. I feared that my desires might show on my face when I asked the question. It was my face, which had now started to light up whenever I lied, or if I was embarrassed and it would be my face that would give me away.

As usual, I walked with Tom up to Campbell Road and then hopped on my bike leaving him to his walk home. My thoughts raced on how I was going to put the question to Mum and Dad. Could I camouflage it in some way? My Mum was no fool even if my Dad wasn't too bright. The only thing I could think of was boosting Dad's ego by telling him how much Tom depended on him to drive our van. How important summer camp was to so many and how he, and only he, could really make it possible. I think he enjoyed his position of importance. I think if nothing else, my Dad, at times, could be really generous. When Dad was being generous, even if it was only with his time, he was at his best. Mum was a different kettle of fish entirely. As I said, she was no fool. With her, all I could hope is that when I told her that I had been asked onto the Summer Camp Committee she would be quite proud of me and pleased with Tom for asking me.

I was home in no time at all and before I opened the front door I asked my face not to give me away. Dad was sitting in his usual armchair watching television.

'I am glad you're home,' Mum said, 'put the kettle on Jimmy.'

I made the tea and came in with the cups for Mum and Dad and then went back for mine and of course some biscuits. I gave Dad some biscuits and the piece of paper with the summer camp dates on it. I knew he couldn't read but I also knew that it was not good to rub it in. He took a look at the paper and passed it to Mum.

'It's the dates for their summer camp,' she said,

'They are hoping to go to Pett Level again.' I had just dunked a biscuit and shoved the whole thing in my mouth when I announced that I had been asked to join the Summer Camp Committee. I was right; Mum was really pleased about it, but not so pleased that it didn't stop her telling me not to speak with my mouth full.

'Mind you Dad,' I said, 'the whole things relies on you. Will you drive the van for us again and take the kit down and bring it back? If you don't do it Dad, it will be impossible.'

He thought for a moment and asked Mum again when the dates were and she told him. 'What do you think Ede?' he said.

'Well it's up to you Jim,' she said.

I realised they were playing with me.

'Of course I'll do it,' Dad said.

'Brilliant.' I said. 'I can't wait to make the announcement this Saturday at the first committee meeting.' I told them that we were meeting at Tom's house at five-thirty pm.

'Mind you, I did warn Tom that I would smell like a walking butcher's shop because I would have to go straight from work. It didn't seem to worry him though and he said I could grab a quick bath at his place, if I wanted.'

'What two baths in one week,' Dad said. 'What's come over you?'

'Nothing,' I said, and I could feel my face starting to glow, 'I just don't like smelling like the shop that's all.'

Dad just carried on dunking his biscuit and getting back to his television.

'Mum, Tom said if I wanted, we could go to the pictures at the Odeon at Mile End after the meeting. I thought that would be great and said OK.'

Nothing was said. So far, so good.

While Dad wasn't paying too much attention, as he was busy watching the box, I thought now was the time to grab the bull by the horns.

'Tom said that I should be able to get a bus home after the cinema and wondered what time I could get back round to his place on Sunday morning to help him prepare the paperwork for everyone in the troop. We have to prepare the cost on how much it will be for each one to go, and put together some information sheets ready to hand out at next Tuesdays meeting.' I went on to say that I didn't mind bussing it home in the week at that hour but I was a bit worried as it was Saturday night and the buses were often full of the louts that had been kicked out of the Blind Beggar.

The Blind Beggar was a pub in Whitechapel Road, where the Kray twins used to hang out and it was notorious for its Saturday night mass brawls. They knew this to be true as we had driven past the pub on our way home from Nanny's and we had seen the mass punch ups outside.

I said in a matter of fact way that I had suggested to Tom that it might be safer if I stopped over. There was a pause for about two seconds when Mum said that she thought the idea of me stopping over was much better as she would rather know where I was and that I was safe. She said she certainly didn't like the idea of me travelling home at that hour, alone on a bus. They didn't seem to give a thought to anything other than that I might get the crap kicked out of me by a bunch of thugs who had probably had far too much to drink.

My Dad added his usual 'Whatever you think is best Ede', waving his hand in lack of interest as he carried on dunking biscuits and shoving them into his mouth. Lassie just sat watching his every move in the hope that he might drop a bit for her - no chance. 'OK then,' I said, 'I'll tell Tom on Thursday at the troop meeting.'
I watched some more television and before I went to bed I took Lassie out for a quick walk around the block.

I lay in bed and I couldn't believe how worried I was about asking and how easy it had been. I just lay there reflecting on what had happened. I somehow took solace from the notion that if they didn't see anything wrong in me staying at Tom's perhaps there wasn't anything wrong in it after all. Of course they were not entirely in possession of all the facts, but I still got some comfort from that thought, and it eased the burden of my guilt as I drifted into a good night's sleep.

Chapter Twenty Five – First Night at Tom's

I arrived at Bow Baptist church early for the Thursday troop meeting and I excitedly told Tom as soon as I arrived that Dad would drive the troop van for us. I told him that Dad said he would let me have the costs in time for our committee meeting on Saturday.

'Oh, by the way,' I said, 'they said it is OK if I stop over on Saturday.'

'That's good,' he said casually and we got on with our evening. Tom's coolness also went a long way to making me feel that there was nothing wrong in my stopping over at his place.

The troop meeting closed in the usual way with announcements and a prayer. I was walking along the road with Tom and we were just chatting away about the evening and we were soon at our parting point, Campbell Road.

I said 'Goodnight Skip,' and as I crossed the road he called out to remind me not to forget the costs from Dad. I gave him the thumbs-up sign and cycled off. When I got in Dad was out - he was round the garage doing something to the car and he had taken Lassie with him. I did my usual and made some tea while I told Mum a bit about the evening and said Skip told me to remind Dad about the costs for the trip.

'I'll ask him when he comes in and write them out for you. Now then,' she said, 'you are working tomorrow so after that tea. Bed!'

'OK,' I said reluctantly without the usual, 'Oh but can't I stay up a bit longer'?

This was no time to be rocking any boats.

I was sound asleep when Dad came in and the next thing I remember was Mum waking me up and telling me to get up for work. It was Friday and as I was on school holidays I had been asked if I would work Fridays as well as Saturdays at the shop, and I had agreed. I thought it would be easy but the opening hours on a Friday are much longer than on Saturday and I found the two days together very tiring. It was hard work.

I had downed some cereal and a cup of tea and before I left, as I was going out the door, Mum asked me to make sure that I had everything clean and ready for Tom's tomorrow night. If there was anything that needed washing, I was to leave it out and she would rinse it through by hand when she got in from work. I told her that I had everything I needed and that all I had to do was shove it into a bag. I gave her a wave as I rushed out the door to work. I still couldn't help but think how it had all been so easy. Still, why not? They totally trusted Tom so I guess I really shouldn't have been so surprised. I suppose my problem wasn't about doubting in their trust in Tom but wrestling with my own guilt.

My first Friday was really busy and for me a real taste of hard work and long hours. I was in at eight and back home again by six-thirty with just an hour for lunch. I got home and my feet were wet from scrubbing down the butcher's blocks and my hands were red from the hot water.

The worst thing for me was that I stank. As if all this work wasn't enough, when I got in I was still expected to jump on my bike and do the usual trip to Samuel's for the fish and chips. I still didn't dare utter a word of complaint, as I was still very much mindful of the coming weekend. I cycled like mad and was there and back with our tea, I am sure in record time. Thankfully, while I was doing this, Mum had checked that I had everything I needed for my stopover at Tom's and she had packed a small bag for me. She told me all I had to do was to put in my toothbrush after I had used it in the morning.

We had soon tucked into the delicious hot fish and chips and I was sitting by the fire and my face was all red, thankfully this time from a full belly and the warmth from the fire. I was full up and tired from my hard day's work, in fact almost too tired to take my bath. However, there was no getting out of the Friday night ritual, even though I said I was having a bath the next night at Tom's. Mum ran me a bath and put some bath salts into the water, which was deep and hot. It wasn't long before my poor aching body was being soothed by the soft hot water. I was soon out and dressed in my pyjamas ready for bed.

I snuggled up with Lassie on the armchair and watched TV for a while, enjoying one of my favourite programmes ON a Friday night – Take Your Pick with Michael Miles. I can still remember how excited the female contestants would get when they opened the box and were told they had won the 'Star Prize' - a refrigerator. Wow!

I was starting to fall asleep when Dad passed me over a piece of paper. He told me to give it to Tom tomorrow. He said he'd calculated the cost of the trip for the van to take the kit down and bring it back. He went on to say that I could surprise the committee by telling them that he would pay for the petrol. I looked at him in his moment of generosity and simply said, 'Blimey, thanks.' He could be really generous at times.
  I smiled at Dad and just went to bed.

As I slipped into my bed Lassie was at my feet. It only seemed seconds later that I was being woken up by my alarm clock. I, like my Uncle Ray, could sleep through an earthquake, so my alarm clock needed to be extra noisy. Thankfully it worked and I was soon up and dressed, digging into my breakfast. I made tea for Mum and Dad and took it into their bedroom.
  I said, 'I am off to work. See you later.' meaning really

'whenever' and I got a grunt for a reply. I left with my overnight bag in hand.

I was soon dashing through the front doors of the butchers to a chorus of 'He's keen!'

The shop wasn't open to the customers yet and I had lots to do. I wanted the day to pass quickly as I was so looking forward to my weekend. I set about preparing my deliveries. It was my job to get the orders ready, weighed, priced and wrapped. I had soon learned how to slice liver, gut chickens and even cut lamb chop using a meat cleaver. I was rapidly becoming an adept little butcher and I really enjoyed the job. The orders were ready and I was starting my delivery round by mid-morning.

The day soon passed and as usual I had scrubbed everything the best I could which was obviously quite acceptable as no one ever complained. Mr Greystone paid me my wages and gave me a shoulder of lamb to take home. As I left the shop I thanked him politely and said 'see you next week'. I rushed over the road to Mum's shop with a shoulder of lamb in one hand and my bag in the other.
'Hi Lil,' I said as I walked past.
'Hello,' she said, 'I hear you are off for a dirty weekend!'
Now ordinarily this sort of comment would have been a fairly normal run of the mill thing to say. However, under the circumstances I suddenly felt as though I had been caught out and that when my Mum saw my red face she would immediately realise what was going on and stop me from going. I tried not to let my panic show but try as I might I went as red as a beetroot. Thoughts rushed through my brain on what I could say to get myself out of this mess.

I couldn't stop myself thinking they must have talked about this and that the cat was out of the bag. What was I going to do? I stood there in silence for what seemed an age. Lil could obviously see that she had embarrassed me, so she said, 'Well I think it's good that you are helping out! Your scoutmaster must think the world of you little bleeders to do what he does, you should think yourselves bloody lucky.' With that the colour started to slowly drain from my face. Mum told Lil that Tom was such a good man and said she was convinced he put a lot of his own money into helping these boys out.

I swallowed heavily and tried not to let anyone notice my sigh of relief. Mum was walking toward me from the back of the shop when she said,
'Now you had better be off, if you have to be at Tom's by five-thirty.'
'OK then.' I kissed Mum on the cheek, gave her the wrapped up joint of meat and said, 'it's a shoulder of lamb. Save me some will you?'
'You're having lunch at Tom's aren't you?' she said.
'Yeah, so what,' I said.
'I am sure that boy's got worms,' she said.
As I rushed for the door Lil said,
'What about me then?' pointing to her cheek. 'I'm not kissing that, I don't know where it's been,' I said and she threw a wire coat hanger at me.
'See yer,' I said with my usual cheeky grin.

As I ran around the corner to catch the bus I had an enormous spring in my step and a massive rush of excitement at the thought that my weekend had at last started. I was free of home and Dad for a whole night, and in the safety of Tom's home to relax and do what I wished. My mind raced along almost as fast as my heart as I turned the corner, and as luck would have it the bus was coming along. It was a warming sight as they were less than frequent and more than unreliable in keeping to a timetable. I jumped onto the platform and we were off. We went right past Mum's shop and I waved at Lil who was still sitting at the front desk, pinning tickets onto the clothes but her head was down so she didn't see me. I went inside and took a seat. I sat there and reflected on what Lil had said and how silly I was to be so embarrassed. Everyone says that when they are going away - nothing was meant by it. It was just me being me. I had coloured up out of my own guilt and I didn't want that to happen again.

We arrived at Limehouse and within minutes I got my connection and in no time at all the conductor shouted out 'Aberdeen'. I hopped off as the bus took the corner slowly into Bethnal Green Road to save me going to the bus stop and then having to walk back again. I was outside Tom's place in about two minutes and gently knocking on the front door. I could hear Tom call out to Uncle downstairs that it was all right as it was just some of the boys coming round for a meeting. The door opened and there was Tom standing in his khaki trousers, beige shirt and highly polished black shoes.
'Come in, you're the first,' he said.
'Thanks Skip,' I said, as I knew Uncle would still have his kitchen door open, trying to hear or see who it was. I went upstairs and Tom's kitchen door was slightly open. I went in. I looked at my watch and the clock on the shelf and I thought I've only got twenty minutes to grab a bath before they get here. Tom walked in and with his usual friendly smile came over and gave me a side-on hug.
'Phew,' he said. 'You were right; you do smell like a butcher's shop. Still there is time for you to grab a quick bath.' And he went down to the half-landing to the bathroom and ran one for me. Through the bathroom was his bedroom where he had gone and he was soon back with a clean towel and he told me that perhaps I would like to unpack my things while my bath was running. I grabbed the towel and headed off for the bathroom. As I passed through into the bedroom, I couldn't help but notice the really old-fashioned gas water

heater on the bathroom wall, the likes of which I had never seen before and certainly never seen since. It had all manner of knobs and levers on it and it roared away as it heated up the water. The bath was just about deep enough when Tom came in to turn off the heater. I was soon undressed and getting myself scrubbed up when Tom walked in and sat on the laundry bin. He proceeded to ask me how my day had been. Ordinarily bath time for me was a private thing, but I didn't mind Tom being there at all. He was interested in me and listened to what I had to say. His sincerity made me drop my defences and I certainly lost my shyness. This was all so different and I loved it.

I was soon washed and dressed and we were sitting in the kitchen when the first of the committee were to arrive. Two more Senior Scouts came and we sat in the lounge to discuss summer camp. Tom told them that he felt in view of the fact that my dad was driving the van it was only right that I be on the committee. I think one or two of them probably thought I was too young to contribute anything sensible but I soon put that right. When we started to discuss costs, I told them that I had said to my dad how important it was for us, particularly some of the younger boys, to get the kit to the site by van and because of what I had said my dad had offered to pay for the fuel costs. I hadn't told Tom about this so everyone was genuinely pleased and I was suddenly more than an asset to the committee.

We agreed the camp would be at Pett Level and when it would be. Furthermore, who would be responsible for doing what. Tom said that he would be preparing an application form for the boys' parents to complete and a leaflet giving details of how much it would cost, what they would need to bring and so on. The meeting went well and it ended at about six-thirty.

I remember thinking to myself as I could hear the others talking to Tom as they made their way down the stairs, 'I wonder if they think it is strange that I am not leaving with them.' No doubt Tom would have had some form of an answer ready. I was still young and still terrified of anyone knowing about me, and my feelings. Of course Tom was in much more danger than me. Homosexuality was not even legal then between consenting adults - let alone us. If we had been caught, heaven only knows what the law would have done with him. He came back upstairs and I was glad the meeting was over as it meant that I had Tom all to myself until tomorrow afternoon. I could relax and enjoy myself. I asked him if he would like me to put the kettle on to make some tea or coffee. He told me to take it easy as I had been at work and that he would do it. He told me we have an hour before we need to leave for the pictures so I should take my shoes off and relax. He probably noticed the hole in my sock but just ignored it. He went to his fridge, which was on the landing outside the kitchen, and quickly came back holding a cooked chicken on a plate.

'Would you like some dinner?' he asked me. As usual I was starving.
'Yes please.'
He soon had some potatoes on the boil and in no time at all we were tucking into a meal. I told him I was back to school on Monday and that I wasn't at all looking forward to it. He asked me why. Tom asked me why! Someone was interested in me! I told him why and he listened. I couldn't help but think that this maybe wrong, terribly wrong, but I was happy. The meal was soon finished and the dishes cleaned and put away.
'Come on,' he said, 'grab your coat, let's go to the pictures.'

The walk to the Odeon took about ten minutes. Tom's long legs would stride out and I would struggle to keep up in a walking pace. We were soon inside the foyer and Tom went and bought the tickets. I did offer to pay for mine but I guess he felt I could do better things with my hard earned butcher's boy's wages. Probably buy a new pair of socks! We watched a film called The Land of the Pharaohs and I really enjoyed it. In particular I remember feeling how glad I was that the greedy Pharaoh's wife was tricked and buried alive with him, however it was a bit on the tough side being a servant or slave. They were also buried alive with him too. It was a great film.

The walk home from the Odeon didn't take long at all and we discussed the film. I was flattered beyond belief that someone was prepared to listen to what I had to say. During those early days I reckon I must have bored the pants off Tom with my endless griping about how unhappy I was. He listened with a tireless ear and he always had a good answer. More importantly he showed me how to look at problems differently and that life wasn't that bad. I used to think to myself 'he doesn't live with my Dad!' If only my Dad was like Tom - if only Tom was my Dad!

We got back in and I was asked if I would like a cup of hot chocolate before I went to bed.
'Would that be with a biscuit?' I asked.
'Of course,' he said, 'or a piece of Angel Cake or a sandwich or, if I have got it, whatever you want!'
'Just a biscuit will be fine,' I said politely. 'Oh and ,thank you very much for taking me to the pictures, I enjoyed it very much.'. My Mum had always taught me that Please and Thank you cost you nothing but take you a long way. He just gave me a wink and his kindness, along with the heat from the gas fire, filled me with a depth of warmth I will never forget.

We chatted some more over our chocolate and then it was

time for bed.

'I have put a small heater in the bedroom and a hot water bottle in the bed,' he said. 'If you want to go and brush your teeth and get ready for bed I will be there in a minute as soon as I have washed up these cups.'

I said 'OK' and went through the bathroom to the bedroom. The room was warm and I was soon undressed and into my pyjamas. I rummaged around in my bag and realised that I had forgotten my toothbrush. Tom came into the bathroom and I told him what I had done and he produced a brand new toothbrush from the little bathroom cupboard on the wall.

'Here you are, have this one. You can leave it here for when you come again.'

I thought nothing of his remark and was soon giving my teeth a good brushing. The toilet at Tom's was outside so it was a bit of a trek. It certainly brought back memories of 49 Morville Street, as the house was a similar layout although smaller.

I was soon back and Tom was tucked up in bed. I walked into the room and he did no more than lift the covers signalling me to get in. I climbed over him to my side, of his four foot 'large' single bed; I was between him and the wall. As I slid down into the bed, I could feel he was naked. He didn't touch me nor ask anything of me - he never did. He just turned out the light and, if anything was to happen, it was left up to me.

The next day was bright and sunny although the view from Tom's bedroom window wasn't anything to write home about. In fact it was the back wall of an old cinema in the road behind. The cinema had long been bought by a Spiritualist group and turned into some form of a church. We never went.

I lay there in bed and I felt great. Tom had got up saying he was going to make some tea but my nose told me it was far more than that - I could smell bacon cooking. What a way to

wake up. I was quickly up and dressed and as I walked into the kitchen Tom asked
'One egg or two?'

'Two please, I am just going to pop downstairs to the loo.' As I passed Uncle's kitchen door I could hear the radio was on and I could see him moving about through the frosted glass. I was soon back to demolish Tom's efforts. I was an appetite on two legs and really appreciated a good breakfast. Everything was cleared away and Tom suggested we take a walk in Vicky Park, which was just around the corner. We crossed the road by the roundabout and as we did I looked up at the small block of flats down whose walls we had long before tipped the red paint. The paint had long been cleaned off and I said nothing to Tom about what we had done.

We walked around the boating lake and fed the ducks. I seemed to talk non-stop and I felt so relaxed I wondered if and when it would be possible to do this again. Tom had told me that if there was anything I wanted to know I was not to be afraid to ask.
'Do you think we can do this again Tom?' I asked.
'Jim,' he said - he called me Jim and not Jimmy, which made me feel quite grown up, 'If you want to, I see no reason why not, but we must be sensible.'
He didn't need to say more than that, as I knew what he meant by 'sensible'. Our relationship was our secret and yet he never once actually told me not to tell anyone. I guess he must have sensed that I knew only too well that what was happening was wrong. Perhaps a part of our relationship was wrong, but there was so much good about it I wasn't about to spoil things. We really got on well together. I certainly felt that my life until then had not been up to much and a lot of the time I was unhappy. In particular it lacked the love of a father. With Tom I felt a freedom and a kindness that I loved. I had found an adult who was humorous, kind and caring and

I never once thought of him as anything other than that. It never crossed my mind that Tom may have preyed on other boys like me. I never once felt vulnerable, I just felt loved. So many times I would wish that my dad was like Tom.

Our walk ended and we headed back home. Tom sat at the kitchen table with a writing pad working out the costs for the summer camp and drafting an information sheet as I prepared the vegetables for Sunday lunch. When I had finished, he showed me what he'd done and asked me what I thought. What I thought! Someone in my life was interested enough in me to ask me what I thought. I suggested that it might be a good idea for one or two boys to go with my Dad in the van to help him unload and that way it would save on their fares. He liked the idea and said that they should still pay and the money could be put in the pot to help those less fortunate in the troop and there were plenty of those. Tom told me that he would get our notes typed up and copied at work on Monday ready for distribution on Tuesday night. The work was done and the rest of the day was spent in a relaxed way.

As usual we talked about how I felt, what I was afraid of and my unhappiness with myself. He told me we all want to be different from what we are, taller, thinner, blonder, or darker and I was no different. He slowly convinced me that I was an awful lot better off than I thought I was and I gained a lot of confidence. The main thing he did was to help me stop blaming myself for my father's outbursts. I was growing up thinking these were due to his disappointment in me. He had adopted me and I was a disappointment. I hadn't turned out to be what he wanted and on top of that I had this terrible problem - which I still couldn't understand - about my sexuality. The weekend went well but far too quickly for me.

I think with the incentive of our next scout meeting, Monday and Tuesday just flew by. As usual I rode like the wind on my bike and I was at the hall before most of the boys. I walked in and Tom was sitting on a table talking with Peter Chandler who was standing quite close to him, laughing, and I experienced my first pang of jealousy. How could Tom be talking to Peter and laughing? Laughing about what? Of course I didn't say anything - I knew it wasn't my place and besides, why shouldn't Tom talk to Peter? No matter how much I told myself it didn't matter, it didn't help my jealousy. The problem was I didn't know which one I was jealous of! I decided neither was mine and that I shouldn't be so daft. The moment soon passed and I never thought like that again. The evening went well, notices on summer camp were distributed and it was decided that we would hold a draw out of a hat for those that could go with Dad in the van. With his quick temper they were welcome to it. I wanted to go by train.

The next few weeks seemed to fly by and now that Mr Lipton had gone, school had become run of the mill and I hated it even more. We never again enjoyed the delight of a permanent form teacher let alone one as good as Mr Lipton. We had a few new teachers straight out of teacher training college or existing teachers from within the school who were simply being moved around for some reason or another. Whatever the reason, I cannot believe it was because, as a class, we were that bad. I seem to remember that we were a reasonably good bunch although it must be said that we did have our fair share of hooligans.

I would find myself daydreaming more and more on how I would get through my remaining time at H.C. Then one day when I was walking through the ground floor assembly hall I stopped to look at the noticeboard. There it was, the answer was staring me in the face, acting.

I had been in a school play in Malmesbury Road and enjoyed

it, so why not again at H.C. The school play that year was called The Sole Survivor and was being put on in October. It was about a few people surviving an atomic disaster. The play's director was our English teacher, Mr Guthridge and his assistant was the Literature teacher, Miss McCarthy. This was a great diversion for me as there was much planning to be done. The central characters of the play were a brother and sister. I auditioned for the part of the brother - and I got it. My sister and I had been left alone in the house and as the story unfolded we discovered we had lost our parents in a major atomic disaster. One of the other characters in the play was a young man who had also survived and managed to somehow stumble on our house. The problem was this character was supposed to be a bit of a psychopath. Now in our school, ordinarily this part would have been easy to cast. We had psychopaths coming out of our ears. However, they cast or should I say miscast, Carl Jackson who was six foot tall, wore a leather jacket, and who was one of the few pupils of that stature who was not a hard nut. In fact just a few days before the play was due to open, he threatened to back out due to chronic stage fright. With a lot of effort we all talked him into doing it and promised him somehow that we would all help him through. The play was set to run for three nights in October and it certainly gave me something else to think about other than whether or not I should sit 'O' levels. Everyone was talking about exams and how important they were. The sting in the tail was, to take them meant staying on until I was sixteen. I had spent the last two and a half years thinking about nothing other than leaving H.C. as soon as I could i.e. at fifteen. I wasn't ready to cope with the thought of another year at H.C. so I put any thoughts of 'O' levels right out of my head.

Chapter Twenty Six - A sole survivor

The rest of the term went quite well and as usual I looked forward to the weekends. I liked working and I enjoyed the independence of having my own money in my pocket. In no time at all the summer holidays were upon us and I had no homework to do except for learning the lines of the school play. We all had six weeks to learn our parts.

A few days after we broke up from school we went on our family holiday, once again in Scotland. I was now thirteen and growing more and more independent and this caused me no end of grief. I would now argue back over things and sometimes, Heaven forbid, I would be right. Sadly, I had to learn that being right was not always in my best interest, where my dad was concerned and it would usually end up in tears. Mine! Of course I could read and write and this didn't help the situation either. We might be arguing over some topic or another and I might use a newspaper or a book to prove a point - just about the worse thing I could have done really. Dad would end up lashing out in a violent temper, this would result in a row between Mum and Dad and once again, I would feel I was the cause. Damn, damn, damn! When would I learn to keep my mouth shut? I was starting to question silently more and more why they had adopted me. I seemed so wrong for them, but I couldn't stop being me. I hated school and I was at times so unhappy at home. I loved to visit a friend's house, but I would invariably end up wishing that my parents were more like his. I couldn't understand why friends had nice comfortable homes that were warm and happy whereas I lived in a cold house, which had a time bomb in it - my Dad!

I spent much of this particular holiday on my own sitting on the rocks at the side of the River Dee wondering what I had done to deserve this and generally feeling very sorry for myself. I hated my real mother for abandoning me to this. However, I was still so much better off than most because I had the best shoes and good food to eat. I just felt so unloved at times and I would rather have gone barefoot just to have my Dad tell me just once that he loved me. My solitude by the river gave me the time to learn my part well in The Sole Survivors. I wanted to ask my mum to help me with the word bashing, as I called it, but Dad had once said, 'I can't understand why you're wasting your time with that fucking rubbish. I bet that school is making money out of what you are doing and they are paying you nothing.' When I told him that they weren't it seemed to frustrate him even more. I felt it best to sit alone somewhere and just keep reading the part until I felt it had sunk in.

Our time in Scotland soon passed and we were heading south for London. The journey home in the car was much worse than in the days of the motorbike and sidecar. We were all inside one vehicle and it was easy to talk and of course argue. We were motoring along through the beautiful countryside when a row developed over my correcting Mum on how to pronounce 'There's a broad brict moonlit nict to-nict'. We had not long left the campsite and Mum just took no notice of me but Dad went on and on at me and the more he went on, the more irate he became. We were listening to some local Scottish radio station in the car when the presenter said quite out of the blue 'There's a broad brict moonlit nict tonict' proving me correct. There was silence in the car and I was ignored for what seemed like ages.

A few days after we were back home I was planning for the scouts' summer camp. I knew this would be fun and so I did my best just to keep out of Dad's hair. As usual in the school holidays I was working Fridays and Saturdays. This gave me more money, much of which I saved in a Post Office savings book. I had become a saverholic. Summer was fun and I was given more freedom now that I was getting a bit older. While Dad was at work I would spend a fair bit of time helping Mum at the shop especially when Lil was on holiday. Perkins never bothered sending Mum down help as they knew full well she could cope on her own, well of course, with my help. If I weren't taking in dry cleaning or at work, I would be at the flat playing with Lassie who was now very pregnant. A few weeks before I had jumped over our back wall to find Lassie firmly engaged back to back with another dog. He had obviously sniffed out his opportunity and made the most of it. Of course in my ignorance I thought he was hurting her so I threw stones at him and told him to 'F' off. They disengaged but his premature withdrawal hurt her and I learned it was better sometimes to leave well enough alone. Lassie was OK but now toting around seven puppies inside her.

When the time was right Lassie made her nest in my bedroom. I had a built-in cupboard in my bedroom, in front of which hung an old heavy lined curtain. This curtain was far too long and had been simply pinned up at the back to shorten it. This made it easy for Lassie to pull it down again and use the excess curtain as her nesting material. She was by now well experienced in the art of ripping away at fabric and so she nested right next to my bed. One night, as I lay in bed I suddenly heard snuffling and whimpering. I put on the bedside light and there was Lass licking away at her first puppy. He was brown and white and for some unknown reason we later named him Peter. For the rest of the night I could just softly speak with Lassie and she gave me the honour of allowing me watch her deliver six more puppies all on her own. I had never seen anything so wonderful and I found it really exciting.

The next couple of weeks were sleepless due to constant whimpering of this small brood. I had to get my sleep so Dad moved Lassie and her pups from my bedroom to a new nest, which he had made in the bottom of our larder in the kitchen. I used to find it fascinating how she would work so hard at cleaning and feeding them. Her work was tireless and soon her nipples and the surrounding skin were bleeding from little sharp claws pushing away at her for more and more milk. Despite what must have been a great deal of discomfort, she never neglected her duty and she was a wonderful mum.

The school summer holiday that year was filled with the fun of watching this little family grow up and play together. They played, fought, and ate and after that they would fall in a heap to sleep. Lassie was great to watch in her role as Mum and for the first time a summer holiday seemed to flash by almost too quickly. It was soon time for me to join my patrol for our summer camp at Pett Level near Hastings. Although official scout camps like Cuffley or Chalfont had proper facilities such as toilets and showers which were much better for the younger ones, I preferred Pett Level as it was a farm, more natural and within easy reach of the sea.

Dad had loaded the scout van and he and Mum made their way in advance of us along with four scouts who travelled in the back. They thought that getting tossed about as Dad took the corners great fun and he obliged by taking corners probably as fast as he dared. The rest of us set off by train giving Dad a good start to ensure that the kit was at the site in advance of our arrival. It was great travelling without having to tote all that kit with us. This meant we could make the march from the station looking like a smart, highly honed troop of soldiers. Well that's what we thought we looked like.

We arrived on site to find that the four lucky, battered and bruised scouts who had been in the van had moved the kit by our cart to our allotted area. Dad had long returned to Bow and we got on with setting up camp. This was done in the usual way with the tents set up in an arc with their entrances facing toward the campfire. At either end of the row of big tents was a small one-man tent - Skip's at one end and mine at the other.

Who would want to share with me on this camp, was the question racing round in my mind. These thoughts seemed to be taking me over and I was getting more and more concerned about my extreme desire to be close to another boy for physical contact. It just didn't seem right, and these thoughts were really beginning to worry me. I was obviously not handling my own sexuality too well. I just didn't understand anything about it. I wanted the physical contact but I always felt so guilty afterwards. I tried to help myself over this problem, by making myself share my tent with someone my own age. Although this worked it wasn't satisfying this need of mine and left me with a feeling of regret that I had missed out on an opportunity. So, I thought I would leave things to chance this year. I ended up on my own and I felt this was a good thing, although in a way I would have preferred being in one of the big tents as I didn't like being on my own too much.

Summer camp was, as always, great fun and if nothing else at least at the end of this one I didn't go home feeling bad about myself for what I had done. For a change I went home feeling bad about myself for what I hadn't done. Neither were easy feelings to handle.

The journey home was physically easy but much more mentally stressful. Mum wasn't with Dad, and I was elected along with three others to travel with him in the van. I am certain that Dad had asked for me, as without Mum, I had to navigate. There was no way that Dad was going to announce that he couldn't read or write. Normally I hated this job, but as we had three other boys aboard, I was sure Dad wouldn't go nuts if I got it wrong. We made the journey back to Bow Baptist without a single wrong turn and it didn't seem to take us that long either. The kit was soon unloaded and we left the van in the churchyard and we went home in our car.

We got home and I received a fantastic welcome from Lassie and her pups, which by now had really grown quite big. Peter was developing a collie type mane and he looked really handsome but, sadly, it was time to let them go. While I was away Mum had found homes for them all, bar Peter, whom she had decided we should keep. Within a couple of days people were calling round to take their chosen dog. It was sad to see them go but nice to have some peace and quiet back in the house again. Lassie was fine about the pups going, I guess because she still had Peter with whom she got on well. Peter was developing into a great looking dog for a mongrel. The problem was, as he got older he loved to get out and roam the streets. I wasn't the only one in our house with hormones rushing around his body!

Chapter Twenty Seven - Enter 1962

It was now September and the summer holidays were over and I was back to H.C. and in heavy rehearsals for The Sole Survivor. The play was to be put on in another school not too far from us, as it had the luxury of a stage. Sets were made and it was time for on stage rehearsals. I will never forget sitting on stage as they opened the curtains and I looked out at row upon row of seats. It was awesome but my thoughts were more on how Carl Jackson would cope. The first rehearsal went well - up until Carl made his first entrance and he took one look out front. There was a huge pause, and we all waited for him to get over his fright and, thank goodness, he was word perfect. The time had come for opening night. My parents said they would try to come but as the curtains were pulled back and all those rows of seats had people in them, it was impossible to see if they were in the audience. The play went really well and received a great deal of applause. What was really sad for me was when all the cast's mums and dads came back stage mine were not among them. Once again I stared into the face of disappointment as I thought I had done so well and all I wanted was for them to see me. I should have known better.

The other two nights went as well, although the girl who had played my sister had broken her leg and a teacher had to stand in for her, reading her part from a script. I hated this as it really took the magic of the play away. There was still no sight of my parents on the remaining nights and when I asked why they weren't there, I was told that they just couldn't get home from work in time. On reflection I know that my Dad would never have gone and my Mum would not have gone without him. I was deeply hurt by this although I never said anything.

The rest of the year rapidly disappeared and it was Christmas time again. Work was chaotic. I spent many hours gutting turkeys and whizzing around on the bike making deliveries and the greatest thing was the tips. In total I was given what seemed to me a small fortune, most of which went in my savings account. It was hard and smelly work but I enjoyed it. I was given a turkey by old man Greystone and his son gave me a couple of quid and, to me, this was big money. I went home wishing everyone in the shop a very Merry Christmas with this bloody great turkey under my arm. I felt as though I was contributing to the running of our home and I liked the feeling that gave me.

Uncle Billy and Aunt Eve came for Christmas with Kathy and Simon and the whole thing went off without a cross word, for a change. I did my usual babysitting bit for both Christmas night and New Year's Eve. I had now long passed the age when Father Christmas had stopped coming and I was given my presents before Mum, Dad Uncle Billy and Eve went round the pub, with my Dad in his ever loving way saying
'Go on then, open 'em.' He made me feel that the presents had nothing really to do with Christmas but were more a consolation prize for having to stay behind to babysit. I may have been aware there was no Santa but they could have put a little effort into maintaining the magic of Christmas. I opened my presents, said thanks, and out they went. The time between Christmas and New Year was spent playing with Kathy and Simon with their new toys or out on my bike. I didn't like the week between Christmas and New Year, as it was always dull. It seemed all that hype on the run-up to Christmas with all that shopping and shouting 'Merry Christmas' would just stop at midnight on the twenty-fifth of December. Christmas was gone and its spirit dead.

New Year's Eve was here again and Mum had been to the hairdresser to have her usual shampoo and set. We would have dinner, which after all the Christmas food, was usually something quite simple like a steak or a pork chop. We would then await the arrival of Aunt Eve, Uncle Billy and the kids. I would once again be the babysitter and they would go to the pub. I was again spending New Year's Eve with Ken and Andy and so entered 1962.

I would soon be fourteen years old and the thrilling thought for me was that I would be leaving H.C. next year. Of course, I hadn't told Mum and Dad about my plans but I don't think they would have said much if I had done. Mum had started to make noises about me being a Singer sewing machine mechanic when I left school. A sewing machine mechanic, me! Well it was obvious why she felt this would be good for me. Mum had spent much of her working life on a sewing machine making shoes and she knew what the mechanics earned and how important they were. I would have a good job for life and my skill would also enable me to do private work. I somehow couldn't see me doing this, but as I didn't have a clue what else I would like to do, for the time being, I just went along with the idea.

The Christmas holidays were over and I was back at H.C although with the thought of leaving next year my attitude changed as I could now see the light at the end of the tunnel. I was also older, taller and I found the older boys a little less intimidating. I also think my performance in the school play gave me a bit of playground cred. I am sure some of the parents must have commented on the play and who knows, perhaps that did some good for me. This improved my attitude toward H.C. but not enough to make me want to stay on for exams.

I was now beginning to worry about something else. When would I mature? Boys at school were talking about coming and wanking. Some of them were bragging about how they could come and a few of them were even giving demonstrations in the toilets. It was quite funny to watch three or four lads in the toilets all going at themselves in a race to see who could get there first and who could spurt the furthest. All I wanted to know was, when would it would be my turn? Of course not for such a disgusting public display, but just to know when. However, my mind was soon to be taken off that problem for a while. I came home from school one afternoon to find Mum in a real state. She had come home to let Peter and Lassie out as usual at lunchtime. Peter and Lass both disappeared over the back wall but only Lassie came back to Mum's calls. Peter must have caught a whiff of something desirable, which overrode everything. I spent hours on my bike looking for him, but it was no use. He was gone. After two or three days of telephoning the local police station and Battersea Dogs Home we resigned ourselves to the fact that he was gone for good. We decided that he had probably been taken by some passing lorry driver, or someone who liked the look of him. We were convinced that Peter was a victim of his own good looks.

I was seeing Tom on the occasional Sunday and sometimes for an overnight. I didn't have to make excuses any more about buses and the dangers of travelling home late on my own. My parents obviously had a lot of confidence in Tom and I took advantage of that trust. It was just before my birthday and Tom had asked me to stay over and told me that he would take me to the pictures. I did my usual Saturday job and I took some meat home for Mum and also a couple of steaks for Tom and me.

I got in and Dad had the fire going so there was plenty of hot water for a quick bath. I packed my uniform for church parade the next day and got myself ready. Mum was still in Perkins' so I told Dad I would pop in to see her on my way and that I would see him tomorrow. He was busy mucking about with something on the floor and it was though I didn't exist. He just grunted 'tarra'. I gave Lassie a pat and left. I poked my head through the door of Perkins' and told Mum I was off and that I had put a shoulder of lamb in the fridge - a new addition to our extremely short list of kitchen appliances.

It was quite an event when that arrived - especially as we really didn't have room in the kitchen for it. It ended up in the bottom of the pantry plugged into one of Dad's self installed plug points. Mum was about to shut the shop so I walked with her back toward our flat and I crossed over to catch the 86.
'What time will you be home tomorrow?' she asked. I told her probably about six o'clock.
'OK, will you want some tea?'
'No I don't think so - I expect I'll get something to eat at Tom's.' With that I kissed her on the cheek and ran over to the bus stop to wait for the bus.

I arrived at Tom's and received the usual welcome. I dumped my stuff and we went out again to the pictures this time to see Ben Hur. The stunts were great but in particular I enjoyed the religious aspect of the film. We walked home eating some chips from a local chippy and on the way home we discussed what we liked most about the film. I said I was really moved by the bit in the movie when poor old Ben Hur was given water by Christ. It sent a sort of shiver down my back. We got home and Tom made us a cup of hot chocolate and we went to bed. I was really tired and I was keen to get to bed. I was in first and when Tom got in, he switched off the light. The bed was warm and the sheets fresh on and they smelled of washing powder. It was to be that weekend that my wish about being mature was to come true. At first I couldn't believe it, but it had happened. The sensation was wonderful. The next day the equipment had to be tested again just to make sure this wasn't a one off, and thankfully it wasn't.

There was no time to languish in bed, as we had to get up for church parade. We arrived at Bow Baptist and as I sat there in the church I had all sorts of thoughts racing through my mind. I looked up at the cross over the altar and once again I recalled the bit in the Ben Hur film that had moved me. As I sat there with eyes fixed on the cross, I wondered what Christ would think of me for what I had done, for what I was doing. I asked why I was the way I was. I asked why was my Dad the way he was. I asked what was it that I had done to deserve so many problems at such a young age and again, why had I been abandoned by my mother? Why did I have to be adopted by someone who had such a quick temper and who at times would frighten the life out of me? There were so many questions, and at times so much unhappiness, but the answers never came.

I was back at H.C. and we were on the run-up to the Easter term. I had done the usual bit in Metalwork by making a steel poker and in Woodwork, a bookshelf. It was one of those rare occasions when Dad showed some approval at my work, especially for the poker and Mum in particular liked the bookshelf. It wasn't often that I received praise but this little bit of approval really meant a lot to me. I suppose all I really wanted was for them to say well done now and then, but as usual that just didn't happen.

I was at Scouts one night and Tom told me he had received a letter from Baden Powell House. The letter informed him that there was a major badge course being held at Gilwell Park Scout Camp over Easter. The letter went on to ask if the 38th could provide someone who could cook well, to go and be part of the catering team for the course leaders. He asked me if I would like to go and represent the 38th. I thought this was such an honour and leapt at the opportunity. Tom stood at the end of the evening in front of the troop and brought us to 'attention' and then 'at ease'. He then told us about the coming events and about the letter he had received. He told everyone that he had asked me to represent the 38th and subject to my parents consent, I had agreed to go. The pride I felt was immeasurable.

The evening ended as usual and I had good news to tell Mum and Dad. I got home and as I walked through the door there was Lassie flopped on the carpet in front of the fire soaking up the heat. Dad had his feet up on the mantelshelf, wearing a string vest and eating a bowl of cornflakes and Mum was glued to the box. I went to make my announcement and was told to be quiet. I pushed my bike through to the back and went to my room to get changed. There was no point in saying anything just yet, as it might just annoy them and their evenge could be stopping me going.

I walked into the lounge with the tea and biscuits and waited for whatever they had been watching to finish. Then I calmly told them my news and asked if I could go to Gilwell Park instead of going to our usual Easter camp at Cuffley. I explained why and that I had been especially selected to represent our troop. I oozed pride as I explained but I got no reaction other than Dad saying that he hoped they like their oats well done. I was quite used to his attitude by now but I still couldn't stop myself craving recognition, but it never came. I just quietly drank my tea and revelled in the thought of being asked to do such a thing and secretly I knew Tom was proud of me.

The weeks soon passed and I was off to Gilwell Park. It was Good Friday morning when Dad dropped me off at the gate. I told him I would ring home on Sunday morning when I knew what time we were finishing, and what time he could collect me. He just said OK, told me to behave myself and gave me a quid (one pound). It was always easier for him to give money; I would have rather had a hug or the odd 'well done' now and then.

The next minute he was zooming off back down the road. I waved but I knew he couldn't see me, as he wouldn't be looking. I felt quite alone and as I walked through Gilwell's gates I momentarily had the feeling that no one really cared about what I did or what I achieved but, thankfully, those moments quickly passed.

I couldn't help realise I was entering the most famous of all the scout campsites. Gilwell was the very first campsite for the Scout Association. I followed the signs for the main office and reported in for duty. After a few formalities, I was shown to a large bell tent, which would be my home for the next three days and which I would be sharing with a couple of other young scouts like myself and six of the course leaders. It would be these men that we would be cooking for, of course with some supervision. I set out my sleeping bag next to one already laid out and in the usual manner placed my rucksack at its head. Then I was asked to meet the course leaders and shown the cooking equipment and the food store tent. There was no cooking to be done on the first day or evening, as it was to be a relaxed day free for fun. The evening meal was prepared for us and served by the course leaders and was done in the form of a huge buffet. Through the day, friendships were forged. There was a lot of laughter but we were soon reminded that there was much work to be done the next day.

I got back to my tent and in no time I was tucked up into my sleeping bag. The tent was full of the strong smell of grass as it filtered up from under the groundsheet and mingled with the smell of the canvas. I was safely cocooned and warm as my thoughts turned to something far more exciting. Who would be in that sleeping bag next to mine? No matter how much I regretted my actions after the event, it just didn't stop me. I found the excitement of it all, an all too powerful driving force to even allow me to think about what I was doing.

It wasn't long before the course leaders turned in and the tent door was closed as the last one entered. At first it wasn't possible to see, but someone soon turned on a small bicycle headlamp torch. With each turn of the knob on the top of the torch you could hear the spring under it being compressed as it was squeezed nearer to make the connection. You could hear a pin drop and suddenly there was a soft light in the tent. The walls of the tent were adorned with shadows of men quickly undressing and clambering into their beds. Next to me was Robert, who was about the youngest of the leaders. Everyone was settled and after a couple of whispered good nights, the torchlight was switched off. Within a few minutes I was lying there, listening to men breathing heavily, some snoring, as they slipped into slumber. Robert hadn't gone to sleep. He was fidgeting about trying to get comfortable when his arm gently reached over and he cuddled me. My delight was only noticeable by my heart rate, which had probably doubled, if not trebled. I was convinced even a deaf man could hear it banging away. I slowly reached up from under my sleeping bag and touched his arm. It was covered in soft downy hair and as I cuddled him back he did not move away from me.

The silence and darkness remained uninterrupted as heavy breathing was suppressed as much as possible. Yet another night of pleasure but only to be followed by regret. The next day I was up bright and early and as happy as Larry. Breakfast was ready and the course leaders arrived to the breakfast table en mass. We buzzed about them like little worker bees trying to please. No one looked at me strangely so I guess no one knew. Robert didn't give me a second glance, which in a way I was glad of, yet I also found quite hurtful. I hated myself for what I was doing, for what I was, but I was enjoying it and that made it even worse. The day passed well and the worker bees cleared up after breakfast, collected wood, and prepared lunch. The whole ritual was repeated and we were ready for dinner. The day was over. Everyone was showered and soon we were providing a sumptuous meal of lamb chops, mashed potatoes, and peas, which, after a day in the fresh air, was soon devoured by all. No sooner had the last plate been cleared we were up clearing away and washing up.

The evening ended and I went to bed and as I walked into the tent the first thing I noticed was that the beds had been re-arranged. Robert had moved his bed away from mine. Why had he done this? What had I done wrong? Why had the sleeping bag on the other side of mine been moved closer? I got into bed and watched as everyone came into the tent and the undressing ritual by torchlight was once again repeated. I could see Robert slip into his sleeping bag. The light went out and it was dark. Soon the sound of gentle breathing would change as the men fell asleep. I lay there looking in Robert's direction, and I too fell asleep.

The Easter course weekend ended on the Sunday, culminating in a huge campfire. There were probably two hundred or more scouts around it and it started off with the organiser giving a speech. He said how proud he was of how well things had gone. The pass rates were high and he was particularly pleased and grateful to volunteers, especially the catering boys who had looked after everyone very well. There was a big round of applause at that point led off by the course leaders. They were clapping us, the caterers, and I was one of the team. The feeling was great. Speeches were over and suddenly one of the leaders leapt from his seat and led us into singing the Quartermasters Stores with a few made-up verses about some of the course leaders and personnel which got huge screams of laughter. The evening was wonderful and I loved it. It ended with the National Anthem. What a night it had been. I said a lot of 'good nights' as I walked over to my tent to discover the beds were yet again re-arranged!

I rang home the next day to arrange to be collected on Easter Monday as planned. On the way back Dad said he had a surprise for me when I got home. The journey didn't take long and I was soon to find out that we had another puppy. Someone had taken it into Mum's shop on Saturday saying it needed a home and Mum had adopted him. He was jet black and Mum named him Rex. I was briefly asked about the weekend but no more than a passing enquiry. Even so, I got quite excited as I told them what had happened -about the campfire and how the speech included a special thank you to the catering volunteers. No one was really paying attention to me as they watched Rex playing with Lassie. He was chewing her ear on the floor in front of the fire. Rex fitted into our lives well except that he had worms. Well, that is what my Dad said when he saw him crap on the floor and then proceed to drag his arse across our living room carpet. Mum said she would get them both some Bob Martin's worming tablets, that would sort out the problem in no time. We all sat and watched Rex and Lass as they basked in the warmth of the fire and so ended Easter.

Due to the Easter weekend,. the next troop meeting was on Thursday I was there early and so was Tom. He was glowing with a beaming smile.
'Well done,' he said. 'Well done Jim.' Bloody hell I thought, what did he know and I coloured up. He then gave me a letter he had received that morning from the camp organiser and I read it. The letter, like me, was glowing, full of praise and actually said that some of the course leaders had in particular wanted to praise me for my valuable efforts and leadership in

my team. Ordinarily I would have welcomed such praise but instead I saw it as a reminder that, in a way, I had let myself down and I had also betrayed Tom.

There were many compliments that evening and quite a lot of swapping stories of events during our separate weekends. Underneath it all I was unhappy and somehow this had to stop. I could not go through life like this. I was hurting inside and I just didn't know the answer. Should I stop seeing Tom? I couldn't just stop, it would look suspicious, but I could cool things down a bit. I thought this is going to take some time, but it must be done.

At times I felt I would do anything for some peace of mind, just to be a little bit happier with myself. It seemed that every time I did something wrong, I was filled with remorse afterwards and I couldn't ask anyone why.

My withdrawal programme from Tom started that night. I told him that I had to dash home to see the new dog - in truth that was the last thing I wanted to do. I zoomed off leaving him to make his way home on his own and I felt dreadful for lying to him. My journey home gave me more time to think and the more I thought, the more I felt of no use to anyone. I felt my father didn't really love me, my mother was dominated by my father and had very little time for me and I was carrying this great big secret. I wasn't normal; something was wrong with me. Suddenly I was shocked by the thought of why the beds had been moved around at the weekend? Had the course leaders talked to each other? My God, what had they said about me? I had just co-operated, what a bloody fool I had been. I have got to stop this, but how? I went to bed and cried myself to sleep.

Chapter Twenty Eight - 38th to 43rd

It was my fourteenth birthday. I got the usual card from Mum and one from Dad, that Mum had written out, and there was money in each. They felt I was past the age of silly presents and would probably prefer to go out and buy myself something. It was good to get the money but I think I would have preferred someone to have taken the trouble to buy me something. It's so easy just to give money.

Things at the scouts carried on as usual and Tom gave me a present for my birthday. He had bought me an LP recording of the Ralph Reader Scout Gang Show. I loved it and I was so thankful that he had thought to buy me something. I felt guilty that I had sort of ignored him a bit. I blamed myself for making him pay for what I thought was my own bad behaviour.

'How are you?' he asked. 'I haven't seen much of you lately.'
'I'm OK,' I said and I asked him if I could pop round to see him. I missed his care and love like that of a dad. I was hurting inside because I felt I had hurt him.
'Would you like to come over this Sunday for lunch?' he asked.
'I'd love to,' I told him. So much for my slow withdrawal plan! Soon things were back to normal but at least I had made one decision. The matter of my sexuality had to be put on the back burner for a while until I was better able to understand it and deal with it.

I was back at H.C. when I found out that I could leave at the break-up for Easter next year, as Easter fell just before I was fifteen. That was lucky. There was much talk of 'O' levels and who would be sitting them but I said 'not me that's for sure!' I hated the thought of exams just about as much as the thought of staying on at H.C. for yet another year. My mind was made up; I was leaving. We were given notices to take home to our parents about 'O' levels and I took mine home to my mother. I told her what it was about. Before she had a chance to open the envelope, I told her that I wanted to leave. There was no way I was spending another year in that hellhole of a school. My mother looked at me and told me that I would be better off if I got 'O' levels, but if I felt that strongly about it she would talk with Dad. If he agree, she would sign the paper consenting to my leaving next Easter. That was it! No big let's sit down and talk about this, nothing. The form was signed and I took it into H.C. with a light heart and a metaphorical hole in my foot where I had unknowingly shot myself.

Tom and I resumed our friendship and soon summer camp was upon us. However, the 38th Poplar was to suffer a bit of a setback. Bow Baptist Church, for some unknown reason, gave us notice to quit the hall. Tom told me we had to find another place to hold our troop meetings. Tom found a new place in no time at all called Kingsley Hall, which was just across the road from Wallingford House, where Aunt Maria and Uncle Steve lived. It wasn't too far away from Bow Baptist so it shouldn't affect too many Scouts hetting to the troop meetings. We moved in, and again much to my surprise and for no apparent reason we were told we were changing from the 38th Poplar to the 43rd Poplar Scout Troop.

Kingsley Hall was, by comparison to Bow Baptist, ancient. It had a plaque outside on the wall informing all that Mahatma Ghandi had visited and Tom took great pains to explain to us all who Ghandi was and why he was famous. I ate like a horse and the thought of starving as he had done was not at all appealing. What a brave man he was.

I never really liked Kingsley Hall as I had done Bow Baptist, but it served us well. As it was an old building I found it a bit eerie and thought it probably had ghosts. The main hall had a parquet floor with a stage at one end. The walls were tiled in a horrible brown colour up to the bottom of the high windows. In between and above the windows was painted in cream. Despite my dislike of the building, I did my best to get on with it and I was appointed storekeeper. We were given a room in the basement, which I didn't like very much. It was accessed by a dark stairway at the back of the stage, which led down to a basement corridor. The one light bulb half way down the hall and the doors each side of this basement corridor gave it a subterranean prison look. Our storeroom was the first door on the right. Just a plain room which I, with a bit of help from Dad, I got it shelved out ready to accept all our camping equipment, tents, pots and pans and so on. I soon had it well organised which meant it didn't require much work to maintain. Eventually I got used to the hall, but I never got used to that basement.

I never asked Tom why we had to leave Bow Baptist or why we changed from the 38th to the 43rd Poplar and I wish now I had. I just hope it wasn't because of some indiscretion of his! The 43rd thrived and our numbers grew as we were much closer to lots of blocks of flats and on the right side of Bow Road for many of the wayward boys there to join our troop and see what scouting was about.

Chapter Twenty Nine - The last family holiday

I was still friendly with my mate Tim, although since he'd ducked out of the scouts I didn't see so much of him. I decided to put that right and I went round to see him at home where he lived in Prioress House. Prioress was quite an old block of flats, not quite as old fashioned as the ones Nanny Taylor once lived in but old fashioned just the same. The flats had the luxury of inside toilets and baths although the bath was in the kitchen and covered with a wooden worktop. The kitchen had an Ascot water heater, which provided the hot water for both the kitchen sink and bath.

Tim was the younger of two children, having an older sister called Polly. I never really spoke with her much, but she seemed OK. She was involved with a bloke called Brian and they were always zooming off somewhere on his motorbike. Tim's Dad was an ex-Navy officer and a softly spoken, quiet man. After leaving the Navy he had become a messenger at Barclays Bank and he seemed quite content with his job. Conversely Tim's mother, Maureen, was not quiet. She was noisy, spoke her mind and ran the house well. If we got in the way, she had no qualms in telling us to get out in her usual very loud way. Bloody hell, I used to think, she frightens the life out of me. Then I got to know her, and the family much better and she wasn't at all frightening. Just frank. She made dresses as a part time job and it amazed me how she could hold a conversation and even shout at us without swallowing one of the many pins she always seemed to have sticking out of her mouth.

When I wasn't at troop meetings or camping with the Scouts, Tim and I went everywhere together on our bikes. We even bought a tandem between us, which we spent ages doing up, at my Dad's garage. To me, Tim was sort of like the older brother I had always wished for. He was kind and a soft sort of a guy, really level-headed and never silly. He was almost two years older than me, and I guess that's what accounted for the difference in his attitude compared to the rest of my mates. He was shaving, a bit, and was going through the spotty forehead stage. It was nice being with Tim as he was so steady. We went camping together, did up our tandem and talked about everything. I ached to tell him my dark secret but how could I. How could he possibly understand what I was going through and tell me what to do about it. The subject was never broached.

My last summer holiday with my parents was in 1962. We went to Scotland and as usual it was a difficult time. I had started to want to stand up for myself a bit more where Dad was concerned but I was much too afraid of him. I started to feel more protective of my Mum as I hated the way he talked to her and treated her at times. While I was scared of him, I felt, while he was having a go at me, he was leaving Mum alone. At least I was doing something.

Scotland is such a lovely place - although a bit wild. It is a great place to find a corner for yourself where you can sit, reflect and think things out without interruption. It gave me time to weigh up my decision to leave H.C. and I still felt positive about my choice. Dad had always been an endless source of embarrassment for me, which, as I got older grew harder for me to handle. I was entering what I called my 'embarrassment' years, those years when for boys, bristles on the chin won't come through fast enough and spots erupt just as you are going out. A time when girls are supposed to become more noticeable, which in itself was a problem for me. Still, I had to maintain my secret and be normal so I would hang around on street corners with my mates and we would delight in shouting out remarks to young girls as they walked by. Things like 'Look at the knockers on that' or to be even more subtle 'Oi big tits, fancy a shag'.

The girls would ignore us, thank God, and we would fall about laughing. My Dad would have been proud of me if someone had reported me for this behaviour. I couldn't help but wonder as I sat by the River Dee where this was all leading. Perhaps I should get a girlfriend; perhaps that would sort me out. So I promised myself to do that when I could. Yet another promise to myself to be more normal.

We got back from Scotland and I went round to see Tim. His mum told me he was out with his girlfriend! Tim had gone and got himself a girlfriend. Shit, I thought as I walked home. I didn't know her, but I hated her already. She was going to take Tim away from me. He was like a brother to me and now he would naturally want to spend more time with her, but thankfully it didn't quite work out like that. I went round the next night and Tim asked me if we were going to Dad's garage to get on with our tandem. 'Blimey'. I thought 'perhaps he's not that keen on her after all'. We cycled round to the garage and he told me about her and what he had been up to while I had been away. Things didn't seem to have changed that much and from the way he described her, she sounded OK and he was quite keen on her already.

Summer closed its doors and we slipped into autumn. We'd got the tandem finished and it looked a treat. We had completely stripped the thing down and rebuilt it. We'd even taken the frame to be re-sprayed. There it stood looking like new and we decided it was time to make her maiden run. We set out for Laindon Hills in Essex, a place to cycle to, which had become a favourite of ours. We were going great guns along the Romford Road when suddenly it started to snow. Not too heavy, but heavy enough to get in Tim's eyes, which was awkward as he was in front. The snow prevented him from seeing a car parked outside the church and we went right up its arse. Tim went over the handlebars and hit his face on the back of the car. I went over my handlebars grazing my thighs. Although Tim's mouth was pouring with blood, thankfully he didn't have his brace in. The dent in the bodywork of the car, above the back window was where he got his teeth straightened out in one go, rather than have to wear that brace for umpteen weeks. The tandem was a write-off as the front wheel had buckled badly but, even worse, the frame had split.

We called home to Tim's Mum and to my Dad and told them what had happened. Dad came out in his car and the tandem was unceremoniously dumped into the boot with much of it hanging out due to its size. It looked quite sad hanging there after all those hours of work, which were now well and truly wasted.

Later in the week we took the tandem to a local repairer's who advised us that because of the bike's age we couldn't get a new front end of the frame. He also told us that due to the position of the fracture it couldn't be welded either. So we had to bite the bullet and write it off, and that was a sad day for us. Still every cloud has a silver lining, as it would give more time for Tim with the new girlfriend. In a way, a double blow for me. Kismet...

Chapter Thirty - Caird & Rayner

Things at H.C. were changing as several fourth year classes were split up. A leaving class was formed for those not taking 'O' levels and for those taking the exams a six form class was formed. I suddenly found myself in a class with a lot of disruptive boys. Some, like me, not willing to sit 'O' levels, but the majority not capable of sitting on a chair properly, let alone sit an exam. There were many antics and I felt sorry for those teachers as they struggled to keep our class under control. Once again I found myself wondering if I had made the right move. I disliked most of my new classmates, as many of them were complete morons.

We had heard, and heaven knows how, that one of our many teachers, a young man, was the son of a vicar. He was given a really hard time by some of the worst boys in the class. Just before this teacher arrived to take his class, half a dozen of the boys put on white dog collars they had made, and one of them had made a wooden effigy of his head, which was thrown up at the ceiling with such force that it made holes in the plaster. The teacher tried to bring the class under control but he couldn't and walked out close to tears. The next minute Mr Guthridge, my old English teacher, entered. He was quite a short man but ten foot tall in voice and command. There was a stony silence as the dog collars were quietly removed. The boy who had made the head was removed from his seat and caned in front of us all. As the cane whipped down onto his hand, he tried not to flinch. We all felt the pain for him and he returned to his seat rubbing each hand with the thumb of the other as if he was trying to disperse the pain as quickly as possible. Then Guthridge stood in the front of the class and told us that we had not only disrupted this class but his too. He warned us that if he were called into this class again he would cane every last one of us whether we were involved in the disruption or not. The vicar's son was replaced and we never saw him again.

Winter was marching on us at a pace and Christmas was around the corner. I was really busy in Greystone's, Mum was rushed off her feet in Perkins and Dad was on short time as the contract he was on was coming to an end. I was enjoying my time working and learning more and more about butchery. I still hadn't really given any time to what I was going to do when I left school so life just tumbled along. Violet Prater asked me if I would help shut up her greengrocers shop each night after school and I agreed. I certainly wasn't afraid of hard work and the extra money would come in handy.

We had been advised in H.C. that those of us in the leaving class were to be interviewed by the Youth Employment Officer (YEO). The interview day came, and I was dressed reasonably smart for the occasion. I had put on a clean off white shirt, which was off-white because it was a nylon drip-dry shirt that Mum had ironed turning it into a sort of yellowy colour. I had even put on a tie, one of Dad's. My trousers were too short for me, and my shoes scuffed. Mum didn't come as she was working so I saw the YEO on my own. He was smart, quite pleasant, and at first keen, however, when you have to interview the sort of kids we had in our school, enthusiasm soon falters. As usual, we were called in alphabetically and being a Wilkinson by the the time I got to see him I think he had mentally shut down for the day. After a short chat and a few quick questions he took a glance at my school report and determined my career and fate.

'So James,' he said, 'it looks like you are good with your hands by the look of your marks in metalwork.' I hated metal work but as he had paid me a compliment, I agreed with a sheepish sort of nod. He told me he felt I should do an apprenticeship to be a Fitter and Turner. I nodded again and he went on to tell me that he would try to get me a job at Caird & Rayner who were based in Limehouse. He immediately got on the telephone to arrange an interview and then gave me a slip of paper with the date and time on it along with some directions where to go. He wished me luck and as he shook my hand he briefly gave me one of his tired old smiles. Before the handshake was over the smile turned back into his officious look as he released my hand and shouted out 'Wilson?' My fate was sealed. I was going to be a fitter and turner in about six years!

It was the end of November when I went for my interview. I got off the 86 bus at Limehouse and made the short walk along Commercial Road to the big green wooden delivery gates of Caird and Raynor. The right hand gate had a small pedestrian door in it, used by their workers. Before I rang the bell, I looked up at the firm's name fixed to the filthy brick wall of the building way above my head. The huge brass coloured letters hung there on their fixings and, like the wall, looked as though they had about thirty years of motor exhaust stuck on them. The smell of newly turned brass and lathe lubricant oozed through the doors, which at first offended my nostrils. It was a dirty smell and filled me with dread as I pressed the bell push. The door opened and I was greeted by a man not that much taller than me. His friendly face had a welcoming smile, which broadened as he invited me in. He looked as though he was straight off a 1940's movie with his centre parting placed exactly in the middle of his Brylcreamed, plastered down hair. His eyes were framed in heavy spectacles; he wore a clean shirt and tie, protected by his brown cover-all coat.
'James Wilkinson?' he said
'Yes,' I little more than whispered.
'I am the foreman here, my name is Mr Richards,' he said, still smiling. I handed him the envelope that the YEO had given me.
'Come in, come in,' he said, in a tone that seemed to understand my nervousness. He put his arm around my shoulders ushering me in. He closed the door and told me that

he had one of my school chums upstairs also hoping to join the firm. I enquired who it was but the name Jackson did nothing to make me feel better. It was Carl Jackson who had wanted to be the school play duck-out. Mr Richards then led me to the waiting room where Jackson was sitting, still wearing the same leather jacket as the last time I had seen him. Mr Richards asked him how he was doing. Carl nodded and said

'OK.'

Then Mr Richards told us he'd have to leave us for a few minutes as he had a small problem in the factory that he needed to sort out.

Aside from the school play, Carl and I didn't really know one another, well other than to say 'watcha' in the playground. He was tall compared to me and much taller than Mr Richards. He may have been tall, but like me he was quiet. It wasn't long before Mr Richards returned and Carl was called in first.

I sat and glanced through a few magazines that lay on the table and in no time at all Mr Richards came back out of his office door patting Jackson on the shoulder and telling him to take a seat. Then he asked me in.

'Now then James,' he said as he closed the door behind me, 'or do people call you Jim?'

I had to think for a moment. At school I was called everything but James, ranging from Jimmy to Wilkie (short for Wilkinson) and at home always Jimmy, as Dad was Jim. If I said Jim would I be treading on Dad's toes, stealing his name? I said, 'Jim.'

'Well then Jim, your Youth Employment Officer thinks you wouldtmake a good fitter & Turner, what do you think?' I was still bathing in the glory of being called Jim (as it sounded so grown up) when I realised I had been asked a question. I didn't expect to be asked what I thought. No one had told me to expect a question but I thought for a moment and said, 'Well I like working with my hands and I don't mind hard work. I already have two part time jobs.'

'Oh really,' he said, 'and what are they?'

So I told him about Prater's and Greystones & Son.

We chatted for a while longer and he seemed satisfied with what I had said. He told me that Caird & Rayner would be offering both Jackson and me a job and that we would work for one pre-apprenticeship year until we were sixteen when, if we proved to be good enough, we would be invited to sign up for a five-year apprenticeship. The hours would be from eight am to five pm, Monday to Friday and I would be paid the princely sum of £2.18.00 per week. He asked me what I thought and I accepted immediately, as I bathed in the glory of being offered my first job. I gave no thought as to whether or not it was what I wanted to do - just that I could go home and say I had got a job.

Mr Richards then suggested that he take both Jackson and me around the factory to see how it all worked. I left his office to find Carl thumbing his way through the same magazines I had looked at. Mr Richards closed his door and said, 'Come on lads', and I was 'a lad!' We were escorted round the works, which was on two floors. On the ground floor there were the heaviest of machines whirring away on metal that had been lowered down to them by the huge overhead gantry crane. The first floor was a balcony, not actually a floor, which ran around the walls of the factory. This housed the lighter machines. We were shown around quite quickly really and in no time at all we were both being ushered out of the front door. Mr Richards said he would confirm our appointments in writing, I said goodbye to Jackson and ran back to catch my bus occupied by the thought that I would soon be a worker.

I didn't go home but went straight round to Perkins to tell

Mum. I couldn't really say whether she was pleased or not but Lil immediately suggested that we got married now that I was earning a good wage. I went scarlet and I was annoyed with myself for letting her do this to me yet again. When on earth would I ever get control over my blushing face? I had a cup of tea with Mum and then went home. Dad was in and had gone straight out into the back yard. I found him hammering away at a bit of metal he had clenched in his vice. I announced with more than some degree of pride, 'I've got a job at Caird & Rayner, I am going to be a fitter & turner. I start as soon as I leave school.'

His reply was short and to the point:

'Good, then we can charge you rent.'

Welcome to the real world, I thought.

I finished dinner and then shot round to see Tim to tell him my good news but he was out with the new bird. It's no good, I thought. I am going to have to get myself a girlfriend, but no time to think about that now.

The next night it was scouts and I quickly told Tom my news and he asked me a question. 'Is that really what you want to do?'

'I guess so. The Youth Employment Officer told me I would be good at it.'

'Oh well, if he thinks you will be good at it then it must be OK!' There was more than a hint of sarcasm in his voice but I still thought he was happy for me. At the end of the evening he said that he was pleased that I had got my first job, but he thought I could perhaps do something a little better than be a fitter & turner. I thought 'better' meant getting 'O' levels so I just said, I am not staying on at H.C. and that was the end of the conversation.

In a few days the letter arrived, addressed to Mr James Wilkinson, and it was on the table, opened and read. When I was living at No. 5 I hated having my post opened, not that I ever got much. Mum always said if it was addressed to James Wilkinson how was she to know. A point I had to accept but it was frustrating never the less.

Christmas was once again here and as usual I was lumbered with Kathy the pain and Simon. Kathy had now become a whingeing, whining little girl: Ow Mummm Simon just pulled my hair, or ow Mummm I'm hungry. She was always ow Mummming. Simon, on the other hand, was funny. He had lost his front teeth and developed a temporary speech impediment due to the gap. He looked rather like an angelic vampire. On top of this he would often get his words muddled up which at times caused great hilarity. Once we were in the car when he told my Dad that he'd left his imbercators on as he smiled through his huge gap wondering what it was we were all in fits of laughter over. This was a year that would sport not one but two great occasions for me, one being my last family summer holiday and the other my last Christmas babysitting, I mean I was now at work, almost.

Nothing really exciting happened that Christmas, oh, except that I had popped round to see Jack and his parents asked me if I would like to go on holiday with them next summer. They were going to a holiday camp in Brixham, Devon. I said I would love to go. I would ask my Mum and Dad but I didn't see a problem. Jack's Dad said that I would also have to ask at work if I could have that week off. I wasn't yet fifteen, I was still at school, and already I was having to consider work. Oh well.

Christmas was the usual round of TV, followed by a disappointing Christmas day lunch with Dad as usual refusing to eat because he had had too much to drink. It was followed by the same old anticlimax of presents and a week later New Year's Eve. For a complete change (I don't think so!) I spent this with Kathy and Simon in bed, leaving just myself and the TV to welcome in 1963. I went to bed wishing myself a Happy New Year. It was just weeks now until I left H.C. After the Christmas holidays, which I hadn't thought about as being my last school holidays ever, I was back at school.

I had written to Mr Richards at Caird & Rayner asking him if I could have time off to go on holiday to Brixham with my friend and his family. He must have smiled when he got the letter due to the way I had expressed my request, which was so school-boyish. He kindly replied telling me that there was no problem with the time period and that he would request that I be paid for the holiday, even though I wouldn't have been with the company long enough to qualify. His reply had been opened. I hadn't said anything about this holiday to Mum and Dad as I felt if Mr Richards said no there was little point in asking at home. Did I ever get that wrong. Mum must have told Dad about the letter and when I walked in the front door I was greeted with
'You should have asked us before fucking asking Mr Richards.' My reply, while correct, got me in even deeper trouble.
'If my letter hadn't been opened I could have asked you properly,' I said, 'It seems as though I have no privacy in this house.' My Dad leapt up at me and frightened me as he grabbed me and in his usual way, spat his words in my face, 'If you don't like it, you can fuck off and find your own place, but while you live under this fucking roof you do as you're fucking well told.' I felt the colour drain from my face as the old lion once again roared..

He hadn't lost the knack of scaring the life out of me, and I had long learned that saying sorry, and playing the grovelling downcast reprimanded pup was by far the best thing to do. He let me go and I just went to my room. I hated him when he was like this but I needed the love of a father so much that I always forgave him for his temper and sometimes violence. I got myself ready to go out and as I walked through the lounge I said I was really sorry and I asked if it would be all right to go on holiday with Jack?

Dad just said, 'Do what you fucking well like.'

He and Mum had obviously had words and that was about the best I was going to get.

H.C. had settled down to regular dreary dull lessons and it seemed as though the teachers couldn't wait to be rid of us. All the attention was focused on those sitting exams and we were made to feel like outcasts. There was only one thing that made me feel better. There was to be a church service on our last day and I was asked to read a lesson. I was given the lesson to study and as I read it I discovered I had a huge problem, with the word 'asked'. I was brought up in Bow, and although my accent was nowhere near as strong as my Dad's I was still an East End boy. For years I had been saying 'arst' instead of asked. How could I stand up in church and read 'And so Jesus arst Simon?'

So I spent weeks rehearsing 'asked', but no matter how I tried, to me it sounded terrible. I would record my reading on my reel to reel and the replay would bring that old blush of mine on in full swing.

My fifteenth birthday arrived and much to my surprise my Dad gave me his gold Rotary watch. He said he always intended to give it to me when I grew up and that he saw my leaving school as being grown up enough. His moments of generosity always left me speechless. I could never understand how at times he could be so nice one minute, and then in a flash, so nasty. I had been given the usual cards by Mum with some money in them, but without doubt I was so thrilled with my Dad's gift. It really made that birthday quite special.

246

The church was full, my parents were at work, as usual, and my turn came to get up and read. As I read I could see the word 'asked' rapidly getting closer as my finger slipped down the page through the passage. 'Asked', came to pass peacefully and nobody seemed to notice. I walked out of that church into the spring sunshine and I had finished with H.C. I felt kind of strange really and thought it must be the same for those men released from prison, except I did not have a black bin liner in my hand! I simply could not believe that I had finished with that dreadful school, yet there were no screams of joy, in fact quite the reverse. The walk home was quiet and in a way sad as I reflected on the last four years. The school play with no Mum and Dad out there to see me, Mr Tetley's slipper and of course, the most memorable of all, being kneed in the balls by one pupil and bullied by another, Tilson! No matter how horrible H.C. had been at times, I knew that the future journey from boyhood to manhood was not going to be a bed of roses either. Still, that was tomorrow, and now it was good bloody riddance to today, and H.C!

I got home and threw my bag on the bed and the flat was empty and silent and as I never liked the feeling of being alone I went round to the shop to see Mum. I walked through the door to Perkins and Lil said, 'Ello worker, Mum's in the back.'

'Hi Lil,' I said, as I shrugged my shoulders and went through to the back of the shop where Mum was ticketing up a pile of clothes.
'Well,' she said, 'how did it go?' I told her that there was no laughing at my 'arst', and somehow that broke the moment and we all laughed. Mum made some tea and said, 'well, at least you have a few days before you start work.' Although she felt I was wrong to have been so eager to finish my four year sentence at H.C, I was also daft to be so keen to commence the next sentence, only this time fifty years! Fifty

years' hard labour, more commonly called work. I think she would have preferred that I stay at school but she knew how unhappy I was and there was little point in forcing the issue. That night after dinner I went round to see Tim and we caught up on all our news. In fact we talked a lot that night and he told me that he was working hard for his exams and that he had really fallen for this girl of his, Christine. He never really displayed much emotion so I felt quite privileged to be told how he felt.

'You gonna marry her?' I asked. He simply said he didn't know, but maybe, one day. The subject was left there. We chatted a while longer and I knew he had more swotting to do so I left him in peace. Tim saw me out and I said good-bye to his dad who was quietly reading his paper and his mum who was working away at finishing a dress. She shouted at me 'good luck at the job,' through a row of pins clenched between her lips.

At the Thursday scouts meeting that week, I told Tom how things had gone at school and about reading the lesson at church. The troop meeting went well and excitement was noticeably growing among the boys over the coming Easter Camp. The evening came to a close and as we poured out of the hall, the Patrol Leaders were appointed for the impossible duty of trying to keep us as quiet as possible. Kingsley Hall was in a residential area and one of the conditions of being allowed to use it was keeping the noise down to a minimum when we left. Not an easy task. Tom locked the doors and I walked with him for a while, taking a short cut through the back streets to Campbell Road. Sadly since we had moved, walking part way home with Tom was out of my way. Yet we still walked together and that gave me the opportunity to chat to him about anything and everything. He was a great listener and I told him how I felt about leaving school and he gave me a different way to think about things. He told me that I shouldn't worry too much as I had to re-adjust. He told me that as I had been at H.C. for four years, like it or not, I had adjusted to it. It would now take a little time to accept that I no longer had to put up with it. How right he was and I felt so much better for the advice. I told him that Jack's parents had asked me to go on holiday with them and how Dad had reacted. Tom never once told me that my dad was wrong, he just listened to me telling him how unhappy I was. That was just as well really as no doubt in a moment of fear or anger I would have said to Dad, 'Tom thinks you're an arsehole' and that would have caused real problems. Tom then asked me if I would like to go over to his place on Saturday after work and we could go to see a movie. I said I thought that would be great and I would ask Mum and Dad but I felt sure it would be OK. I said good night and hopped on my bike for the short ride home to No. 5. Thoughts about right and wrong flashed through my head - but only momentarily. This was not a time for that. I wasn't going to let right or wrong get in the way. Once I started thinking like that I would get depressed and just now I felt OK

I got in and wheeled my bike through to the garden and made some tea. Dad was glued to the box and Mum was sitting at the table doing some paperwork for Perkins'. The programme Dad was watching finished and I posed the question: 'Any objection if I go over to Tom's Saturday, we are going to the pictures'. Tom had long been thought of as a 'nice man', so staying over was no problem, but there was another problem brewing.

'Tell 'im Ede,' Dad said as he slurped his tea. I looked at Mum and wondered what was coming.

'Well,' she said, 'it's about housekeeping, now that you are going to be working.' I breathed a sigh of relief and said that I hadn't really thought about it. She told me that they had discussed it and that thirty bob a week should cover things. I exclaimed, 'Thirty bob! I'm only earning fifty-eight bob a week! That'll only leave me twenty-eight to spend.

'Plus what you get at Greystones and Praters,' Mum said. I nodded, thought about it for a few seconds, and agreed. I knew the idea of housekeeping would have been Mum's. Dad may have been hard on me at times but he was never mean. He would have spoken out in my defence but my Mum would have insisted arguing that how else would I value money. Of course, she was absolutely right. It was agreed that as Caird and Rayner kept a week in hand I could pay from the end of the second week.

I sat down and again I posed the question about seeing Tom on Saturday but without the fears any more of them seeing my staying over as a bit odd. They had long come to accept Tom and thought of him as nothing less than a very 'nice man'. Mum reminded me not to be home late on Sunday as I had work the next day. Work! It sounded so nice. I would be a little more independent and that thought filled my heart with warmth and excitement. Unknowingly, I was already starting to lose that sadness at leaving H.C. The hollow was quickly being filled with other things, like work on Monday morning. What would it be like?

Saturday at the shop had been good - I had loads of deliveries and the tips were welcome. I had been long trusted just to get on with my workload, which had grown a lot from when I first started there. The day flew by and I was told as usual to help myself to some pieces for the dogs and to take a shoulder of lamb home for the weekend as he gave me my wages. I was never greedy when it came to taking things like that although I had learned how to compress the bits for the dogs to make what I had taken not look too much. Of course bits for the animals were just scraps that couldn't really be used for anything else, given that it was Saturday. Nevertheless I respected their trust in me.

'G'night all.' I shouted as I left the shop, and rushed over the road to Perkins'. I went in and there was Lil, sitting there at the desk, head locked into conversation with Mum. Obviously there was some juicy gossip going on and when I tried to find out what it was, I was told it was women's talk. I had long learned to accept that answer without question. I just lowered my voice and said, 'OK woman, here's your weekend meat ration, see you tomorrow.'

I gave her the shoulder of lamb and bits for the dogs and went to leave the shop. I almost got to the front door when Mum shouted out, 'Don't be late home, you've got work on Monday.'

'OK,' I said, and I left, bathing in what I hoped was an element of pride in her voice. I left the shop ten foot tall.

My time at Tom's was great, as always. He did much to prepare me for what to expect at work on Monday. He told me about cards, and what they were. I had so often heard Dad say that someone at work had been given their cards, but I never thought to ask what he meant. I was probably too frightened at the thought of being told to mind my own Fucking business, and that he wasn't talking to me. In our house there was a definite barrier between children and adults that was not to be crossed. The rule was, children should be seen and not heard.

Cards were National Insurance Cards, which were stamped by the employer to prove that contributions had been made, thereby entitling the holder to treatment on the National Health Service - and now I would actually have my own cards. He also told me about things like holiday entitlement and how most companies calculated it. He told me so much and it was without doubt a great help. There surely is nothing worse for the employer than to have a new, fifteen-year-old employee, asking on his first day about holiday entitlement. Thanks to Tom, I had no need to ask. Still, no matter what Tom told me, he could not fully prepare or protect me against what to expect on my first day at C&R. I got home not too late from Tom's and Mum said she had made me some lunch for the following day. It was in the fridge. My jeans were clean and there was a clean shirt in the wardrobe. I was ready for work tomorrow.

Chapter Thirty One - First day work nerves.

I was up at six-thirty on Monday morning, dressed and breakfasted and yelled 'Bye' to Mum and Dad as I rushed out on the stroke of seven o'clock to run and catch the bus to Limehouse. Only a few minutes passed before I saw it trundling towards me - a welcome sight, as I didn't want to be late on my first day. The journey wasn't that long but I managed to get the bus that was ahead of its scheduled time. That meant that the driver drove at a pace that I could have matched jogging. Still, we arrived at Limehouse with plenty of time to spare. I ran to those great big green gates and my watch said seven-forty am.

Just along from Caird and Rayner was a small café full of workers having breakfast on their way to work. I had plenty of time so I went in and bought myself a mug of tea. There I sat, with my baby face, drinking tea among a load of workmen. I must have looked as though I had just finished my paper round. My stomach was all over the place with first day nerves. I downed the tea quickly, and walked back again. The pedestrian door was unlocked, and I pushed it open to find Mr Richards talking with one of the men.
'Oh, hello, Jim,' he called out to me. He finished his conversation and then walked toward me putting out his hand and I shook it.
'Now then,' he said, 'I'll just show you where to clock in, Carl is already in!' He would be, I thought, probably grovelling upstairs, getting in with the men. Carl was lucky as he was taller and broader than me. His stature would give him credibility. I on the other hand was much shorter and looked about twelve years old and I was filling more and more with dread. We walked over to the big brown clock on the wall. I knew about clocking in because Dad had always done so on the building sites. Mr Richards told me that I had to put my card in the slot at the bottom of the clock, pull

down the big brass handle, which would stamp the time on my card. The rack to the right of the clock was for cards 'out' and to the left for cards 'in'.

'Are you OK with that,' I was asked. I just nodded. If you are late by five minutes you are docked a quarter of an hour and no matter what, do not clock anyone else in or out. That is a sackable offence. I looked down the cards, and there I was at the bottom, tail end Charlie once again, Wilkinson! I pulled out the card and stamped it at 7.55 am and then put it into the 'in' rack on the left. 'Now come in and let me introduce you to the man who will be showing you the ropes,' Mr Richards beamed.

We went upstairs to the gallery, which housed the lighter lathes and a small brazing forge around which the men were sitting along with the already well-in Carl Jackson.

'Hello, this is Jim Wilkinson.'

There were several men huddled around the opening of the forge and one of them was showing Carl how he could toast his sandwich, if he wanted. They had made a long-handled sandwich holder out of wire, which held the sandwich as it was popped into the hot furnace. It was toasted in no time at all. I also noticed that next to the forge were two metal drums, one full of oil and the other of water. These were the coolants used to temper the metal being worked on in the forge.

I was introduced to the man with whom I would be working, sitting there in his filthy overalls, oily boots and flat cap rolling a fag.

"Ello son,' he said, and I nodded. I didn't like being called 'son' but I was too scared to say anything. Of course they called Carl, Carl, but then they bloody well would. The klaxon sounded eight and the men went to work.

'My name's George,' my instructor told me as he walked toward a lathe and I followed behind like a lamb going to the slaughter.

'You will be working here on this lathe and on these nipples,' he said as he pointed to a box of large brass nipples on the floor. He picked one up and as he did he looked me up and down.

'Son you're gonna need a box to stand on. There's one over by the forge,' he said as he pointed. I obeyed and in seconds was standing next to him small box in hand.

'Now then, I'll show you how to set this up and turn a thread onto it,' and he quickly put the nipple into the chuck of the lathe. The blanks were cast, so they were not exactly straight. George started the lathe up and the nipple wobbled all over the place. He then tapped the nipple with a lead hammer a couple of times and there it was, spinning in the chuck without so much as a quiver let alone a full-blown wobble. There were years and years of experience in his lead hammer tapping. Once it was spinning true, the thread could be turned into the metal. He wound two knobs on the lathe simultaneously. One bringing the cutting tool in and the other bringing it across the nipple until it was in line ready to cut the thread. He then engaged the clutch and the lathe went automatic. It cut in the thread, but it had to be stopped at the right point otherwise the cutting tool would continue across and cut into the flange at the back of the nipple. That would ruin the nipple and probably the cutting tool as well. Such responsibility! George took out his newly threaded nipple and put a blank into the chuck for me to have a go on. He also gave me the soft lead hammer and told me not to try to thread the nipple unless it was square in the chuck and that was it, instruction over and he left. I stood on the box looking at this nipple revolving and wobbling all over the place. I hit it but George deliberately hadn't tightened the chuck properly and the nipple flew out of the chuck and over the back of the machine. Joke number one. I stood there hammer in hand and very red-faced. I managed to retrieve the nipple and by lunchtime I had threaded a whole two nipples, much to the hilarity of all. Of course things could only improve and the afternoon was much better. I managed three, so things were looking up! I washed my hands just as the five o'clock klaxon sounded. My last act for the day was clocking out just before I stepped out through the green door. The air outside was full of traffic fumes but to me it was better than the smell in the factory. I had actually got through my first day even though my chest ached from the fear I had felt. I ran to the bus stop, shouting out, 'See yer tomorrow George.'

On the bus journey home I found myself sitting among all the other workers, talking about their day. There was I, a worker, and I allowed myself a brief smile.

When I got home, Dad was in the garden mucking about with some scaffold tubes making a frame for a new trailer.

'Well?' I said.

'Well what?'

'Ain't yer gonna ask me 'ow I got on?'

'Oh yeah,' he said showing as little interest as he could, looking down one of the tubes to see if it was straight.

'Owd yer get on then?'

'It was OK,' I replied and I then told him what I had done, but I didn't tell him that I was crap-scared.

'I think I'll just pop round to see Mum,' I said and left him with his tubes and his under-whelming lack of interest. I ran around the corner and it was very quiet. Both of the butchers were closed (half-day Monday) along with the baker's. Mum was in the grocer's buying a few bits and chatting about something or another when I walked in.

'Ah here's my baby,' she announced, and I immediately lit up like a beacon.

'How was work then?' she asked and proceeded to tell them in the grocer's that I had started work as an apprentice fitter and turner. We left the shop and when my face had just about returned to its normal colour,. I said that I wished she wouldn't call me 'her baby' in front of everyone. Normal boy's' embarrassment I guess. We walked home and Mum got on with tea.

The next day I was up early, made my own sandwich and was clocked-in and sitting by the forge, this time ahead of Carl. The men arrived and chatted away to each other, pretty much ignoring me. Then one of them suggested I could toast my sandwich and have it with my tea. I so wanted to fit in that it didn't matter that I was going to eat my lunch early. I didn't see them wink to each other. The sandwich was placed into the homemade toast rack and inserted into the half-open forge doors. I could feel the heat on my face suddenly stop as two of the men slammed the doors shut and wound up the gas, full pelt. It took about a minute to incinerate my food. They didn't laugh at the burnt food but at the fact that I had been idiot enough to do it. The embarrassment was more than I could bear. I bet they wouldn't have done that to Carl. The day passed without any other incident and I sloped off at lunchtime to the café and bought myself sausage, mash and onions as a consolation for being such an idiot. I got home at the end of the day and said nothing. The rot had started, but I was keeping it to myself.

The coming weeks at C&R were dreadful. I hated it as they never left me alone. I had been sent on the usual joke errands including being sent for a 'long weight'. Even that to me seemed plausible. We used weights on the lathes to pull heavy metal through the chucks, so why not a long one. I was too trusting of my so-called workmates. I had been brought up to respect my elders and betters and never to be cheeky. Here I was having spent all my short life learning to respect them and they were gaily taking the piss out of me for it. On my eleventh week they (my fellow workmen) announced that I had to now undergo the 'initiation ceremony'. Of all people, Carl was to inform me that this meant having my trousers forcibly removed and thrown over the balcony to the floor below. The only way to get to them was to run past the office window where all the girls worked. If that wasn't bad enough, he then told me that the girls would try to grab me and remove what was left. My heart sank and the fear in me was more than I could cope with. I got through to Thursday, clocked out and never went back. I told my Mum and she told me that I should write in and explain why I had left otherwise the bosses might just think that I had just walked out because I didn't like the company. I followed her advice and got a very polite letter back with my salary cheque. There was no apology, no invitation for me to return or statement saying they would look into this. My first proper job had proved to be a disaster. I hated Caird and Rayner and I was glad to see the back of it, but what next?

I went to see Tim and I told him what I had done. He said they sounded like a bunch of prats and he thought my decision was a good one. I felt so much better when Tim said this. He wasn't an experienced adult, he was just a boy like me, but he was like my older brother. We did laugh at the thought of my sandwich in the forge though, and then the chapter was closed.

Chapter - Thirty-Two   The lluf emit Rechtub (The full time butcher)

On Monday morning I took myself off to the railway arches just off Campbell Road because someone had told me that one of the car repairers there was looking for a trainee paint sprayer and panelbeater. I went along knowing absolutely zilch on what to expect. I got as far as the front door, but the pungent smell of the spray paint immediately got the better of me so I made a quick 'u' turn and went back home. I got in and Mum was in having a sandwich for lunch and she asked me where I had been. When I told here she made no comment as she could see that I was trying, albeit badly, to sort myself out. She told me that she had been speaking to Mr Greystone about my experience at Caird & Rayner and that he had asked to see me.

'If you run, you might just catch him before he closes,' she said, 'it's half day today, remember?'
I got to the shop just as it was shutting.
'Hello Jimmy,' old man Greystone said. 'Mum was telling me what had happened at your job, I am sorry it didn't work out for you. You know we're looking for a young lad to join us to train as a Blockman. You've already got lots of experience and I would be delighted if you would work for us. We would pay you four pounds a week and of course you will still get your meat allowance.'
Four pounds!!! I accepted immediately.
'Good,' he said as he locked the door. 'We'll see you at eight am tomorrow then, don't be late!' he winked at me and left.
Thanks to Mum, I was back in work although I had lost the status of Jim and gone back to being Jimmy. To be honest I don't think I was ready to be a Jim. There was plenty of time for that.

I went round to see Tim that night to tell him my good news, but he was out with Christine. His Mum invited me in but I politely declined and asked her to tell Tim that I'd been round and that I would call in to see him the next day, on my way home from scouts.

Tuesday was the first day in my new full time job. It was so easy as I knew where everything was and the shop was like home to me. Everyone was friendly and lots of the customers knew me. I was soon cutting up top-bits and hindquarters of beef, and halving pigs and sheep. I still had all the cleaning to do but the best for me was the odd occasions when I was allowed to serve the customers. I just loved customer contact, especially as East End women were such great fun. I was happy.

Scouts that night was better than it had been during the weeks I was working for Caird & Rayner when I was so miserable. I had told Tom about my problems but he wasn't a wizard and couldn't make things right for me. I had to be my own wizard and resolve my own troubles. Thankfully I'd done so and once again I was happy. We closed Kingsley Hall after which, I zipped round to see Tim. His mum was expecting me and had tea and homemade cake on the go. Tim and I swapped news and we laughed about the thought of me being a paint sprayer, especially considering the dreadful job I had made at paintingbits of our tandem. Work, and Tim's girlfriendwere really pushing us apart and there were not too many more camping trips ahead for us as we drifted in opposite directions.

On Sunday I went round to see Jack and his folks who reminded me that it wasn't too many more weeks before we went away.
'Shit,' I said. With all the performance of leaving Caird and Rayner I had forgotten to ask Mr Greystone if I could have the time off. I reassured them that it would be OK and we

settled into showing me how to play Cribbage. We would while away so many nights in the future, pegging away fifteen for two and one for his glorious knob. Jack's dad would smack his lips together when he would lay down a good hand and there was always tea and biscuits at nine pm. Terribly old-fashioned for a young boy, but I enjoyed their company and Jack and I always got on famously.

The very next day I asked if I could have a week off in the summer as I had been invited away on holiday with Jack's Mum and Dad.
'You only started yesterday,' Colin Greystone said. I told him I was sorry but I forgot to mention it to Mr Greystone senior last week and that I had paid my deposit weeks ago and that I hoped it would be all right. The dates were noted and a reluctant OK was said, and I was left to get on with my work.

I was seeing less of Tom outside of scouts now because of other things happening in my life; however, when I did see him it was great. We would talk about everything I had been up to and I was happier. I was less troubled by my dad as over the years I had grown more adept at avoiding the trouble and keeping out of his way. At least now I was old enough to spend a lot of time either out or privately in my bedroom. Now and then he would accuse me of 'treating the place like a fucking hotel', as he would put it. He could be so aggressive at times and I never understood why, so I was still very mindful of living with a time bomb. I had come home from work one night and he was in a foul mood. We were sitting at the table eating dinner and Mum was trying to make light of things and she was talking about Perkins'. Then for no apparent reason he just went apeshit. He threw his dinner across the room and he said he was fucking sick to the back teeth of hearing about fucking Perkins' and there was an enormous row. The language was foul and Dad just seemed to accuse her and me of anything and everything. At this point I tried to slip into my room to let them get on with it, but Dad grabbed me and threw me into the chair and told me to finish my fucking dinner, pushing my face into my plate. At this point Mum told him to leave me alone and then suddenly, as if by magic, the row became my fault. I sat there too frightened to move, panic stricken. My Mum grabbed her bag and told him, as she stood at our open front door, that she was sick of him, his temper and the way he treated us. The front door slammed and she left. I just sat there with my mouth wide open, my face covered in mashed potato. My Dad hit me in the back of the head and said, 'I thought I told you to eat your fucking dinner!'

I dare not say a word. There was a tea towel on the table that I used to wipe my face and I tried to force some food down my throat. It was like trying to swallow lead as my now terrified stomach refused to accept food. Mum didn't come home for three days. She slept on the floor in Perkins' and came home when Dad had gone to work to wash and change her clothes.

For the first two nights Dad was arrogant and kept saying 'She can fuck off' and then he hit the Scotch, and the more he drank the more violent he became and I was the only one in the house he could vent his anger on, now that Mum wasn't there. I missed scouts and all I could do was go to work. The third morning, he had calmed down a bit and asked me where she was. As I worked across the road from her he reckoned I must know where she was staying. I had long been told about telling tales out of school or squealing as we called it in H.C. However, I was also terrified of him so I said, 'I think she is staying at the shop.'
With that remark, he went round and did his usual begging and pleading for forgiveness. He was so unable to express himself properly that his pleas were always pathetic really. Anyway, she came home and all returned to normal - that's if

you could ever call what went on in our house 'normal'.

Not before time, my summer holiday come around. Jack and I caught the coach from Victoria Coach Station to Brixham, in Devon. It took eight hours and was an overnight journey and we were both very excited about it. Jack's Mum and Dad had travelled that Saturday morning, but Jack had agreed to travel with me, as I had to work. We were nuts with excitement, and on the way the coach driver stopped at a pub for us to have a drink. Jack and I went to the toilet and there on the wall was a condom machine. There was much hilarity at the prospect of buying a packet of three, 'Johnnies' as we called them, but the thought of his parents finding these things was enough to bring us down to earth. We arrived in Brixham at eight am tired, hungry and without the Johnnies. There was the expected welcome for Jack and me from his parents and there I was at my first seaside holiday. We decided to hit the beach but, being so tired, we immediately fell asleep and slowly cooked for a few hours in the sun. Eventually, we woke up and thanks to some pretty fierce sunburn could hardly move a muscle. After three days of cream upon cream we were able to walk again without looking like a couple of robots. What a riot that holiday was too, with Donkey Derbys and the never ending Tannoy system announcing prizes to the first man in reception wearing a nappy or his wife's clothes, and so on and so on. I had never seen such a thing and to me it was hilarious. The nights were even more fun. Every night there was entertainment followed by dancing to a live band. At the right time, children were adeptly tricked into leaving the ballroom by the entertainment officer. He would get them all to blow hard to put out the ballroom lights and as they did they were switched off in batches. Then he would ask them to go outside with him to blow out a nearby lighthouse! They went outside, the lighthouse was blown out, well intermittently, and then they were scooped up into the arms of waiting mums who were soon to return knowing that their children were safe under the watchful eyes of the patrolling nannies. Meanwhile Jack and I studied the birds! I got up the courage to ask one girl to dance with me, and she tried to teach me a quickstep. I was clueless but I was much better with the March of the Mods! After all, the only dancing I had seen was on the TV in Come Dancing or at the odd family wedding. The holiday to me was a fantastic change compared to camping and the fear of Dad losing his temper. I am certain Jack's dad didn't have a temper. He was always calm and his mum was also very quiet. This helped me make up my mind that I never wanted to go on holiday with my parents again.

I got back from holiday two weeks later on the Sunday afternoon and things at home were no different. Dad was round his garage doing something to the car. The dogs went nuts as I walked through the door. Mum was watching TV, which she switched off to the announcement that she was pleased to see me. That came as a bit of a surprise as Mum was never one for showing much affection or emotion, unless it was over an old weepy on the TV. She asked me how I had enjoyed myself and I said it was fantastic. I told her about everything (except for the Johnnies) and she was pleased that things had worked out well for me. I asked her how things had been while I was away. She said OK really and on that note told me I had better unpack. She told me that she had saved me some lunch if I wanted her to re-heat it but I told her that I wasn't really hungry after the trip. In truth, Jack's mum had made us a lunch for the coach trip and I didn't want to offend her. I unpacked and dumped my dirty washing in the old tea chest at the end of the bath, which stood as our laundry basket and then I crashed out.

I was asleep when Dad came home so I didn't have to face him straight away. I woke up in the evening and made tea for everyone.

'Watcha Dad,' I said.

'Have a good time?' he asked. I said I did but I didn't labour on how wonderful it all was just in case he tried to turn my obvious pleasure into an argument. I wanted to tell him how easy going Jack's dad was, but didn't dare. Other than telling him I had enjoyed myself he wasn't really interested. He was glued to the TV screen so likewise I just watched some TV and then went back to bed, with my usual statement, 'Work tomorrow, g' night then,'

With Mondays being half-day at the shop, I had the afternoon to myself. I popped into Perkins' to see Mum. I walked through the door to the usual 'Ello darlin' from Lil, 'ave you missed me?' she asked.

'Like a toothache,' I said, as I ducked the coat hanger she threw at me. Mum asked me if I would do her a big favour. I said suspiciously that I would try, if I could. She said she'd asked Dad if he would mind if she went hop picking for two weeks in September. He said he didn't mind and then she asked me if I would look after the flat, the dogs and Dad. I tried to hide my reluctance as I thought Dad, God help me. I could never say no to Mum - she deserved all the time to herself that she could get.

'Of course,' I said, 'no problem,' as my heart sank into my boots. I spent the next three months worrying about Mum going away.

I saw Tim that night, just catching him before he went to see Christine. He was pleased to see me and we spent ages talking about what Jack and I had been up to. We had a good time, sharing my holiday experiences and then he asked me to go downstairs with him to see what he had bought. There it stood, gleaming on its stand: a motorbike.

'What do you think?' he asked and I said it looked fantastic, but did it go? He quickly gave me a demonstration round the block and I said, 'I can't wait until I am sixteen when I can have one.'

He said 'see you soon,' and whizzed off and I jumped onto my not-anymore-so-interesting bicycle, and went home. I watched some TV and then bed. Work tomorrow and scouts tomorrow night.

I arrived at Kingsley Hall and everyone seemed pleased to see me. My Second had done a good job in my absence and Tom and I had a short chat with the promise to catch up properly as soon as we could. The night was over and Tom and I walked part way home together. I told him about the Johnnies, the fun of the camp and our efforts at trying to pick up girls. He listened well and asked lots of questions. He said nothing about the girls and said that I should go on one of these holidays again. He told me I was different and that he'd never seen me so happy. I guess outwardly I was, but inwardly I was still wrestling with my sexuality. I was still confused over wanting to spend time with him and yet always afterwards thinking it was wrong. I wanted to stop all this and get a girlfriend but for a reason I didn't understand, I needed Tom and when I was with him, I was content. At those times I felt my life had no problems in it, well except for the one looming up in September when I would have to look after Dad. We parted company and I went home.

Chapter Thirty Three - My first love

The next day my life was to change forever, or so I thought. I had worked the morning and when it was lunchtime I went across to Perkins to see Mum before going to the local café for lunch. Just before she closed for lunch, a woman walked in with her daughter to drop in some dry cleaning. Her daughter was a really nice looking girl and somehow I got involved in the conversation as I was standing at the counter next to Mum in my oversized butcher's coat. Mum introduced me, and Deborah, being not at all shy, introduced herself but said she preferred being called Debbie. It was all so unusually laid back and somehow I managed to ask her if she fancied going out with me one night. She agreed; she actually agreed! Debbie wrote down her telephone number and gave it to me and as they walked out of the shop I stood there, chin on the floor. I took no notice of Lil as she said, 'I guess that's me dumped then is it?'

A couple of days later I telephoned Debbie and arranged to go round to see her. Her mum and dad were very nice and raised no objections to us spending time together listening to records in her bedroom. Debbie to me was wonderful and I was completely taken with her. Her favourite record at the time was The House of the Rising Sun, and even though for a single it was quite a long record, she played it over and over again. I loved the record and I loved her.

Debbie and I had seen each other occasionally for a couple of weeks when her mum kindly invited me round one Saturday for lunch. They lived in Poplar, not very far from dear old Hay Currie. I cycled round on the butcher's bike, still wearing my white coat. I passed H.C. and looked at it for the first time without hating the place, as it no longer posed a threat. I arrived at Debbie's out of breath and very excited at the prospect of seeing her again, although if I am to be honest, most of the time she didn't seem to care that much about me. We sat at the table and her mum had cooked me a fry-up, which had everything on it, eggs, bacon, sausages, tomatoes, and mushrooms, the lot. I was ravenous and it looked great as it was placed in front of me. However, her mother had put the plate not fully on the table, sort of half on, half off. I politely said thank you and then, watching the beautiful Debbie, plunged my fork into one of the fat sausages in preparation to cut into it. With that, the plate did a somersault off the table, flipped between my legs and landed face down on the floor. I felt I could have died of terminal embarrassment. Her mother immediately said it wasn't a problem, but I must have looked such an idiot. The food was delicately scooped off the lino floor, which was clean enough to eat your dinner off anyway and put onto a clean plate. No amount of suggestions to cook me another meal would work. I insisted that the food was good and that I would eat it. It was and I did. It was about forty-five minutes later by the time the redness had just about gone from my face.

My time with Debbie wasn't often enough and one night she told me that she and her family were spending the coming Saturday night with her Aunt who lived on the Isle of Dogs and she asked me if I would I like to join them.
'I'd love to,' I told her. I couldn't believe it. Debbie had asked me to spend the night with her, well, more or less. I cycled home from her place that night as though my bike had wings on it, ah, love's young dream. Saturday just wouldn't come round quickly enough. I told Mum about the invitation and Dad made some disgusting remark about me getting my leg over, which was typical of him. I finished work, had a bath and threw a few things in a bag. I then cycled to Debbie's Aunt's place following her directions which, like her, were perfect. I knocked at the door and was invited in by her mum who then, with approving tones, introduced me to her Aunt.

'This is Jimmy, Debbie's new boyfriend.' How sweet that sounded!

They were all very nice, but Debbie in truth was years ahead of me. I was fifteen going on twelve and she was fifteen going on twenty. The evening passed by quickly enough and it was time for bed. I was sleeping on the couch downstairs and Debbie was upstairs in a bedroom by herself. I had not long made my bed and snuggled down on the couch when she came down for a glass of water, and everyone must have known what she was up to. She crept into the lounge and asked me to go up to her room a couple of minutes after she had gone back up. I didn't dare question her. What was I supposed to say, what kind of a boy do you think I am! I lay on the couch and my heart raced away waiting for those few minutes to tick by. I got up, in my pyjamas ,and crept upstairs. Debbie opened her door and I went in and she quietly closed it behind me. We were safe in the room and no one knew we were there, or so I thought. We lay on the bed together side by side looking at the ceiling. My left arm was around her neck and she took my hand and placed it onto her left breast. I could not believe what was happening to me. I turned to kiss her and then there was a knock at the door.
'Debbie, are you awake? Is Jimmy in there?'
I lay there frozen in silence, terrified. It was her mother.
'Jimmy, I think you had better go back to bed.' her mother said and continued, 'I think you had better get back downstairs right away.'
I could have leapt out of the window and run away into the night. If I had I would not have seen Debbie again. I kissed Debbie and said I had better go and quietly went back downstairs.

The next morning everyone got up and it was as though nothing had happened, and in truth, nothing had. I was plied with a good breakfast and there was a lot of chitchat. I felt terribly uncomfortable and I couldn't wait to get out of the place. With each mouthful of food I was dying inside, as I thought any minute now someone is going to say, 'And what were you up to last night then?'

The weekend passed and after that I saw a lot less of Debbie. Her choice, not mine. Blinded by desire, I just didn't see that she was tiring of me. In fact I don't think she was ever really interested in me at all. I think I was just a stopgap. Debbie really needed someone older than me, and much more mature.

It was summer and Debbie and her family were due to go away on holiday to a beach chalet they had rented on the Isle of Sheppey. Debbie invited me to come down to the chalet on the Saturday night to see her and, of course, stop over. She said she would miss me terribly while she was away and the night before she went we kissed goodbye - a goodbye kiss filled with such passion that I was sunk and lost to her forever. How could I possibly say no? The Saturday came and I was packed ready to go. I caught the train and it was an awkward journey and I thought I would never get there. She met me at the station and I was really happy to see her, but sadly, it wasn't the same for her. The magic of the night before she left had long gone. It had been replaced by another magic and I can't remember what his name was. She didn't warn me about him and as we walked into the little lounge of the wooden hut there he was, hand outstretched to say hello to me. As Debbie introduced me to him, I shook his hand clueless to what was happening. Later that evening Debbie and I went for a walk in the moonlight on the beach and I was put squarely into the picture and I hated her for what she had done to me. Why drag me all that way to suffer such terrible bloody indignity. She certainly wasn't worth fighting over and besides, he was a big guy, older than me, taller than me, better looking than me and much more what she wanted.

That night Debbie went to bed after kissing what's-his-face goodnight on the porch - for some time I might add. I just sat in the lounge on the sofa like a prize prat. She waltzed in, said she was really sorry, kissed me on the forehead and said goodnight. I said sweet sod all. I never slept a wink that night and I was up and gone long before anyone woke in the morning. How could I have been such a bloody fool? I got back home and told Mum. I didn't dare tell Dad, as I didn't want him laughing at me. I felt so ashamed that I had been such a stupid idiot. Mum did her best to console me but even when she said it is better you find out about it now than later, it didn't help me much. I was devastated. If this was what girls were about, then you could keep them.

Chapter Thirty Four - Burnt Bacon

I was fifteen-and-a-half when Mum went away hop picking for her two-week break without Dad. The thought of what was ahead filled me with dread but I had to get on with it. At least the weekends would be mine, as he would go to see Mum Friday night and come back on Sunday. My job was to look after him and the dogs during the week.

The first week wasn't too bad as for some reason he was on his best behaviour. Perhaps Mum had spoken with him. Even one night when he was in a bad mood he was OK. That was the sort of night when Mum might have put dinner in front of him and he would probably have said, 'I don't fucking want that' and pushed it away.
I sensed that this could happen to me, so I told him, 'Before you say anything, that's all there is and I am not cooking anything else.'
He was so taken aback, he just laughed at me. I had got away with being cheeky, which made me wonder why Mum hadn't said that to him. However, it was not to last. All hell was to break loose on the Thursday afternoon of the second week. It was half-day closing for me at the shop and I had brought home a piece of salted belly of pork to boil for his tea. I had just put it on when one of my friends knocked at the front door. I opened it and I got head-locked into conversation with him. I told him about my holiday and Tim's bike and so many things when he suddenly saw smoke pouring over my head.
'Shit! The bacon!' I went into the kitchen and there it was, lying there at the bottom of our big aluminium saucepan sizzling. It was black, the saucepan was black and it wasn't long before Dad was due home. I quickly threw some water into the saucepan and shot out to one or two of the local shops that didn't close on a Thursday afternoons, but no bacon. But I did manage to buy some sausages instead, still frozen. Sausages in hand I rushed home again. I opened the

front door I could hear Dad in the kitchen. The panic hit me like a sledgehammer, and the fear was back. I hadn't felt like this for ages. I knew I was for it. The atmosphere had been building up between us and it was just a thing like this that would cause a major problem.

'What the fuck's this?' he said, pointing at the saucepan in the sink. I told him what had happened and that I was really sorry. Sadly no amount of sorrys was going to get me out of this mess; sorry just wasn't enough. I said I had been out and tried to buy another bit of belly of bacon for him but that the shops were closed but I had managed to get some sausages, holding them up to show him. He snatched the frozen packet from my hand and threw them so hard against the back door that they cracked a pane of the safety glass.

'That's it,' he said, and I knew I was for it. He came at me and shoved me so hard against the kitchen door I thought that had broken as well. He then told me I was fucking useless, slapped me in the face, walked into the lounge, and sat down to watch TV. I didn't know what to do. I put the sausages under cold running water to defrost them and then cooked them.

I gingerly walked into the lounge with a plate of well-cooked sausages, mashed potato and fried onions and he ate it in silence. I was too upset to eat so when he'd finished I washed up and went out on my bike. I went to Samuel's and got myself some chips. I was fifteen years old and I didn't think I should be landed with all this. I wasn't married to him so why should I be treated like shit. I hated him at times like that and once again it was time for that tired old question, 'Why me?'

Mum came home and she looked great. Although it was only hop picking, she'd had a wonderful time. I was so pleased to see her. I was pleased to hand over the responsibility of Dad. Love Mum as I did, I hated doing her job, looking after her impossible husband, my terrifying father.

During the next few weeks, things at work were not great. Old man Greystone wasn't in the shop anywhere near as much and compared to him, his son, who was slowly taking over, was a pig. He was rude and sometimes talked to me as though I was something nasty stuck to the sole of his shoe. I already had one man in my life doing that, there wasn't room for another one. I finished work one night and, crossing over the road as I usually did, I noticed a sign in the window of A G Hedges Butchers: Butcher's Boy required - Apply Within. I looked back over the road to Greystones to see if there was anyone watching me and as far as I could see there wasn't, so I slipped inside.

That part of Devon's Road wasn't exactly huge and of course the Manager, Ben Smith, knew me. I quietly spoke with the cashier, Carol Smith, no relation to Ben, and she got him to speak with me. We instantly clicked and immediately Ben offered me a job. Starting salary £4.10.00 a week plus allowances and I accepted on the spot. I ran home and as soon as I got in I told Mum. At first she was a bit disappointed as she felt that old man Greystone had been good to me, but she told me that if I felt it was better, then that's what really counted. I went into work the next day and told Colin Greystone that I wanted to leave. I then made the mistake of innocently but honestly telling him that I had got a job across the road at Hedges. He went to the till, gave me my wages and told me to get out. I took off my white coat and left. I was completely shocked by this action and at first I just couldn't believe it. I went across the road to Perkins and told Mum what had happened and she said I shouldn't worry about it, as Colin was just a prat. As long as I had Mum on my side I somehow felt I was right. I knew that if I was wrong, she would tell me. I had a cup of tea with her and soon calmed down again. It seemed I was always being manhandled - either physically or verbally - by someone bigger and older and tougher than me. I hated the way things were.

On the way home I called into Hedges and told Ben what had happened and he said it makes no difference - you still start here on Monday morning. He told me to take the few days off that I had been paid for and enjoy them. I did just that and I started at Hedges the following Monday. Compared to Colin, Ben was fantastic. Naturally for the first couple of weeks I felt really awkward when I walked passed Greystone & Son's shop window.

A. G. Hedges was in one of the older shops in Devon's Road sitting between Prater's and Monty's, the hairdressers. It had a small shop window and an open entranceway with a roller shutter that was only ever closed when the shop shut. This meant that working in the shop in winter was freezing cold, but that didn't worry me a bit. Between Hedges and Monty's was a side alleyway, which led to our shop's side door, which served as our entrance. The shop had an 'L' shaped counter at the back of which was the walk-in chiller. The upstairs was old and neglected and had at some stage been living accommodation. Accessed by an old wooden staircase, the walls of the upstairs could have no doubt told a tale or two, if that were possible. The back of the shop was quite run down and was where we stacked all our packs of white wrapping paper. The floor was concrete and slopped down to an open drain. Next to the drain was a water tap under which was an old wooden barrel. At least twice a week this was tipped over to wash the back down. That was unless the barrel was being used as a brine tub for a few days. Then it was full of old hands of pork or joints of silverside of beef, or brisket. Ben would make up the brine solution and with our old brass brine pump the joints would be regularly injected with the solution, ensuring that the meat was salted throughout. The injecting was one of my jobs. I used to get the pump and attach a big long brine needle that had several holes down one side of it. The pump was huge and heavy and when full was not exactly easy for me to handle. I used to have difficulty with it as I tried to get it to suck up the brine before I would stab one of the joints to inject it. Slowly they would absorb the solution and when Ben told me they were ready, the joints would be put into the window for sale. It was all a bit basic, but salt meat was popular in the East End especially silverside or brisket, which were served with mashed potatoes and pease pudding.

Contrary to any of today's laws on hygiene, the shop had a couple of cats, which were always having kittens. It seemed that when one cat wasn't pregnant the other one was. We were always looking for homes for kittens and they always went. None of this putting them in a sack and drowning them lark, which I knew a lot of people did. There were many problems with these cats, the least of which was that they liked to sleep at night on the wrapping paper left on the counter. As well as that, and much worse, they had another favourite hobby - crapping in the sawdust store. These were the days when butchers used to have real sawdust strewn on the floors. That was done when the butcher's shop was scrubbed clean. A clean butcher's shop with fresh sawdust on the floor looks and smells great. However, the problem for us was keeping the sawdust fresh. Our sawdust was stored in a cupboard under the stairs that led to the flat above. If the rough old wooden gate was left open at any time, even for the briefest of moments, the cats would be in there scratching their hole to either piss or crap. I would clean and scrub the place and when it came to scooping up a bowl of sawdust I would often get hold of a cat's turds. If ever there were times that I hated bloody cats, it was then.

I enjoyed working with Ben and Carol - even though they took the mick out of me they were still great fun. Ben was an excellent teacher and I learned a lot working side by side with him. He even taught me butchers' back slang, which was quite useful. Ben knew his customers well and if an old lady came in that didn't have too much money he might say in back slang, 'Serve the old lady in the shop and if she wants it, give her the old leg of lamb in the window at half the price,' which, in back slang was, 'Everse the dlo nammow ni the posh. Less her the dlo gel of bmal at flach the ecrip', and I'd nod and do what he said.

We had a lot of fun with back slang. In fact we had a lot of fun in that shop, full stop.

We were soon on the run up to Christmas and it was a really busy time. Probably due to the lack of freezers, not many people bought frozen turkeys in those days so we sold hundreds of fresh ones. A big help to us, which also secured a lot of our business, was the fact that Ben ran a Christmas club. I cleaned hundreds of turkeys that Christmas and for me the hardest part was drawing the feet of the bird. We had a post in the back of the shop on which was screwed an iron foot drawing implement which was V-shaped. The bird's leg would be cracked, the foot placed in the V and then the bird twisted a few times, which hopefully would start to draw the sinews out. It was then a matter of weight. Mine not the turkey's. On the really big birds, I would swing on the damn thing until the sinews finally gave way, releasing the foot complete with sinews out of the leg. The foot would be left in the V and I would often end up on my arse on the floor, with the bird in my lap.

Chapter Thirty Five - Hello Lynn

It was just a couple of weeks before Christmas when a girl walked into the shop to buy some meat. I hadn't really paid her any attention, but Ben had noticed her interest in me. She came in a couple of times that week and although Ben had told me about her, I was really too shy to do anything about it, especially in front of them. I also think I was still smarting a bit over Debbie. Eventually Ben took it upon himself to play cupid. The next time she came in, he and Carol disappeared leaving me to serve. As I did, Ben shouted from the back of the shop, 'Go on then, ask her if she wants to go out.'

I looked at the door behind which they were hiding with a face that was as red as the meat in the window. What else could I do but follow my instructions. I asked and she said OK.

Lynn was a bit younger than me, and although you might not think it possible, definitely more immature than me. I felt quite sorry for her when she told me that she had been raised in a Dr Barnado's children's home. I knew what it was like to have a difficult childhood so immediately we had something in common, but was that enough? When she was old enough to leave the home she had gone to live with her grandfather and uncle in a block of flats not far from our shop. We went out a couple of times before Christmas, but I felt uncomfortable with her really. She wasn't my cup of tea so I told her that I was too busy on the run up to Christmas to go out much. I told her I worked late most evenings at the shop gutting poultry so going out wasn't possible. Sadly she didn't take the hint and simply waited until the Christmas rush was over.

It was Christmas Eve, the work was done and the shop scrubbed clean. We were having a cup of tea and laughing as

Ben paid us our share from the staff Christmas tips box. To me, my share was a lot! Then he gave me my wages telling me that Mr Hedges had said that he was very pleased with me. Furthermore, at Christmas, it was customary for those that worked at Hedges at Christmas to be paid double wages in reward for their efforts. That included me and I was over the moon. I had worked really hard, and well appreciated the bonus and the compliment although I was a bit overwhelmed by it all. We exchanged Christmas presents and I left wishing them both a very Happy Christmas.

Mum was in the kitchen preparing our own turkey for cooking. I told her my news about the tips, wages and about what Hedges had said about me and she seemed happy for me. I promptly hid my money in my bedroom and announced that I was saving up to buy a motorbike. At first Mum wasn't too keen on the idea but it was one of those occasions when Dad was on my side. He had always loved motorbikes and this was not a time to be running them down. He told Mum that he was sure that I would be OK and passing my test would prove it, and so the gauntlet was thrown down. I could have a bike but I had to pass my test as soon as possible. As a learner on 'L' plates I was not allowed to carry a pillion passenger and they knew that the temptation as a learner to put a mate on the back might be too great. I had to pass my test. I had been given the go ahead and I felt the test would be a doddle.

I had run a bath to try to remove the smell of meat and turkey guts but the latter actually gets into your system. So much so that when you fart the smell is like the inside of a turkey. I lay there soaking and thinking about my new bike. I had seen a Honda 125, Benley Sports in Eddy Grinstead's near Limehouse and really wanted it. Somehow, I would get it. The bath was warm and my hands, having endured the terrible cold of winter and frozen meat, felt like they were defrosting. My dream of the bike was interrupted when I heard a knock at the front door. It was Lynn! I could hear Mum tell her I was in the bath as she invited her in and that was the last thing I wanted. Next came the knock on the bathroom door with Mum telling me Lynn was here. I told her to tell Lynn to get herself off home and that I would be round to see her later. Mum did just that and after a few minutes she left.

I got myself ready and I went round to see Lynn at her flat. They had made some effort to decorate the place for Christmas, but it hadn't worked. The place had no atmosphere and the decorations had failed miserably in doing their job of brightening the place up. I thought our home wasn't too Christmassy but compared to Lynn's place ours was like Santa's Grotto. I couldn't help but feel sorry for her as she hadn't had the easiest of lives and now she was living in this flat with her old granddad and her really strange uncle. I had never seen the likes of his behaviour but I now believe it was due to what is now known as Obsessive Cleaning Disorder (OCD). If Lynn and I were sitting in the kitchen he would come in and wash his hands, for about half an hour! He would just stare at the water as it ran over his hands as he rubbed them together. On one occasion when I was round there, I had been a bit nosey and looked into his bedroom. He was out and as I passed his door I noticed that it was slightly open. I opened it slowly and peered in and immediately noticed that he had sprinkled powder up the walls. I asked Lynn what it was and she told me it was ant powder. Apparently he had a thing about ants, so I didn't ask any more questions. Anyway, both her uncle and grandad were out and Lynn had definite plans for me, plans that involved some passion. I was invited upstairs so that she could give me my Christmas present! I had been caught once before in a bedroom with a girl and there was no way I wanted her grandfather, or even worse her weird uncle, catching me. She assured me that they were in the pub with the folks from work and that it would be ages before they came home. Any other healthy young boy of almost sixteen would have jumped at this opportunity but I was hesitating. I felt like the proverbial lamb being led to the slaughter. We went into the bedroom and things got amateurishly exciting. There was no actual sex, but I found that she could definitely arouse my interest and thank God for that I thought. Having been brought up in Bow London E3, by a really 'gawd blimey' heterosexual father, how could I possibly announce that I fancied men? Who on earth would understand? By now I had heard a bit about poofs and even worse about the queer bashing that was going on. People made jokes about woofters, poofs, poofters, queers, Nancy boys, shirt lifters...the list of names was endless. I didn't fancy the idea of having to announce that I was one of them. I felt if I did I wouldn't be one for very long, as my Dad would surely lay me out. I would be thrown out of the home. Home as it was, was still where I had to live.

So, thank God for Lynn as she made me think that I might not have a sexual problem after all. Perhaps I had been worrying for nothing. It may not have been the most successful of sexual opportunities, but at least I'd been excited by her, and perhaps that was something to build on. I thought that I had to stop thinking about men and, as much as I enjoyed Tom's company, I had to stop all that nonsense and get on with life. Grow up, get married, and have kids. That's what people do in the East End, not keep looking at men - and certainly not do what I'd been doing. So, once again wrestling with myself, I was ashamed of what I had done and frightened of what I might become. I left Lynn's in a real state of physical excitement and couldn't wait to get home and jerk off. So I found myself a nice romantic brick wall to get behind for a Christmas wank. Yeah, this was being normal and I could tell anyone what I had done and it would be acceptable. In a way

I was excited at the fact that at last I could talk about what I had done, there was no need for secrets. I didn't have to be ashamed.

Christmas passed quietly and this time with no Uncle Billy, Aunt Eve and the Kids. For some reason, it was time for a change. They had gone to Nanny Taylor's and without having to babysit I was able to get out. The problem was where to go? I was too young to get into a pub for a drink. Although I was almost sixteen, looking almost twelve was no help. I did go round to the Widow's Son pub with Mum and Dad Christmas morning though and try as I might I just couldn't find a drink that I liked. The 'in' drink among the young was Vodka and Lime, which I tried but found bloody awful. Still, it was trendy, and of course normal, to drink it so I drank the stuff. Anything to be normal!

1964 entered and this time I enjoyed it with the family in a pub. Although I couldn't legally drink, being among my big East End family in an East End pub, who gave a toss? Not the publican, that's for sure. We were spending far too much money for him to care that much and so, for the first time, it was a different but very happy new year.

Thankfully Lynn was not to last and I never again got behind her bedroom door again. In short she drove me nuts, as she was all over me and worse still, wherever I went, she followed. I even found her outside Kingsley Hall one night waiting for me to come out. We would walk home together and if I had my hand in my pockets she would slide her hand into my pocket to hold my hand and that really annoyed me. I didn't need a girl in my pocket or for that matter my life that much, even if I was a supposely hot-blooded almost sixteen-year-old. Lynn had to go, but she was so persistent, how? The answer was my motorbike! I told her that I was saving so hard to get one, that I wouldn't be able to go out with her any more. Lynn then offered to help me buy it! I said no, and besides when I got the bike, I would want to be out on it all the time and on 'L' plates I couldn't carry a passenger and it might be weeks, months or even years before I passed my test. Finally she got the message, and I got my life back.

It was great to be able to enjoy scouts again without her lingering about outside waiting for me. I had missed my part walks home with Tom and even if I was going to be making the effort to be 'normal' like everyone else, I could surely talk to Tom, there wasn't any harm in that. I never went round his place and I tried to keep my eye open for a girl. I think my biggest problem in the girl department was the fact that I looked so young. What girl would want to go out with a boy that looked twelve? I had some growing up to do.

Chapter Thirty Six - BGO 933B

The day arrived and I woke up to being sixteen at last, but it was the first birthday I'd had on which I had to get up to go to work. I got up to find my usual two birthday cards on the table and in each was money. Enough to top up my savings and make a good deposit to buy my Honda motorbike. I screamed out with great joy, a huge thanks and I could imagine my Dad lying there with a big grin on his face.

I couldn't wait for my next half-day off to go and put down my deposit. Mum and Dad had to come with me because Dad had to sign the Hire Purchase papers as guarantor. I was under the age of twenty-one (the age of consent) and Mum had to fill in the forms in the pretence that Dad had left his glasses at home - his tried and trusted excuse for not being able to read or write. With deposit paid and papers signed, I was told it would take a week for everything to be cleared by the finance company. A whole week!

That week seemed to pass agonisingly slowly and it felt like an age before I went back to Grinstead's to collect my new bike. I could barely contain my excitement when I got off the bus at Limehouse. I ran across the road only to have to wait yet again in the shop while they ensured that all was ready. Finally I was led to the back of the premises and into the workshop and there she stood. , Leaning on her stand and gleaming with highly polished blue paintwork and sparkling chrome. Boldly standing on the front mudguard was the registration plate BGO 933B. I oozed with pride as they attached some 'L' plates for me and I was given a run through on what did what. I impatiently listened to instructions on how to carry out a minor service and to a few do's and don'ts. The bike was innovative with both kick and electric start actions. I wheeled her out into the courtyard, sat astride, turned the key and pressed the start button. The engine spun into life , whirring almost silently. This bike was a dream and I carefully rode her home via the back streets to avoid the traffic and to get used to how she handled. This was the most expensive thing I had ever owned and I just loved it.

I got home and parked under our lounge window, chaining it to a convenient downpipe. Dad was home first and I couldn't wait to give him a ride around the block. He thought it was OK but he preferred the throaty roar of his old Arial Huntmaster. Then it was his turn to drive her and how could I say no, even though I wanted to. Surprisingly he drove her well and slowly and carefully went through the gears until she was purring away. We got home and he never asked to drive her again. I actually think he respected the fact that she was mine. Mum came home and was not really interested at all. Later that night I went round to Tim's and he gave her a quick once over before he went round to see his girlfriend. He too, thought she was exceedingly quiet, she was supposed to be, she was modern.

Life for me was much better and I quickly booked my driving test, as promised, and hoped that due to the waiting list it wouldn't come through too soon. The letter arrived with an appointment for August. It was now the beginning of April and I had four months to get my act together. I had to learn to drive by the book and even more commit the 'Highway Code' to memory, so I knuckled down to the job.

At first I continued going to scouts on my pushbike for fear of someone stealing my beloved new Honda from outside the hall. I could take the pushbike inside, but not the Honda. My efforts to try to avoid male contact or temptation had obviously become noticeable by Tom who asked me to walk part way home with him. I had even tried to stop doing that. I just didn't know how to handle my own situation and with me it was either famine or feast. We walked our usual route through the back streets, cutting through the little alleyway at the end of which we would normally part company.

Tom said he wanted to ask me something and immediately I was embarrassed, as I felt guilty over the fact that I had really been ignoring him.

'How would you like to come with me to Holland for the day?' he said.

'Holland!' I said loudly, 'for the day, you're kidding!'

'No I am not,' he said, 'there is a special day trip return package to the tulip fields and Kuykenhof Park and I wondered if you would like to come along. We will fly from Southend Airport to Rotterdam where we'll be met by a coach to take us on the tour. The day includes lunch and we would be back home in time for dinner.'

Holland! I thought and I was excited at the prospect of flying. I had never flown before and my excitement knocked out all my efforts to try to put some distance between us. I leapt at the chance, but as always it was subject to Mum and Dad saying yes, but I never thought for a moment that they would say no.

'You'll need a passport,' he said as he went on to tell me that I would be better having a one-year passport, which is issued by the Post Office as opposed to a ten-year which would take a lot longer to get.

'Yes please, I'd love to go,' I said and the distance between us once again just melted away.

As soon as I got home, I asked Mum and Dad if I could go - and there wasn't a problem where Tom was concerned. The next day I went to the Post Office for a passport application form, which had to be completed by a parent, as I was a minor. The passport photo had to be of an exact size and was done by a local photographer with a special camera, smiles not allowed. It was in duplicate and I had to go to a professional person who knew me to verify that the photos were actually of me. I went to our doctor who charged me two shillings and sixpence for the pleasure. The form, photos and fee were submitted to the Post Office and the passport issued on the spot.

Chapter Thirty Seven - My first great loss

A couple of weeks later Tom and I were on the train for Rochford, the location of Southend Airport. We boarded a small twin-engine turbo prop, bound for Rotterdam. There were the usual announcements and safety drill and we were soon revving up at the end of the runway. As the engines revved the props tore at the air in front trying to move us as they fought against the aircraft's brakes. Suddenly the brakes were released and the battle to lift tons of steel and us into the air commenced. Of course the plane won the battle and as I looked out of the window I could see the ground falling away below us and I clung onto the armrests. We climbed and white cloud sped passed the window I was looking through. In a few minutes we had hauled ourselves through the bank of cloud into blue sky above. The cloud below looked like it could be walked on and that was comforting and I slowly released my death grip on the armrests of the seat. I had seen this so many times in all those war movies but now I was actually up here.

It didn't take long to get to Rotterdam where thankfully the weather and the landing were good. We were soon through passport control to be met by our tour operator who showed us to our waiting coach. The lady tour guide on board was good and told us all sorts of things as we went along. She even managed a little joke with her funny accent, telling us that she was with her husband one day when an Englishman asked their age. The husband said he was Dirty and his wife was Dirty too. We all laughed politely.

Keukenhof was a wonderful park with a lake full of flamingos and flower displays that were breathtaking. I had never seen flamingos before and I was amazed at how pink they were. In fact, I had never seen anything like the offerings of this park before. This was my first taste of overseas and I was hungry to see more. I had caught the travel bug.

We had a light lunch and on our way back to Rotterdam we stopped at a roadside stall selling huge garlands made from the heads of tulips. The driver told us the heads are cut off to develop the bulbs so I bought a garland for Mum. I wore it around my neck all the way home and I was nearly ill due to the rich smell, which was almost unbearable.

Tom left me at Mile End underground station, no doubt with my voice ringing in his ears telling him that I had a fantastic day. I was on cloud nine as I continued on to Bow Road underground and the walk home. I got in and was greeted with the usual lack of interest by Dad, who didn't like flowers at the best of times. It wasn't the flowers that I wanted him to be interested in but the story behind them. I knew I was wasting my time so I didn't press the matter. Ignorance is bliss, so they say. Mum on the other hand was fascinated by what I had to say although as far as the garland was concerned, she would have preferred the stems as well. The excitement of my first flight and trip to a foreign country certainly camouflaged the fact that I had failed yet again to get myself away from Tom. I had not consciously taken advantage of his generosity nor had I thought I could put distancing myself from him on hold until after the trip. I liked Tom very much and the physical side of things was just a small part of our relationship.

A couple of weeks later when I was working away on the butcher's block I looked round to see Tim standing there in our open doorway. He had the engine block off his motorbike in his arms. We had not long had a motorbike repair shop open along by us and he had taken the cylinder head in for a re-bore.
'Hy yer,' he said and I looked up to see him nod his head over

toward Greystones saying,

'How's life since you crossed over?'

'Crossed over! I'm a butcher, not a bleedin spy!' We laughed and he said as he walked away that he was going home to put his head back on. He was almost at the corner when I shouted after him,

'Get it on the right way round this time, the ugly bits point to the front,' and I could hear him laugh again.

'Yeah, ok,' and as he marched off he shouted back, 'Come round soon.'

I walked back into the shop and carried on with my work.

It was later that week towards the end of our troop meeting when I over heard two of the boys talking.

'Did you hear about Tim Rushton?' one said.

'No.'

'He's dead!' said the other.

I couldn't believe my ears. I mean it couldn't be Tim. Not the Tim Rushton I knew, it must be someone else. As soon as the meeting was over I shot out of Kingsley Hall. Thankfully I had taken the Honda and was home in a minute. I burst through our front door, as I would never normally do. Dad was sitting in his chair quite quiet and Mum looked at me and could see by my face that I knew something.

'Come in Jimmy,' she said.

'We've had a visitor this evening. It was Tim's sister Polly with her boyfriend.' and at that point any hopes in my heart were crushed by the heavy realisation of truth. It was my Tim, and I was stunned into silence as Mum told me that he had died in the bath the day before. I just couldn't believe it. How? Why? Mum said, in her way to try to soften the blow, that Tim had apparently died of hardening of the arteries and advanced sugar diabetes. I shook my head and my eyes stung as they brimmed with tears. I didn't want to cry. I didn't want my Dad to laugh at me.

'Mum, he was in the doorway of the shop this week with his engine block in his arms! How could he have a bad heart, he was strong Mum. He is only seventeen.' I stood there shocked into silence and I could hear my own heart beating in my ears. The room was cloudy as I strained to look through my tear-filled eyes. This was the first time I'd experienced death and the dreadful feeling of loss it brings. I was stunned but I didn't cry. Although I was shocked by what I had been told, the reality of what had happened hadn't really sunk in. I wanted to do something, but I didn't know what. Mum suggested that I buy a sheath of flowers and go round and see Tim's mum.

The next day at work I struggled to tell Ben what had happened and what Mum had suggested. Ben was so understanding and told me which florist to go to, and to tell them he had sent me. They made me a magnificent arrangement of flowers ready for collection when I finished work. We closed at five-thirty and Ben just rubbed my head and said

'Go on, I'll finish up here.' His kindness caused a lump in my throat, which felt as big as an apple and it was almost impossible to speak. With head down I walked to the florists and then home.

Dad and Mum were both in but I didn't really say much to them. I just quietly had a bath and put on my best clothes. Although the thought of Tim dying was beginning to sink in, I was still, in a way, dreading going round to his mum as I knew that as soon as I did, there would be no doubt. I would no longer be able to hang on to the remote possibility that this was all a big mistake. I walked to Tim's place so as not to damage the flowers and as I stood outside his front door it took me a couple of minutes to pluck up the courage to knock. I felt almost as though I had been frozen in time. My hand reached for the knocker and its light rap soon brought

Tim's mum to the door. I stood there in silence, clutching the flowers, unable to speak. His mum took the flowers from me, passed them to Pat and without a word she put her arms around me.

'Come in Jim dear,' she said, and I just stood and sobbed in her arms. She gave me the time I needed and then gently led me into the lounge where Tim's poor dad was sitting in silence. The atmosphere in the room was heavy with grief and I was a part of something I didn't want to be a part of, and it hurt! Tim's mum made some tea and brought out one of her home-baked cakes. Like a pillar of strength she led the conversation about her son, my friend. We all talked about him, the many things we had done and I couldn't believe he wasn't with us anymore. I expected him to walk out of the bedroom any second. I wanted to hear him say goodbye. During the conversation his mum said that Tim was lying in the Chapel of Rest at the Co-Op Funeral Parlour in Crisp Street and how good they had been to her. I asked if it would be possible for me to go there and see him.

'Of course dear,' she said. So on my next half day off, I went along, on my own. The man at the undertaker's was very nice as he said in his soft understanding tone,
'I understand you have come to see Tim Rushton.' Mum must have telephoned him and told him to expect me. I barely whispered yes, as he put his hands on my shoulders.
'It's OK,' he said, 'would you like me to come in with you?' I told him I was OK and that I would like to see Tim on my own. We walked to the back of the funeral parlour, down a wood-panelled corridor to the door, which had a cross on it. He gently opened it and there in front of me was a highly polished coffin on a trolley. I went in and he quietly closed the door behind me. There was peace in the room mingled with the smell of flowers. I walked over and there he was, sleeping. Sleeping as I had seen him do, so many times when we had gone camping together. He looked beautiful and so at

rest and to look at him, it was still hard to believe that he was actually dead, but wish as I did, he didn't move. Then with final acceptance, my eyes filled with stinging tears, I said my goodbyes. Someone, my Aunt Maria I think, had told me to touch him, and I did. His forehead was cold and felt smooth like marble. I told him I would never forget him and then I kissed him on the forehead and said goodbye.

The day of the funeral passed and life went on. I knew Tim and life going on was, as he would have wanted.

Chapter Thirty Eight - The failure

I once again renewed my vow to try and be more normal. I needed to get myself a steady girlfriend and give the summer camp this year a miss to avoid any temptation. Unfortunately, I didn't really go out much to socialise and I was too young for pubs and clubs, so there were not too many places I could really get to meet girls, well except through work. Still, I was only sixteen so there was no rush.

When the time for summer camp came round I just couldn't resist it. There was so much I loved about the scouts and I didn't see why I should give it up just because of what I saw as a bit of a weakness in me. I asked Ben if I could have the time off, he agreed and off I went. The gear went in the van driven by Dad and I went down on the bike. It was to be my last time at Pett Level.

It was a good summer camp and I enjoyed it. Tom was never pushy and talked to me as though nothing at all was wrong. He never asked me why he hadn't seen me or why our walks after the troop meetings had ended. Although to be fair, since I had decided to go to troop meetings on the new bike, I could hardly push it along beside him as we chatted and I couldn't carry him because I was still on 'L' plates.

Summer camp was good and I was enjoying passing on to the younger boys the many things I had learned. Tom and I had time together to chat and I told him what I had been up to. He wasn't at all surprised and nor did he try to discourage me. He promised always to be there for me whenever I needed him even if it was only for a chat and he told me there was no need to stay away. There was never any pressure from Tom and he was a great listener. It's just that he never really gave me the answers.

We got back from camp and I had to get on with work and more importantly ready myself for the rapidly approaching driving test, which was to be at the Ilford driving test centre. The day came and the instructor introduced himself to me and he must have wondered if my feet could reach the floor when I was on the bike, as I looked so young. My baby face was the cause of being stopped on many occasions by the police, when I would have to produce my driving licence. In a way this problem made me take heed of the law, as I knew that as sure as eggs were eggs if I were to break it, I would be caught within minutes.

The examiner quickly told me what to do and I could feel him watching me as I nervously set off for the round-the-block trips. He watched me drive down one street and then he would run along the road to watch me turn the corner and come up the other side of the block.

As I approached the end of each road with great caution, I would make sure that my look each way was obvious, before setting off again. He was out there somewhere, watching my every move. After the practical part of the test came the traditional questions on the Highway Code.

'When can you overtake on the left?' was one of the questions but I had studied the book so much I was convinced there wasn't a question he could ask me that I didn't have the answer to. I eagerly answered his questions and the test was over. He made all sorts of notes on his clipboard and then with a pleasant smile on his face told me that I had failed! I was devastated, as I thought I had done really well. He told me where I had gone wrong and of course like any sixteen-year-old, I didn't agree with him although I didn't say as much. My years of being browbeaten by Dad had taught me not to question adults. I dealt with the frustration of this blow by thinking the examiner was nothing more than a doddering old bloody idiot who should have been retired years ago.

Thanks to him, I now had to go home and tell Mum and Dad the news.

The drive back home wasn't easy as my eyes kept straying down and staring at the 'L' plate still fixed to the front of the bike. It shouldn't be there; it bloody well shouldn't be there! What would Mum and Dad say now? I was not looking forward to seeing them. I stared ahead and I could hear my Dad telling me exactly what I had done wrong, just as though he was sitting on the back of the bike with me. He would go on and on and I would have to sit there and listen to him.

I got back to the flat and waited for them to come home. I knew they wouldn't take the bike from me but I wasn't ready for a lecture either. I was still upset at failing so I really didn't need my failure being rubbed in. Dad got home first as usual. He had seen the 'L' plates on the bike and his first words were, 'Failed then, what did you do wrong?'
I told him what the examiner had told me and then Dad completely took me by surprise, as he was nice. He told me he thought that I drove the bike really well and that we all make mistakes. I was shocked as I was expecting a verbal barrage. Mum came home from her day at Perkins' and she was equally sympathetic. It was almost as though they had discussed beforehand how they would react if I failed, but they were never that prepared for anything. Dad always shot from the hip and all too often I was the one in the firing line.

I had taken biking so seriously and as I was told at the beginning, I had not carried anyone who didn't hold a full licence. Mum said that I should put in for another test straight away but this time at a different test centre. I did exactly that and requested East Ham. The reply came back quite soon and the slip of paper gave me a date in November, which was surprisingly quick. Life had to get back to normal, as normal as my life ever was and I had to get over the disappointment of failing my test. I think what really made it worse was the fact that my Dad had passed his tests for the motorbike and for the car first time. The best distraction I had for getting over any troubles was work, as I loved my job. There was always fun to be had with Ben or Carol and our wonderful East End customers.

One of those unforgettable fun days happened once because one of the Hedges shops, that had been selling groceries as well as meat, had closed down the grocery section. The stock of cleaning materials from the shop was distributed among the Hedges chain and we, amongst other stuff, received a case of Ten-Day washing-up liquid. One night after we had finished work and the shop was clean, I was putting the finishing touch to the shop floor with the usual shit-littered sawdust when Ben called me upstairs. I put the bowl down on the block and went up to find him. He had taken the light bulb out and it felt like I was walking up the stairs in the Psycho movie. He and Carol were lying in wait for me with a bottle of Ten-Day in each hand. I got to the landing at the top and then they began the Ten-Day fight at the Hedges Corral! I couldn't believe what they were doing to me and ran down to get my own ammunition. We battled it out and in the end everyone was saturated in washing-up liquid, of course me more than either Carol or Ben. It was just a crazy time and with much laughter we left the shop. It was tipping down with rain outside and our laughter grew uncontrollable as we started to bubble up. Ben rubbed my hair and immediately my head turned into a foam ball. I couldn't believe what had happened. Carol laughed as she ran across the road, heading off home down Campbell Road where she lived, her usually perfectly coiffed hair flattened by Ten-Day. Ben had to drive home to East Ham and swaggered his usual way to his little car. I was home in thirty seconds but because there was no fire alight, we had no hot water so I had to have a strip-down wash in cold. The antics of the day convinced me that both Carol and Ben must be nuts.

It was thanks to many of these silly days, jokes and pranks that the three of us grew together more like a family than just three people who worked together. At times, they teased me something terrible but even that had a purpose and it worked. They knew that I had to learn to cope with the harder things in life, like disappointment. They knew I had to be tougher to cope so I think they, in their own inimitable fashion, set about toughening me up. Their plan worked and thanks to them I learned how to deal better with what life could throw at me. I even learned how to deal with the crushing blow that Carol had found herself a boyfriend called Terry, who was a good looking motor mechanic. Like me, he wasn't very tall, but his jet-black wavy hair gave him the handsome Italian look. I could understand why Carol fell for him and thankfully my disappointment was short lived.

November soon came round and mentally I approached my driving test a lot differently than before. I was so much more confident, but not cocky. I did the test and at the end, answered the questions put to me. I stood there next to the bike during his brief pause while he checked his notes on his clipboard. Then with the same smile on his face as the other examiner had had he told me I'd passed my test. What a relief. He gave me my pink slip of paper, congratulated me again, shook my hand and left. It took a couple of minutes to sink in and then I set about taking off the 'L' plates. I had passed!

I was now able to carry passengers and until the local police got to know me, they seemed to target me even more. I still looked very boyish, but at least thankfully my voice was well and truly on its way to breaking. Each time I was stopped I delighted in slowly looking for my little red book with the crown on the front. The officer would open it and, with a grunt, hand it back, telling me to be on my way.

I could now give Tom a lift home after scouts, which was a pleasure as he had done so much for me. Yet he never counted on a lift and sometimes would insist on walking, as he never wanted me to feel obligated. He knew there would be times when I wouldn't want to or that I had other plans. It was after one such lift when he once again asked me to go abroad with him, this time to Belgium.

'Come in,' he said, 'I'll make us a coffee and we'll discuss it.'

I locked up the bike and went in. We sat in his little kitchen as he heated up the milk for the coffee and he told me about his plans.

'We'll fly to Ostend and stay in a hotel. From there it will be easy to go to Bruges, which I am told is like Venice,' he said. He went on to tell me that there was also a tram like a train that ran along the coast and we could catch it and go to a place called Blankenberg. I listened and the thought was exciting. He told me he could get a cheap weekend break through work that would get us away at the end of November. 'How does that sound?'

Once again excitement ruled and I agreed. I was also now going on seventeen and I knew that there would be no problem with Mum and Dad. Still I would sort of ask them nevertheless.

November 24th was Mum's birthday and, remembering her comments about her preference for flowers with stems, I went to the florists and arranged for a bouquet of flowers to be sent to her at Perkins'. Mum never really showed any emotion but when I popped in to see her at lunchtime I could see she was happy. A week later I was in Ostend. I had arranged to have Saturday and Monday off work and as always Ben was accommodating but he did raise an eyebrow and say 'Oh!' when I innocently told him I was going with my scoutmaster.

That was the first time anyone had expressed any suspicion

about what I was doing. It took just one lift of that eyebrow and that small word 'oh', to remind me that what I was doing was wrong. I had committed myself to this weekend and I had to put his suspicion behind me to deal with later.

Tom and I once again set off by train to Rochford to catch our flight from Southend airport. I think the sheer excitement of flying and the trip outweighed any doubts I had about what I was doing and it was easy to put guilt to the back of my mind. We arrived at Ostend, where we were met and coached to our hotel, which was next to the station. It was my first time visiting a hotel, let alone staying in one. I had seen hotels in films and on the television and in real life but I had never actually been in one. We had a twin room, which had central heating, which was another first for me. The bathroom was huge and there was constant hot water, unlike home, where we always had to light a fire, summer or winter, to have a hot bath or at Tom's where the water was heated by that old fashioned gas heater.

We did things economically like eating in cheap cafés where the food was good and the experience exciting, as I had never really eaten out before. Well, save for pie and mash or the full English breakfast in a transport café while we were en route to our annual camping holidays. You could hardly call eating a full English breakfast amid a bunch of greasy lorry drivers 'fine dining'. The whole weekend was exciting and Bruges was exceptional. Tom had told me that it was like little Venice and what a beautiful place it was too. We went to Bruges by coach and got off at the main square. It was bright with winter sunshine, which enhanced the beauty of the buildings, in particular the huge church and the town hall. Before we left, we went on a canal trip and I savoured the beauty of Bruges, a place I will never forget. It was all so different from Bow.

The next day was again so different. We walked out of the hotel into a dark grey rainy day. Tom first looked up and then to me, he shrugged his shoulders and said,
'Blankenberg.'
Without too much difficulty we soon found the tram stop and waited for the next one to arrive. Blankenberg, compared to Bruges, was quite forgettable. Still, even Blankenberg in the rain was exotic, compared to hop picking. The trip wasn't entirely wasted as I did buy Mum and Dad a souvenir - a revolving lighthouse, the top of which turned, due to the heat coming from the light bulb inside. Just the sort of thing a real English tourist would buy.

The excitement of the weekend was only once briefly interrupted by the thought that I had let myself down once again; I had allowed our physical relationship to re-establish itself. The momentary interruption by the image of Ben's eyebrow and his softly spoken 'oh' soon faded. Sadly the excitement of the weekend was not to last, I think mainly because I felt I couldn't really talk about what had happened. I thought others might also raise an eyebrow and think 'oh' if I said I had been away for the weekend with my scoutmaster, Tom.

As I was getting closer to seventeen with each passing month I was growing more and more concerned about myself, and what I was doing. Sod Ben's eyebrow! Thankfully with all the work on the run up to Christmas, which was rapidly approaching, there really wasn't too much time for me to think about things like that. I would soon be up to my neck in turkeys. For just three people working in a butcher's shop, it was such a busy time. Turkeys were delivered in their dozens by Hedges' lorry. The shop window was dressed with a variety of birds and decorated with laurel and the shop itself with a selection of colourful Christmas decorations. In fact, the shop looked more Christmassy than home. It was a hard slog, at the end of which was the usual financial reward. Christmas Eve finally arrived. The shop was clean, and the front shutter firmly shut down. The chaos was over and we savoured the quiet and the smell of the fresh sawdust on the floor. Ben had opened a bottle of wine and we had a Christmas drink together. Then Carol announced she was getting married next year, Terry, the good-looking car mechanic, had won his prize. By now, I had met him a few times and felt he was a nice bloke so I was really happy for Carol. We left the shop with good wishes to each other, and we went our separate ways to either enjoy or hate Christmas, like people do.

I was still an in-between and in spite of being a seasoned traveller and having passed my driving test, I still couldn't legally drink in a pub. The few friends I had were ensconced in their own Christmas happiness and I was out on a limb. I did go to the Widow's Son, around the corner for a drink before Christmas day lunch with Mum and Dad. Thankfully there was no Uncle Bill and Aunt Eve or the kids. So instead of spending News Year's Eve in front of the box again with Ken and Andy doing their Hogmanay stuff, this time I went out to a pub with the family and celebrated, East End style, the arrival of 1965.

When the festivities were all over, I went back to work and was glad of it really. The holidays had been uneventful and I had spent far too much time in front of the TV with nothing much else to do. I was weeks away from seventeen and feeling more and more that I wanted someone to share life with.

Chapter Thirty Nine - The Dixons

It was quite early in January when a young girl walked into our shop for the first time. As she stood in the queue I couldn't help but notice her thick long brown hair as it hung over the black velvet collar of her green overcoat. She was about five feet tall, quite thin, ghostly pale and wearing hardly any make up. Quite a plain Jane really but she did have a real sparkle in her eyes. With both Ben and myself serving it was always a lottery who would get to serve whom in the queue but as luck would have it, I served her. She shyly whispered her order to me with a voice that was quite croaky with a bit of an Irish twang. At first I thought she had a cold and with that soft Irish accent, I thought she sounded a bit like the singer, Ruby Murray.

I had soon served her and was onto the next customer. As she left the shop, the 'all seeing' Ben had noted my interest in her and before she had barely gone, out of the blue he said to me, 'Why don't you ask her out?'
'How the bloody hell do you always know what I should do?' I asked him.
The answer went without saying - he knew me well. The next time she came into the shop, I served her but this time with Ben and Carol making their retreat to the back of the shop more than obvious.

I was shy and fearful of rejection, especially in the shop in front of Ben and Carol. The clock was ticking and I had seconds to find the courage to ask this girl if she would like to go out with me. So to play for more time, I served her as slowly as I could. I got to the point where I was taking her money and I could imagine Ben and Carol almost falling through the back door with their ears pressed so hard against it. I then managed to say, in my newly broken voice, 'Do you fancy going out one night, maybe to the pictures?'

She thought for a second or two, which seemed like an hour and simply said, 'O.K.'

Now my heart was up and running.

'This Friday?' I said, and she nodded.

'I'll meet you by the crossing,' I said as I pointed to the pedestrian crossing just along from the shop. 'Seven o'clock?'

'OK,' she said, smiled and went to leave.

'Oh,' I said, 'I'm Jim, and you are?'

'Barbara,' she whispered, and she left. The shop went quiet and then both Ben and Carol fell through the door in fits of laughter. They couldn't wait to tell me that I was about to go out with a girl that only said 'OK!' but at least she knew her own name and, just for a change, I went red in the face.

When I got home I told Mum about Barbara and our date and I told her not to tell Dad well, not that night anyway. The next day was Thursday when most shops in the area closed half-day. I went to Whitechapel where there were lots of Jewish tailors and bought myself a new jacket and shoes. I got home with bags in hand and as I walked in, Dad was lighting the fire when he asked me about this 'tart' I was going out with on Friday! He always referred to girls or women he didn't know as 'tarts'. I was embarrassed by his remark and all I could say was 'She's not a tart, her name is Barbara.'

I went to my room to hang up my new jacket and I heard Mum come home. I asked her what was for dinner and she told me sausages, mash and onions - another one of my favourites. Thankfully that night Dad didn't make any more rude comments about Barbara. Here I was, aiming to be as normal as I could, trying to be what I knew he would want me to be and all he can do is call the girl I was about to go out with a tart! I had my dinner and I went to the scouts. I didn't tell anyone about Barbara, especially Tom, as I really didn't feel it was the right time. I decided just to see how things went.

Friday was the longest day in the shop and this one really did seem to drag by. We closed at six pm. Thankfully Ben wasn't one to want to be in the shop for a minute longer than was necessary. We were usually all washed up and scrubbed down perhaps, save for a few meat dishes, in advance of pulling down the front shutter. The last bits never took long to put away and we were nearly always cleaned up and out of the shop by six-fifteen, as was the case that night. It was a typical cold, dark winter's evening and I rushed home knowing that Dad would have been in a couple of hours by now, with the fire alight and the hot water tank dripping with heat. I rushed through and ran the bath taps.

'What's his panic?' he asked Mum.

'Barbara,' she replied. I was shaved - well bum fluffed as Dad called it - washed and dressed by six-fifty-five.

'How do I look?' I asked. Mum told me I looked OK. Dad once again told me that I smelled like the bottom of a whore's handbag and on that note I went out. I walked over to the crossing and waited outside the bakers. Barbara arrived on the dot of seven.

'Hi,' I said, 'want to walk to Bow Road or wait for a non existent 86?'

'Let's walk,' she replied. We had only walked a few yards when I put out my elbow for her to hold my arm, and she did. She was holding my arm and we were talking. Wow!

'Barbara what?' I politely asked, 'and how exactly did you get that husky voice of yours?' She told me that her surname was Dixon and that she'd had these nodule things growing in her throat. They had been removed so many times it left her voice like this. In fact she told me that they had left an open hole in her throat for quick access in an emergency until they knew the things were definitely not going to grow back again. With that she pointed to a plaster on her throat. At first

I thought this was a joke, but when she talked you could hear air escaping through it. No joke! By the time we got to Bow Road I had also discovered that she was two years older than me. There was me, with my baby face, going out with a girl who was also blessed with a young face and almost nineteen. In fact she would be nineteen in February and I would be seventeen in March.

We caught a bus along Bow road and we went to the Odeon cinema. I had got us balcony seats and during the interval between the short and the main film the ice cream lady came round. I asked Barbara what she would like.

'Vanilla, please Jim.' She called me Jim! We were sitting in the back row of a block of seats and as I walked along the row, everyone got up to let me through. I then queued up in front of the usherette. The queue moved slowly and, by the time I was at the front, the lights had gone down and the next film was about to start.

'Two vanilla tubs,' I asked but she told me she only had Neapolitan left.

'Hang on,' I said

'I'll ask,' To save time, instead of making everyone get up again, I slipped along the back of our row, leaned over and whispered into her ear,

'They've only got it three colours,' She looked around at me, but it wasn't her. I was whispering into the wrong ear! Even worse, I was leaning in between this girl and her boyfriend and he didn't look too happy about it. Once again my face was on fire and this time I am sure you could have fried eggs on my cheeks. I just went back and bought the ice creams available and then made everyone get up again so I could take my seat next to Barbara. I never ever told her of my mistake and for years that counted as my most embarrassing moment.

We caught a bus back to the top of Campbell road and we

walked home from there. I walked her right to her door and said goodnight. I wanted to give her a kiss but I was just too bloody scared. I got home and everyone - well Mum and Dad - were in bed. I quietly slipped through the lounge and got to bed quickly. I needed my sleep, as Saturday was an early start at the shop. I lay in bed thinking about Barbara and that bloody ice cream and I decided that I liked her.

The next couple of weeks went well and I saw quite a lot of Barbara. I had even met her mother, Ethel, who came with her into the shop one day and invited me round on Saturday for lunch. She was stout - a bit like my mum - but that's where the similarity ended. Like her daughter, she had thick brown hair although in her case, not long. She certainly wasn't an attractive woman and, where I was concerned, she was only as friendly as she felt she ought to be for her daughter's sake. Saturday arrived and she cooked me a meal, the likes of which I had not tasted before. I politely said thank you and told her it was nice. By now she had developed this sort of sneer when she spoke to me, which I found terribly irritating. The left side of her top lip would ascend to almost touch her nose. She looked like any second she would burst into an Elvis Presley number. I told my Dad about this look and he said, 'She has probably got a bit of shit stuck under her nose. Don't you fucking worry about it,' and that was the extent of my Dad's good advice.

Barbara's father, Harry, was a quiet man of very few words. He was small, bald, extremely polite, and I got the feeling straightaway that he did not really rule the roost. He had a strong Northern Irish accent and had once been a painter and decorator although now he was working for the Post Office. He was doing shifts, sorting the mail out at London's main sorting office at Mount Pleasant.

Barbara had a brother called Paul who sadly was a Downs

Syndrome boy - or Mongol as they were called then. He was about nine years old and would repeat anything he had overheard. He told me things his mum had been saying to his dad - things that did not bode well for my future in that household. I think the problem was the fact that Barbara had been engaged once before and, although the engagement broke off for reasons I do not know, I was always made to feel that I was a poor following act. In fact, I had no act at all. I was sixteen, she was almost nineteen and her mother really thought of our relationship as a joke. The attitude of Barbara's mother's toward me was plainly obvious and based on a firm foundation of contempt. As it was meant to, her attitude toward me made me feel really uncomfortable when I was in their home. What a silly woman she was, as the more she was against me, the more determined I became. Barbara was the first girl that I had gone out with that showed any interest in me - well except for Lynn, who almost drove me nuts.

I was doing really well at Hedges and Mr Hedges - who was then President of the Meat Trades Association - requested that I go to college one day a week on day-release to study for a Meat Trades Basic Certificate at the College of Distributive Trades in Smithfield. At first this suggestion annoyed Ben and for a while caused some problems between us. I don't think he liked the idea of me being paid for one day off a week to 'piss about' as he put it, while he had to do my work. Despite the way Ben obviously felt, I accepted Mr Hedges' offer and went to college for two years. I sat the exams and achieved 'A' level passes in Maths, English, Science, and Meat Technology – Practical & Theory.

*   *   *

Two years later, on graduation day (for want of a better way to describe it) the certificates were handed out quite ceremoniously at The Meat Trades Association hall at Smithfield. Of course my parents weren't there but then why should they be? - I was now almost nineteen. When my name was called out I walked to the rostrum and Mr Hedges himself handed my certificate to me. It was a very proud moment for me as it was my first certificate for education and it meant a great deal.

Much had happened during the last two years, most of which I found tough to deal with. Thankfully Ben had got over the day release thing as he had long seen that I wasn't pissing about after all. He spent a great deal of time with me honing my skills on meat preparation and I had become a very proficient butcher. Good butchery is quite an art and I took great pride in getting things as perfect as I could. In the end, I think Ben was very proud of my achievement.

Carol had married Terry and she continued to work at the shop with us while they saved up a deposit for their new home.

In the spring of 1966 Barbara and I got engaged to be married. Sadly, this caused a great deal of unrest and trouble in her house. Her mother still felt that I was a joke and, at best, a very poor second to the previous fiancé. I had long resigned myself to the fact that nothing was ever going to happen to change that. During the last two years Barbara's mother and I had a few arguments - mainly over the way I felt they treated her. She was almost twenty-one and they were behaving as though she was fifteen. I felt that they had tried everything to try to split us up - even to the point of moving house!

Her mother had somehow managed to get a council exchange to a place called Abbey Wood, near South Woolwich. To get to Abbey Wood by bus from Bow was just about as easy as cycling up the Thames, and so Abbey Wood to me became a hellhole. The Honda had long gone due to lots of mechanical problems. Hondas were quite new in the UK then, so spare parts took an age to get. The bike spent more time at Eddy Grinstead's than at my house, so it had to go. It also just wasn't suitable, as Barbara's parents would never have let her get on it.

The Dixon's move to the back of beyond prompted me to look for an old banger. I found one in a little second hand car dealer's just around the corner from Tom's. It was an Austin A30 and up for sale for the princely sum of forty-five pounds, which Dad loaned me. I immediately got myself a part time job in a pub to earn the extra money to repay him. I practically lived in the car and Tony Keeble's brother, Bert, taught me how to drive. I even took my test in the car. I shall never forget the test examiner's face as we walked out of the driving test centre and I pointed out my car to him.

Of course, originally Dad tried to teach me to drive but one evening we were going along and I hadn't done something exactly as he had told me to. He then took a right swing at me, knocking off the interior mirror and busting my mouth open. At that point I drove him home and told him to get out. That's when I went round to see Bert and he agreed to teach me, and what a great teacher he was. He had a great sense of humour and although learning was serious he also made it fun. Sadly, on the day of my driving test, Bert was working so I had to ask my Dad to go with me to the driving test station. He agreed and then nagged at me all the way to the test station until my nerves were so on edge I felt there was no way I was going to pass.

The test examiner and I walked over to the car and we got under way. It wasn't long before I felt that I had really cocked things up. I rolled back on the hill start and clipped the kerb on my three-point turn. He asked me to pull into the kerb when we got back to the test station so that he could be polite and finish the test off with the statutory questions from the Highway Code book. The questions were posed and I answered them. The driving test was over and the inspector sat in the passenger seat with his clipboard propped up on the dashboard while he went through all the boxes he had ticked or put crosses in.

I sat and waited for the inevitable. Then it came. I got the bloody 'test examiner's smile' that I had seen before at the end of my motorbike test. Then he said that he was pleased to tell me that I had passed.
'Passed!' I said, 'Why?'
Now, how much of a prat can one be? I am now questioning the ability of the driving test examiner. Never mind, it was an honest question to which he replied, 'Why, why?'

Oh, very cute, I thought. I mention my faults and he changes the pass paper for a failed paper. Still I had started this, so I mentioned my faults - for driving that is.

He then told me that I had corrected them so quickly he was happy with my overall ability. Fair enough, I thought, so I thanked him and happily took the pink slip of 'pass paper'. He got out, thanked me again, shook my hand and walked off. I locked the car up to go and get Dad, who was sitting in the test station in the waiting room. I looked in and just said, 'Come on then.'
We walked to the car, and I had left the 'L' plates on it. When he saw them he got in the car and he started on me again with 'I told you that you would fail.'
He went on and on about the way I did this and the way I did that. I let him go on for about five minutes and then in fake exasperation I just stopped the car, got out took the plates off threw them into a bin on the pavement.
'I won't be needing them again,' I said. 'I passed.'

And that was my little moment of glory. He was silent for the rest of the way home. The other person I really pissed off by passing my test was Barbara's mother. She had instigated this move to this most inaccessible place and now I was mobile. I could take Barbara out again only now with ease, which really made passing my test first time something really special.

As far as Barbara was concerned, my Mum and Dad were supportive of me but they were not really happy that I was engaged at such a young age. They consented to the engagement on the condition that I wait until I was twenty-one to get married. I really had no choice, as I still needed their consent because I was under age. They had made it very clear that they would not give consent for me to marry earlier.

I had also finished with the scouts. I had reached the lofty position of Assistant Scout Master at the age of eighteen, but at the St George's Parade that year my photo was in the East London Advertiser. There I was marching along, eighteen years old, and at that point I decided it was time to grow up and to leave that all-male environment. So, with a heavy heart, I left. It was a sad day for me but I had to move on. Tom was now finally in the wings. He had long been aware of the fact that I had got deeper and deeper involved with Barbara. However, just like Tom, he always left it to me to call the shots. I just stopped seeing him. I guess that was cruel on him but, for me, it was the only way - cold turkey.

I had at last taken hold of my life. I was leading a normal life and I could hold my head up in the East End. I was convinced that all this had been a phase I had gone through, perhaps out of desperation for some fatherly love. I was almost nineteen and I no longer needed that love. Now I had to stand on my own two feet and I felt there was no need to mention any of this to anyone, as it was firmly in the past. It was gone and I never wanted it to return.

It was Easter 1967 when Barbara and I tried to get away together for a thoroughly decent weekend. Of course Barbara knew her mother would see this proposed weekend as disgusting and, accordingly, she was too scared to ask if she could go. After much pressure from me, she finally posed the question to her parents just a couple of days before the weekend. The fan was spinning and I was squarely under it. I was accused of everything disgusting you could possibly imagine - yet disgusting wasn't on my mind. I can honestly say it certainly wasn't on Barbara's mind either. She was too upset at what her mother had said for her to go to work the next day and, instead, spent the day with my Mum at Perkins. When I got home from work, much to my surprise, Barbara was at home in our flat with Mum. She told me what had happened and we went together back to her house in Abbey Wood to face the music.

We arrived at the house and, as soon as we got in, a row started. I was told that there was no way that their Barbara was going to be allowed to go away with the likes of me for a weekend. Of course, I felt that I should be told why but I wasn't really prepared for what followed. Vicious words just poured from her mother's mouth, during which time her father just sat there and said nothing - as usual. Her mother attacked me verbally over anything she could think of including accusing me of taking Barbara's money. She told me I never spent any money on her daughter. At that point - like an idiot I tried to list some of the things I had bought Barbara, but on reflection it was all too pathetic really. I tried to stand my ground but I had never been good at that and Ethel ate me alive and in the end Harry asked me to leave and I did. I stood outside the house and wondered, now what? I waited outside for a while and then Barbara came out. She told me that she'd had enough and that she was leaving home. I was really surprised and I asked her if she was sure she knew what she was doing. She said she was and in a way I felt guilty that I was the one who caused her to stand up for herself. She went straight back in and got her coat, walked out and joined me, which I think, sadly, broke her father's heart. Barbara had left home and we were walking along arm in arm and I wondered what next? I really wasn't ready for this and all I could think to do was to go back home and tell my mum.

Barbara was allowed to live with us and with some reluctance the wedding date was brought forward to the 19th of August 1967, when I would be just nineteen and a half. Whether I was really ready or not was no longer an issue. I felt because of her mother's actions I was now committed to marrying her. It was either that or just handing her back again. At the time I never once thought that my situation with Barbara was bad - I loved her.

Barbara had telephoned her dad at work, telling him she was going to marry me and she asked him if he would give her away at the church. I am sure in his heart he wanted to, but to do so would have been at the cost of peace and quiet in his own marriage, so he declined.

During the next few months Ethel tried what she could to stop us getting married. She wrote to Barbara telling her that I was the son of a prostitute and that she obviously didn't know what she was doing. We must have her chained to the sink, as all we wanted was someone to do the work and that we, the Wilkinsons, were just a load of lazy bastards. This letter sent my mother scurrying off to a lawyer in a cloud of temper. She wanted to nail Ethel for these slanderous remarks but the lawyer advised against it. If this wasn't bad enough, there was worse to come.

One evening we were sitting in the flat and there was a knock at the front door. It was the Vicar. I asked him in but he said that he had Mrs Dixon and her sister with him and that I should ask my parents if they could all come in for a minute. Now I had seen my Mum lose her temper once at hop picking and, while I loathed violence, this I had to see.

I went in and told Mum and Dad what the Vicar wanted. Dad said

'Bring 'em in then,' and Mum promptly got up and went out into the garden and would not come back in. I told the Vicar and he went out and spoke with Mum. I have no idea what he said, but albeit reluctantly, she came back in and just sat and glared with pure hatred in her eyes at the two women at the other end of our lounge. The Vicar then dropped the bombshell!

'Mrs Dixon,' he said, 'has advised me that your son's adoption is not legal and therefore, you are not in a position to give him consent to marry. Is that true?' A bombshell indeed - even my jaw dropped. Without a word, my mother got up and went to her bedroom. As she passed Ethel, she nearly knocked her off her chair. In less than a minute she re-appeared with my adoption papers. The Vicar looked through them and told Ethel that all was in order. I was legally adopted and, apart from her now unproven claim, asked if there was any other reason why she felt we should not marry? Ethel sat for a few seconds and said that I had brainwashed her and I had taken all her money. The Vicar reminded Ethel that Barbara was twenty-one years old and could make her own decisions. With that the two women and the Vicar got up and left. The last thing that happened was Ethel poking her head back in saying to Barbara

'You have broken your father's heart.' and as she finished the word 'heart', her sister had grabbed hold of her and pulled her out, shutting the door.

We all sat and looked at each other in disbelief and no one knew what to say. It had all been such a shock seeing Ethel let alone what she had said. What a night.

Understandably, I had my doubts about what was happening - who wouldn't? Once again I found myself in an impossible situation. My hand had been forced by Ethel and, thanks to her dreadful interference, I was now getting married. The alternative to this was to send Barbara back home again. This was an option I was not prepared to entertain and I suddenly felt quite alone.

I suppose I could have gone and talked things over with Tom, who I knew would welcome me with open arms. In my heart I knew what he would say: 'You must do what you feel is best.'

But this wasn't a time for Tom. I had to find my own way. I regarded my early sexual experiences with men as no worse than my experiences with women, such as they were. Why should any of them be important? I had never heard of the word 'homosexual' and no one had told me about such things. I felt that what I had done was wrong but I didn't want to do it any more. I didn't want to live that sort of life. No, Tom was best being left where he was. I wanted to be normal, get married and have a good sexual relationship. It was time and I was getting married.

Chapter Forty – Wedding Bells

There was a knock at the door - it was Bert.
'What are you doing there gazing out of the bloody window?
Have you seen the time? It's eight-thirty! Do you want some
breakfast? You can have whatever you want - the condemned
man's last request!' he said as he mockingly hanged himself
from the doorframe by his tie.
'Shit, is it eight-thirty already?' I said.
'Is the bathroom empty?' I shouted as I rushed down the hall.
'We've got to get to the pub and collect the booze and deliver
it to the hall. I've also got to get to the barber's for my haircut
and what else Bert? My mind's gone blank.'
'Just get ready, Mum's doing us some breakfast and then
we'll get on with what we have to do.' Bert hadn't changed.
He was still the same as when he'd taught me to drive. Rock
steady and great at what he had committed himself to do. He
was my best man and there was no way he was not going to
be the best. We scoffed down bacon and eggs, which his mum
had cooked and got down to the jobs in hand. By noon the
booze was at the hall and I had been to the church to make
sure everything was OK. Barbara's mother had threatened to
wreck the wedding - so of all things, we had to have the
police present. I am surprised my family turned up with the
Old Bill standing either side of the church doors.

I had got my hair neatly cut and put on my suit, which I had
got cheap from Burtons. It was discounted as it had been in
the shop window. I was to be the second dummy to wear it!
Everything was set and Bert and I went to All Hallows
church. Sure enough, there were police either side of the door
and, as I went in, one of them asked me who I was. When I
replied 'the groom,' I prayed that, unlike the days when I first
started driving, they would believe me and not ask to see my
birth certificate. That would have been just too much.

Everyone was arriving and the church was soon full of my family and our friends. The talking stopped and everyone stood as the organ struck up Here Comes The Bride. Barbara walked down the aisle with my Uncle Ray, Mum's brother. Sadly, Barbara's mother had dug her heels in and her dad was not allowed to give his daughter away. How unforgiving can you be? Both Barbara and I were well and truly wound up at the thought of her mother bursting in any second and upsetting everything. At the point when the priest asked the congregation if there was anyone present who knew any reason why we should not be married, you could have heard a pin drop and I just held my breath. Silence continued and so did the service. It didn't take long to hear the words 'I pronounce you man and wife,' and I was so relieved. I could now get on with my life with Barbara. We would get our own house and have a family. I loved kids and I wanted four or five of them.

We left the church for the reception, which, as receptions go, was pretty poor. Everyone had their fill of food and drink and they danced the night away to a live band. My dad ended the day as he had started it, drunk! He was drunk when he got to the church and in all of our wedding photos he looked like he was out of his brains. The reception ended and Mum and Dad invited some of the family back to our flat to continue celebrating our union. Well that was the excuse. So our first night together had to be put on hold, as that too was to be at the flat. Of course, going to bed would have been impossible before the last guest had gone and, by the time that happened, my Dad was unconscious in an armchair. Mum was exhausted and just said goodnight She went to bed leaving him where he was. I told Barbara to go to bed while I cleared away the last few things and let the dogs out. It had stopped raining and it was getting light. As I looked at the brightening sky, I could feel my new wedding ring on my finger and I knew this is what I needed. It was what respectable people did. It was what East Enders did! It was right and it would be the making of me. I would be a good husband and, hopefully, a good father.

I thanked God for giving me this opportunity and for keeping Barbara's mother away from the church. I threw my cigarette end on the flowerbed, called the dogs in, locked the back door and went to bed. Barbara was sound asleep and I wasn't at all surprised. It had been an incredibly long and stressful day - thanks to her mother. I crept into the room, undressed and slid in beside my new wife. As I put my arm across her I could feel her incredibly soft skin and in no time at all I was drifting into sleep. My last thoughts were about tomorrow and all the problems the future might bring. I had come this far so what could tomorrow throw at me? Anyway, who's afraid of tomorrow?

WHO'S AFRAID OF TOMORROW?

Jim believed that after what had gone before, life could present nothing he couldn't cope with. He'd overcome his problems with being adopted, mainly attributed to growing up with his illiterate and, at times, violent father. He'd even managed to keep the relationship with Tom a secret. It was now time to move on and he revelled momentarily in the victory of his battle for a new life with Barbara. Sadly, such happiness was short-lived with the realisation that he'd only won the battle - not the war. There was still much to cope with as he tried to make the best of his marriage. Life for Jim and Barbara was far from easy as they started out living with his parents and it would not be long before Jim was keeping another secret. This time the secret was about Barbara's complete frigidity. Trying to be patient and understanding, Jim confronts this problem but finds himself flanked by two others. To one side, the fights with his father, as they refurbish the old house Jim and Barbara have purchased and to the other side, Barbara's anger with him at her surprise pregnancy.

There is the overwhelming high at the birth of their baby daughter and the misery caused by their huge financial struggle. Then things really deteriorate with the invasion of their life when Barbara's secret efforts to re-unite with her family pay off. Jim hits a real low due to the complete lack of a physical relationship in his marriage. He once again experiences the feelings he had as a boy - of being unloved and unwanted. Convinced that things could not get worse in his life, he meets David. The sexuality issues of the past will pale into insignificance as the problems of today overtake Jim's ability to cope. Feeling trapped, alone and depressed even suicide will be a consideration. Had Jim known what lay ahead, he would certainly have been afraid of tomorrow.